Problems with Preterism

Problems with Preterism

An Eschatology Built upon Exegetical Fallacies, Mistranslations, and the Misunderstanding of a Genre

BRYAN C. HODGE

WIPF & STOCK · Eugene, Oregon

PROBLEMS WITH PRETERISM
An Eschatology Built upon Exegetical Fallacies, Mistranslations, and the Misunderstanding of a Genre

Copyright © 2022 Bryan C. Hodge. All rights reserved. Except for brief quotations in critical publications or reviews, no part of this book may be reproduced in any manner without prior written permission from the publisher. Write: Permissions, Wipf and Stock Publishers, 199 W. 8th Ave., Suite 3, Eugene, OR 97401.

Wipf & Stock
An Imprint of Wipf and Stock Publishers
199 W. 8th Ave., Suite 3
Eugene, OR 97401

www.wipfandstock.com

PAPERBACK ISBN: 978-1-6667-9831-9
HARDCOVER ISBN: 978-1-6667-9830-2
EBOOK ISBN :978-1-6667-9832-6

10/20/22

To my children, Jonathan, Alexander, Peter, Lily, Andrew, Edmund,
Samuel, Lukas, and Athanasius, through whom I continue to
be present upon the earth and who exist as a reminder that the
inheritance of God's people is the land of the living and that all who
hope in Christ are not merely meant to retreat to a spirit realm but
will return again to possess this world.

καὶ βασιλεύσουσιν ἐπὶ τῆς γῆς
"And they shall reign upon the earth." (Rev 5:10)

Contents

Preface | ix

Introduction | 1

Chapter 1: Exegetical Fallacies in General Eschatological Interpretation | 4

Chapter 2: The Genre of Apocalyptic | 13

Chapter 3: Three Arguments that Clarify the Timing of Biblical Eschatology | 33

Chapter 4: Three Arguments That Clarify the Nature of Biblical Eschatology | 47

Chapter 5: Preterist Prooftexts concerning Time References | 141

Conclusion | 211

Appendix: A Critique of Preterists' Three Strongest Evidences that the Book of Revelation Is Written before A.D. 70 | 213

Bibliography | 269

Preface

This book is a result of countless hours of discussion with preterists who were seeking to understand whether they had interpreted the biblical texts correctly. I want to thank my fellow elder, Jeff Stackhouse, for encouraging me to write this book that he believed was very much needed in this debate. I would also like to thank the members of my church, Trinity Reformed Church of Las Vegas, for their encouragement and support while writing it. A special thanks is to be given to my wife, Allison, who formatted the book and organized my bibliography, all while doing the really hard work of raising our children while I write these books. Finally, this book would be so much more of an incoherent mess if it were not for my editor, April Khaito, who worked tirelessly on ironing out its deficiencies. Any remaining imperfections are purely my own.

I have decided to use the term *preterism* instead of *full preterism* throughout this book to convey the idea that I am not only attempting to correct the misuse of Scripture by full preterists but also the misuse of Scripture employed by full preterists and partial preterists alike. It will become clear that the exegetical fallacies and mistranslations employed to support preterism in general are errors of which all types of preterists are guilty. The distinction between them has to do with their ultimate conclusions concerning the "already, not yet" of apocalyptic literature. Where partial preterists anticipate an end, macrocosmic event as predicted in Scripture, full preterists do not. In my reading of partial preterists, I have found it is not that they understand the genre of apocalyptic literature so much as it is that they often come up with what would be the interpretive conclusions of a correct analysis of the genre due to that hermeneutic.

By presenting apocalyptic speech concerning localized, socio-political events as typological, the partial preterist gains a sufficient understanding of apocalyptic speech to arrive at a more correct paradigm than the full preterist. While not capturing the whole picture of what apocalyptic speech is expressing, at least the partial preterist's analysis allows the incorporation of the idea that apocalyptic texts often combine and speak with the voice of two events rather than one.

That being said, their understanding of the genre could use some work, and their repetition of exegetical errors and inferences from imprecise English translations is just as rampant as that which is found in the literature of full preterism. In fact, partial preterists tend to interpret the texts in question with the same exegetical fallacies employed by full preterists across the board. Due to these similarities, this book will address the interpretations of all kinds of preterists regardless of whether they are partial or full.

Introduction

The problem with studying eschatology is that it takes more than a cursory knowledge of one's English Bible and a couple years of basic Greek to really get a grip on what exactly biblical eschatology is attempting to convey. One must be informed linguistically, logically, textually, and historically if he is to make a biblically feasible argument. This knowledge must then be applied to a comprehensive knowledge of what each biblical book is teaching, not just about the end times but about all of the underlying theology that informs it. Unfortunately, this necessary knowledge and skill is often ignored by many who wish to speak on these subjects, and like a misshapen bow that cannot fire straight arrows, one's theology can become as malformed as one's deficient interpretive methodology allows.

The amount of divergent literature on eschatology is, at least in part, a testimony to this fact. The most popular literature, unfortunately, is not always the most informed. Whereas the literature produced by scholars tends to be more responsible, or at least aware of the necessity of employing a logically sound methodology of hermeneutics, it rarely trickles down to the masses. This becomes a further problem in that the bulk of books written on the subject are from laymen with little to no formal education concerning proper exegetical methodology.

Instead, the laity of the church is largely inundated with wild theories of the end times that have little in common with the biblical witness. Word studies that are not governed by sound linguistics create for lay audiences imaginative stories that connect previously unrelated texts which are now used to present whatever eschatological picture the artisan of such studies wishes to paint.

Due to this pandemic of poor exegesis, the details of the texts studied are largely ignored, since one does not need the grammar, syntax, and surrounding words in the context to provide the correct nuance to the words under examination. This has led to unwarranted assumptions about these texts that dismiss their literary and historical contexts as the rightful pool into which one must wade in order to understand to what these words refer. Instead, the fanciful pictures of a modern eschatological reconstruction provide the referents for words like "antichrist," "parousia," "666," etc.

The tendency to overemphasize the placement of biblical eschatology in the context of futuristic stories, which may indeed have some remnant of typological truth therein, has led some readers to react antithetically by producing historical stories as their sole context instead. In fact, the same unsophisticated view of literature now serves a preterist eschatological reconstruction that also ignores the details of the texts cited, uses the same poor methodology in its word studies and exegesis, and largely replaces the context of these texts with its own fanciful pictures, which have almost nothing to do with those painted by the exegetical details of the biblical texts themselves.

Again, there is a little truth in both views, but this little amount of truth is used to give credence to a large amount of error. Indeed, it is said that theological error often stems from emphasizing one truth to the exclusion of another. Certainly, futurists have ignored the contexts of particular relevant passages, but so have Preterists. The truth of the matter is that neither group has got it right because both have emphasized certain truths to the exclusion of others. What these biblical texts actually teach us is that these things, in a way, have *already* come to pass, and in a way, they have *not yet* come to pass. They have come to pass in multiple ways, are coming to pass now, and will continue to come to pass in the future. However, it is left to the texts themselves to bear witness to this fact, as they are thoroughly exegeted with a robust methodology that listens to language responsibly, rather than seeing it as a handmaid to support our preconceived eschatological paradigms.

It is important at this point to define what I mean by *preterism*. Preterism, in short, is a belief that most, or all, of the texts in the New Testament that speak of Christ's return actually refer to the consummation of the new covenant age and the end of the old covenant age as it is signified in the destruction of Jerusalem and its temple in A.D. 70 and not necessarily to an event that will end the wicked world and establish Christ's physical kingdom upon the earth in the future. Partial Preterists believe that most of these texts refer to the destruction of Jerusalem in A.D. 70 but still make room for a few of these texts to refer to a larger coming of Christ in the future. Although this work will share some agreement with partial preterism, it will be my purpose to show that most of the eschatological texts in the New Testament do not refer to this event at all. Hence, neither full preterism nor partial preterism have employed solid exegetical methods when dealing with the vast majority of the texts, and thus are committing similar mistakes when it comes to the interpretation of these passages.

As such, the purpose of this book is not to explore every preterist argument, or even every preterist idea, but rather to identify some of the exegetical fallacies, misunderstandings of genre, and mistranslations that are being committed in order to establish the eschatological paradigm of preterism. In the process of doing so, the context of the passages preterists use will be brought out to provide a deeper understanding of what these texts are actually talking about. As we examine and interpret the text, a more robust eschatology will emerge, one that explains all the data in its respective contexts, rather than one that must explain away passages and provide new contexts to make them "fit" into the preconceived paradigm. Hence, this book will also present an argument for that eschatology as superior to that of a preterist interpretation.

Chapter 1

Exegetical Fallacies in General Eschatological Interpretation

There are quite a few exegetical fallacies employed to support various eschatological paradigms.[1] A particularly pervasive fallacy surrounds the use of word studies. When a speaker uses words, he does not at all assume that his words will be taken out of context or cemented to referents that exist in other contexts, yet this is precisely what biblical interpreters do all the time. The following discussion highlights certain lexical fallacies often employed in preterist hermeneutics.

Illegitimate Referential Transference

This fallacy occurs when a word is observed to refer to a particular event or object in one context and then argued that it refers to the same event or object in another context even though that context may be completely absent of said referent. An example of this fallacy would be if someone were to say that the word *man* must refer to an electrician in both of the following examples, simply because the word *man* refers to an electrician in the first context.

---

1. Although there are works that seek to define these fallacies in detail (e.g., D. A. Carson, *Exegetical Fallacies*; Moises Silva, *Biblical Words and Their Meaning*, etc.), I have attempted to generalize these fallacies into larger categories for pedagogical purposes.

A husband says to his wife on Friday, "The electrician is coming to fix the lamp. The man will be here this morning."

A husband says to his wife on the following Wednesday, "The man is coming to fix the sink this afternoon."

It is clear by the context of the second example that the word "man" refers to a plumber, not an electrician. Yet, because the word "man" is used in both contexts, the mistaken interpreter employing this fallacy would think it refers to an electrician in the second example also. The reason he does this is because he has confused the distinction between reference and meaning. The word "man" does not *mean* "electrician." It *refers* to an electrician in a context that makes it clear that the speaker is referring to an electrician. What this means is that the word "man" does not carry some possible meaning of "electrician" that one can merely plug into any text. "Electrician" is not one of its many meanings, as it is merely a referent of the word that context must provide.

This fallacy is compounded by the way laymen read lexicons. Older lexicons committed this same fallacy, and newer ones merely outline what a word *refers* to in various contexts that make those referents clear. The lay reader comes along and often thinks that the lexicon is giving him numerous options from which to choose the meaning of a word in any given text, but this is deceptive, as the work is merely showing what the word refers to in various contexts that contain those referents. In other words, when used in the context of an electrician, the word "man" can refer to an electrician. The lexicon will then have an entry where the word refers to an electrician. This does not mean that one of the meanings of the word "man" is "electrician," so that any time the interpreter sees the word "man" in any other context that plugging in the meaning "electrician" is somehow a viable option in selecting the correct translation. The idea that he has various possible meanings of a single word when, in fact, all words have a limited semantic range that stretches only so far from what is considered its *unmarked meaning*, is therefore erroneous.

Root Fallacies

There are a few different types of root fallacies. The one relevant to this study is a cognate fallacy, where someone assumes that a word's cognates have the same meaning as the word itself. A cognate refers to a word that is associated with another word through derivation. For instance, some have tried to argue that the word *mnēmeion* "tomb" in John 5:28 means the same as its cognate *mnēmosunon* "memory." One can see how the two are related in that a tomb is a memorial. However, it is clear that *mnēmeios*, both in general and specifically in John 5:28 refers to a physical grave in which the body resides. Context, not cognates must be allowed to determine meaning.

None of this means that the information derived from such fallacies cannot be helpful. Sometimes words do carry similar meanings to their cognates, mean something close to their etymologies, or convey what their constituent parts convey separately; but this all must be born through the study of a word in the unique context in which it first appears and not by assuming its meaning apart from the context by which its specific referents are supplied.

The Unmarked Meaning

The "unmarked meaning" of a word in linguistics is the most common meaning of a word within the group that speaks that particular language. When one hears the word "dog," for instance, a four-footed creature is pictured as the default meaning of the word. However, if further context is given, the word can be stretched in its meaning and refer to something other than this furry animal. This stretching of the word is what is called the semantic range. Much of the time, although not always, its further uses can be traced back to the unmarked meaning, showing it as the core meaning of the word that limits its semantic range. However, since context is king, a context can stretch any word beyond its limits if it so chooses.

It should also be said that the "unmarked meaning" is not what these words and phrases *sound like* they are saying to the modern reader. The original audience and author determine what would be considered the unmarked meaning. The modern reader may be simply replacing the ancient context, and referent found therein, by his own modern context and the referent *he* thinks of when he hears the word. The text, however, is not written to the modern reader, and so, this ends up being a way the original context is replaced with a foreign context.

For instance, John Noē argues that Daniel should be read with a "straightforward approach."[2] He favorably quotes what I would consider one of the greatest exegetical errors committed by a modern interpreter, "when the normal sense makes sense, seek no other sense." The immediate problem, of course, is in answering the question, "What is the *normal sense*?" To whom is it the normal sense? Context is vital in determining what is meant. The ancient setting is a context, and the literary setting is the primary context, but what the modern interpreter thinks a word or

---

2 Noē, *Beyond the End Times*, 102.

phrase sounds like is not the context at all. Instead, that is a type of exegetical fallacy called context replacement (see below). Ironically, to employ this methodology is to take these texts out of context, which is the furthest thing from a "straightforward reading" as it would be understood by the author or original audience.

Therefore, the unmarked meaning is the unmarked meaning for the original audience, not the twenty-first century interpreter. This mistake is made by numerous interpreters who attempt to argue that since a text *sounds like* it is saying X to me, it is saying X to the original audience. The problem, of course, is that the only thing that contributes to the correct interpretation of a text is what it sounded like to the author and his intended audience, not what it sounds like to the modern reader.

Understanding the unmarked meaning comes into play when the context does not change what would be understood by the original audience as the most common meaning of the word or phrase. For instance, it is often argued by Preterists that the term "heaven and earth" either refers to a covenant or the temple. This is simply false. The unmarked meaning of these terms refers to literal heaven and earth, and only in certain contexts that make it abundantly clear by what is present in those contexts do they change their reference and refer to something else.

For instance, the phrase "shake the heavens and the earth" can refer figuratively to the upsetting of the present order and creating a new one, but this is only the case when the word "shake" is involved. The imagery is that of an earthquake and how it moves things around. It has little to do with the phrase "heaven and earth" when it appears separately from that context. Therefore, to conclude that the phrase "heaven and earth" has the same connotations as "shake the heavens and earth" is to fail to understand that the phrase loses its referent without the component of it shaking.

Context Replacement

One of the biggest exegetical fallacies committed by those seeking to support their theological paradigms is that of *context replacement*. In fact, one might argue that most, if not all, of the exegetical fallacies presented in this book can be summed up into this one category. Essentially, the fallacy attempts to change what is said by changing the context. If one wants a word within a particular text to refer to something other than what it refers to in its present context, he must give it another context with new referents. The biased interpreter will construct a new context for a passage, verse, or word by piecing together other texts of scripture, speculative background material, and his or her own reasoning, then replace the existing context with the reconstructed one. What this practice does is allow the interpreter to make the passage appear to say what he wants it to say, whether supporting his paradigm or simply allowing a passage that contradicts his paradigm in its current context to be read as consistent with it. Since context determines the meaning of the words used, this has the power of completely changing the text to say something different, and even the exact opposite, of what it originally said.

For instance, if I were to take a simple statement from a child's reading book, "the cat sat on a hat," and give it a different context, I can make it say anything I want it to say. I can do this by saying something like, "The word "cat" was often used at the time period this book was written to refer to the entertainer Sammy Davis Jr. He was 'the cat' and often used the phrase in reference to himself. Given the slang of the time period, the term likely refers to him. The phrase "to sit on something" often meant to conceal something as in the phrase, "to sit on a story." The word 'hat', of course, often referred to one who played many roles in life, as in the phrase "he wore many hats." This context, then, tells us that this sentence should be understood as, "Sammy Davis Jr. concealed the fact that he had diverse talents in life."

The context, however, existing in pictures found within the book, tells us that this is referring to a literal cat sitting on a literal hat. What I must do, as a biased reader, to maintain my interpretation in light of this fact is ignore the context and replace it with the reconstructed one above. This happens quite a bit with lay interpreters of the Bible. In fact, it is the very reason that massive books, and even a whole series of books, articles, and YouTube videos must be created to convince others of a reconstructed interpretation of a single passage. Pages upon pages, volume upon volume, video after video, consisting of all sorts of "context" from other texts and the interpreter's own surmising—often built from a straw house of false inferences—are created before he ever touches the text at hand. This happens because the interpreter must construct the context he is using from somewhere other than the actual text in front of him if he is to change what the text is clearly saying. Instead of using sound exegetical methodologies that pay careful attention to its actual context, authorial intent is bypassed, and the interpreter can now make the text say anything he wants it to say. This is precisely why it is called eisegesis, a forcing of one's own perspective into the text. The interpreter is pouring a context into the text in order to reinterpret it. What he is essentially doing is rewriting the text by supplying another context for it while keeping the actual words used but now devoid of their original meaning.

What perpetuates this fallacy seems to be an approach where an interpreter views biblical texts as an ancient puzzle that must be interpreted through a key found elsewhere in the ancient or modern world, either in other biblical texts or in some other ancient source (e.g., Josephus), or within a history book or newspaper. Whatever text is used to supply the new context, the idea is that the ancient author's words and world are so radically different than ours that they cannot be understood by the modern reader but rather must be deciphered through a cryptic key found elsewhere in order to unlock what it is being said. What ends up happening is that the context of what is being said, i.e., the very thing that would tell us the author's ancient concepts of this or that, is ignored in an effort to conform what has been written to meet the expectations of a theological paradigm or presupposition supplied by the modern reader. The great irony, then, is that context replacement accomplishes the exact opposite goal of investigating the ancient concepts of the author, and instead, forces what he says into the preconceived notions of the modern theologian. As a result, the one who employs this fallacy keeps the original form of the text intact but changes the referents, and therefore the meaning, by supplying a foreign context that its author did not supply within the text itself.

One only needs to examine the way that a preterist handles 1 Corinthians 15 or Romans 8, or how a Futurist often handles the Olivet Discourse. Words are twisted to refer to things outside of the context, foreign details are added to the context from elsewhere, and before one knows it, the passage now refers to a completely different event or situation than the one presented if just the context were allowed to speak without these additional foreign referents.

Preterists commit this fallacy quite often, especially when they appeal to the stock language of apocalyptic speech. It is often argued that if the same language and events are being used in the Olivet Discourse as in the Book of Revelation or elsewhere, then they must be describing the same event. This is nothing short of a wholesale dismissal of the unique referents in the Book of Revelation and other texts in an effort to conform them all to the event (i.e., the destruction of Jerusalem) to which the Olivet Discourse refers in the Synoptics.

Likewise, when dealing with 1 Corinthians 15 and similar texts, an entire narrative of spirits rising out of Hades is constructed to replace the actual referents to the resurrection of the believer's mortal body in the text. The actual text is ignored, and the new context is placed over it so that each statement made in the original text can be conformed in some way to that fabricated narrative.

This fallacy can be seen in a book by full preterist Daniel Harden that critiques the partial preterist view of R. C. Sproul that suggests there is more than one *parousia, a term typically used to refer to the second coming of Christ.*

> Actually, full preterists consider themselves "consistent" because of the way they handle phrases like parousia, the end of the age, and the day of the Lord. When Sproul, earlier in his book, talks about how the New Testament writers meant consistently the same thing by such phrases as close at hand, near, and at the door, part of what strengthens his argument is the fact that these phrases don't need to be constantly qualified. There was only one event that was considered paramount to these writers, so that when they gave these time statements, they knew just what was in close proximity.[3]

What Harden has expressed here is a fallacious methodology where words retain the same referents regardless of context. What this means is that the context of each text is to be molded to the same singular referent rather than be allowed to provide its own individual referents. Therefore, this type of methodology ignores the individuality of each context, and the referents that would inform the reader of its uniqueness, in an effort to make one biblical text the context of all others. This destroys the ability for the Bible to use language to communicate anything else besides a singular event, even if it were attempting to do so.

Harden continues to argue his point this way.

> The full preterist view concerning the phrases *parousia*, the end of the age, and the day of the Lord follow the very same guidelines. If there were more than one parousia, the New Testament would have been much clearer in detailing just which parousia was intended. No such qualifications are given. The lack of qualifications naturally leads to either (1) an intentional (or unintentional) confusion for the readers, or (2) the fact that no such qualification was needed, for there was only one parousia, end of the age, and day of the Lord that was being discussed throughout the New Testament. The full preterist simply dismisses the first possibility as unacceptable and works from the second, that only one parousia was ever taught.[4]

This statement by Harden demonstrates the problem in full preterist exegesis. The different referents found in each context *do* show that there

---

3. Harden, *Overcoming Sproul's Resurrection Obstacles*, 7.
4. Harden, *Overcoming Sproul's Resurrection Obstacles*, 7.

are different events described as the *parousia*. The problem is that the methodology described above does not allow for each context to make that distinction clear. Preterist hermeneutics constantly refer back to the Olivet Discourse as the context for whatever eschatological text is being read, as a result, the individual texts are never interpreted in their own contexts with their own individual referents. The illegitimate referential transference and context replacement fallacies ensure that no matter the context, the text will always refer to the same event, thus begging the question as to whether each use refers to the same event.

Fabricated contexts are placed over these texts in order to make them yield to the interpreter's paradigm that has been constructed from some other place. The referents do not come from exegetical observations of these texts themselves in their own contexts, but usually from a single text or idea that then must dominate all other texts and ideas in Scripture.

What I am essentially arguing is that these are paradigms that exist due to an inadvertent mishandling of the text. In other words, the interpreters are twisting Scripture, albeit while in their own minds attempting to be faithful to what they think Scripture teaches. Sadly, what they are really doing is deceiving themselves into believing that Scripture says something that it really does not. This is why proper exegesis is so important, otherwise the interpreter will spend his life defending positions that he thinks are sacred but, in fact, are false realities created by faulty interpretive methodologies.

But Doesn't Scripture Interpret Scripture?

The overriding assumption in preterist interpretation is supposedly the hermeneutical principle of *Scriptura Scripturae interpres* "Scripture interprets Scripture," or as Luther put it, *Sacra Scriptura sui ipsius interpres* "sacred Scripture interprets itself." This is an important principle that governs a believer's hermeneutics when it is understood. However, often it has been the catalyst through which many false teachings have been forged when it is misunderstood. What the phrase should reference is a sound exegesis of each individual passage taken separately in its own context, then compared and contrasted with other passages that are exegeted in the same way in an effort to give fuller clarity to the wholistic picture Scripture provides to its readers. Properly done, this gives clarification and nuance to an individual's theology. What often happens instead, however, is that one text is taken out of context and placed within the context of another, so that the fallacy of context replacement changes the referents involved, and the original authorial intent of the clipped text is distorted and lost.

An example of this is demonstrated in a common misinterpretation of Christ's statement in Matthew 7:21. The text states that "not everyone who says to me, Lord, Lord, will enter into the kingdom of heaven, but only the one who does the will of my Father who is in heaven." The question becomes, "What is the will of the Father?" Interpreters run over to John 6:40 to provide the context for the statement in Matthew 7:21, "For this is the will of My Father, that everyone who beholds the Son and believes in Him will have eternal life, and I Myself will raise him up on the last day." Utilizing the fallacies of illegitimate referential transference and context replacement that the common interpreter thinks are legitimate exegetical methods, the misguided interpreter concludes that "the will of the Father" is just that God wants people to believe in Jesus Christ. As long as they have faith, they should consider themselves a part of the kingdom of heaven. However, it becomes clear in the context of the original statement in Matthew 7:21 that the phrase, "the will of the Father" is talking about the outworking of faith in refraining from the hateful deeds of sin and producing loving deeds, i.e., the fruit from that faith, that Christ has been teaching throughout the entire Sermon on the Mount in Chapters 5–6. In vv. 15–20, the conversation is about staying clear of teachers who evidence their lack of allegiance to Christ by their deeds. Those who lack good fruit, and instead have evil fruit, are false teachers, and those who follow them are going down the wide path that leads to destruction in v. 13. Going down the narrow road that leads to life, in v. 14, is not following the conduct of these teachers. Hence, in v. 22, Christ tells all who claim to have faith in Him as Lord but are characterized as those who do *anomia* "lawlessness" to depart from Him since He never had a lordship relationship over them. What this means is that the will of the Father in Matthew 7 is focusing on the works that are produced by faith and not the faith itself. When John 6:40 is used as a context for Matthew 7:21, it is not a faithful act of using Scripture to interpret Scripture, but rather an act of using one text of Scripture to ignore what is being said by another text of Scripture. Hence, Scripture itself is being used to commit the fallacy of context replacement. As the reader will see throughout this book, this fallacy is commonly committed in the attempt to support a preterist viewpoint by utilizing Scripture that often may otherwise, in context, say something else or even contradict it.

Chapter 2

The Genre of Apocalyptic

Apocalyptic is a genre of literature that is used in biblical texts like the Book of Revelation or Daniel. The genre has peculiarities to it that include cryptic language that uses a variety of symbols taken from mythology, numerology, or biblical history that need an interpreter, given divine wisdom, who is often supplied by the text itself. In this genre, it is common to find the author use time as a means to communicate his message, namely, that the current localized situation the author is addressing in his work is placed within the larger context of creation and history. A subgenre of apocalyptic literature is apocalyptic speech, where less cryptic symbolism is used but the local event referenced is still placed within the larger context of all of creation and history, referencing, as context for the event, where all creation is moving, i.e., the end and restoration of all things.

This leads us to discuss a similar contextual fallacy when one misidentifies the genre of a text. In the case of apocalyptic literature, or the subgenre of apocalyptic speech, the modern reader is often simply not familiar with the literary mechanisms they employ to communicate their ideas.

One of the key mistakes made in preterist interpretations of apocalyptic is that they believe it functions in the same way that regular prophetic literature or even narrative speech functions. Since apocalyptic authors often refer to their works as "prophecy," it is assumed it must function the same way as straightforward prophetic speech. This common way of thinking about apocalyptic is expressed in Keith Mathison's comments on the Book of Revelation.

> The book is a prophecy (1:3; 19:10; 22:7, 10, 18, 19). It is an apocalyptic prophecy set within the form of an epistle, but it is a prophecy nonetheless. Why is this important? It is important because it means that our approach to the other prophetic books of the Bible should provide us with some guidance in how we approach this last prophetic book of the Bible. We should approach it and read it in the same basic way. We do not read any of the Old Testament prophetic books as a whole in an idealist manner, and there is precious little in any of them that could be approached in a historicist manner. We recognize that these prophecies were given to specific people in specific historical contexts. Many of the Old Testament prophecies deal with impending judgments upon either Israel or Judah or the nations that oppressed Israel. They also contain glimpses of ultimate future restoration. In short, we take a basically preterist approach to the Old Testament prophetic books, recognizing that they speak largely of impending events, yet also deal at times with the distant future. Given that this is the way in which the Old Testament prophetic books are approached, it seems that our presumption should be in favor of the same basic approach to the prophetic book of Revelation.[1]

In discussing Daniel, preterist John Noē rhetorically asks, "Doesn't a straightforward approach to Daniel's prophecies and the preciseness of their literal, exact, chronological, and sequential fulfillment make more sense than a view that interrupts the time context?"[2]

Noē continues to argue that the futurist approach does violence to the text by stretching out a time between the 69th week and the 70th week in Chapter 9. The great irony of Noē's critique of the futurist position is that Noē himself is doing the same thing. The futurist attempts to stretch out what is said into the distant future, but Noē is also attempting to stretch it out to the future by placing it in a first century A.D. context when these things are set in a second century B.C. context. If the futurist interpretation is Scripture-twisting, as Noē claims, then certainly his interpretation is as well. Hence, his interpretation is neither straightforward nor chronological, and this is due to his confusion of the genre of apocalyptic speech with genres that are more "straightforward" (albeit even those are "straightforward" only in the sense that the ancient, rather than modern, reader would have understood them a particular way).

---

1. Keith Mathison, *From Age to Age*, 652.
2. Noē, *Beyond the End Times*, 102.

The problem with this type of reasoning is that apocalyptic speech does not typically present itself in a "straightforward" manner if, in fact, "straightforward" means "literal, exact, chronological, and sequential fulfillment," as Noē suggests. A few observations of apocalyptic speech would be helpful here. (1) Apocalyptic speech usually focuses on the present situation in light of the future climax, whether imminent or distant. It uses the future end of the fallen world as a framework to discuss the past and present, but the future end is not itself the main subject of the speech, which is often why a variety of conflicting images are presented of the future. Hence, the author utilizing this genre is not typically attempting to describe the future sequentially or chronologically connected immediately after the present. Instead, the future event may be separated from the present socio-cultural situation by a substantial amount of time. (2) Apocalyptic speech casts itself as prophetic literature as a literary device, not because it is true prophetic literature laying out a future chronology. As stated above, it often describes its "predictions" *ex eventu* as a literary device to vividly communicate its message. Hence, an author, such as the author of the Book of Enoch, who lived in the second century B.C., projects himself back into the persona of the antediluvian figure of Enoch in order to "prophesy" about the past event of the flood and link it to the end-of-the-world event that the author sees happening in his present or anticipates in the near future. This is why there exist apocalyptic texts that are written in the persona of Adam, Abraham, Moses, Elijah, Ezekiel, etc., none of which are actually written by those authors in the various time periods in which they lived. The future to these famous characters is often the present of the actual author. Only the future eschaton, i.e., that which concerns the macrocosmic end, remains as future both for the author and audience alike. (3) The amount of symbolism used in larger apocalyptic literary works (as opposed to smaller units of apocalyptic speech that may be absent of the imagery[3]) far exceeds that used in

---

3. Greg Carey notes the distinction between "primary" and "secondary" apocalyptic texts. "One distinction involves what we might call primary and secondary forms of apocalyptic discourse. Primary apocalyptic discourse appeals to the speaker's direct reception of revelation. The phrase "appeals to" is essential. Many instances of primary apocalyptic discourse feature pseudonymity; that is, they purport to relate the first-person revelatory experiences of prominent persons from the past. Almost all of the great literary apocalypses reflect this pattern. Enoch, the seventh-generation human who "walked with God; then he was no more, because God took him" (Gen 5:24, NRSV), surely did not compose the literary apocalypses attributed to him, but they rely upon the figure of Enoch for their authority. Nor did Jesus' disciple Peter compose the Christian *Apocalypse of Peter*, in which Peter perceives the souls of all people in the palm of Jesus' right hand (3:1). Primary apocalyptic rhetoric involves the highest possible claim to authority by purporting to describe direct revelation from the heavenly realms.

Secondary apocalyptic discourse does not appeal to immediate revelations but

regular prophetic speech, which can be substantial within itself. Hence, an interpreter of the symbolism is usually provided within the work, appearing as a prophet or angel, in order to guide the reader through any particular symbolism the author wishes to emphasize, precisely because he has not laid out a "literal, exact, chronological, and sequential fulfillment" of events.

Where it is important to note the idiosyncrasies of apocalyptic speech, it is also helpful to understand the similarities between apocalyptic literature and its prophetic forebears. Both use macrocosmic language that describes the end of the present world when they describe events that exist on a microcosmic level, such as the destruction of a nation or current system. This is not hyperbolic language that has no root in an actual cosmic event to come as some, like Mathison above, seem to imply. Instead, apocalyptic speech incorporates a real event that the ancients believed would occur at the end of history into its description of a current catastrophe. The imagery from this event is employed to provide a framework for smaller events that mimic its catastrophic destruction and the reordering of the current system within history. This is part of the creation language used in these texts to convey creation as a present process leading to a future consummation rather than seeing creation and re-creation as singular events in the past or future. Creation is not merely a singular event that happened at the beginning of the world but rather a continual event that happens throughout history. Hence, the renewal of creation and destruction of chaos is not merely a singular event in the future but an event that occurs throughout history. Because of this, socio-political upheavals and religious renewal are tied to the creation of the world and God's people within it. This includes the removal of chaotic forces from the world. These microcosmic events mimic and work toward the event that will put the world in a final state of creation when all chaos will be removed and the world and God's people will be perfected. Because they are a part of that process, both the microcosmic, socio-political event and the macrocosmic consummation of creation in the future can be discussed as a singular event together. This is not merely hyperbolic speech in the sense that the exaggerated elements are non-literal but rather an ancient view of the world. Instead, events that occur in daily life, and that are particularly noteworthy in history, are a part of the creation of the world, and all of these events picture and work toward

---

instead relies upon the interpretation of primary apocalyptic texts or to "common knowledge" that has emerged from apocalyptic discourse's cultural repertoire . . . Primary apocalyptic discourse usually, but not always, finds its expression in the literary apocalypses, while secondary apocalyptic discourse can make a home just about anywhere" ("Primary and Secondary Apocalyptic Discourse" in John J. Collins [ed.], *The Oxford Handbook of Apocalyptic Literature* [Oxford University Press, 2014] 222, 224).

the consummation of that creation. This is why a speech that uses language of finality in the global destruction of the wicked and its empires can be applied to a localized destruction that is neither global nor final. This is not *inflated* speech so much as it is *confirming* speech. The microcosmic event confirms the macrocosmic event as a drop of water from the sky confirms that rain is coming. That drop is a part of that rain but is not the whole of the rain itself and certainly not the storm to come. For this reason, any period of time between the two events is removed from comment and the two events are placed side-by-side, even interwoven into one another, as though the one was the other.

A failure to understand this type of speech leads to a failure in understanding both the language used in the Old Testament prophetic books as well as later apocalyptic speech in general. Hence, some discussion of this unique worldview and speech seems necessary.

The Ancient View of History: Creation and Re-Creation

The modern view of history is sectioned off into segments. Events are bracketed off as points in time that are only mildly related to the ancient past or distant future. The modern individual speaks of events as singular occurrences hedged in by the time in which they occur. However, the predominant view of history in ancient time is that of a continuous outworking of creation that is leading to re-creation. All of history is a stream that flows from initial creation into the final creation. All events in history are sparks from one of these two fires that reside at the beginning and end of the present world, commencement, and consummation. All events, like this stream, come from a source and are flowing to a goal. Hence, events like the Israelite exodus from Egypt or return from the exile can be described in the language of creation because they are creation events. This does not mean that the language is merely hyperbolic and does not have its root in an actual creation event at the beginning of time. Obviously, the macrocosmic event of creation has first priority in that its occurrence began the process for subsequent microcosmic creations to take place. It means, instead, that the microcosmic creation event, such as the exodus, is linked to the macrocosmic event, i.e., a fulfillment of God's initial creation of the earth/land and the people encountered in Genesis 1 and 2. The same can be said of the return from the exile or the death and resurrection of Christ. Creation language is applied to these events, not because it is all figurative and there is no literal physical creation of the world, but because they are literally a part of that macrocosmic creation event. Thus, these events both reflect and are a part of the very process of the *literal* creation event.

In this regard, one could simply express the concept in these terms: there is not merely a completed creation event that exists in the past, nor a singular re-creation event that will take place in the future. Creation is taking place now. What came before is a part of the present, and what exists in the present is a part of the completion of the creation event that is still to come. Every event, every ritual, every movement of the day is a part of this process. Creation, therefore, is not a past event. It is a past, present, and future event, and these all exist as a unified whole, one in which all the other microcosmic events of history can be framed, spanning the entire history of the world. Ultimately, the creation of the cosmos, including humanity, is one macrocosmic event that consists of numerous microcosmic events, as a sea is made up of many droplets of water; and yet, every droplet can be described as a part of that sea since it is, in fact, one and the same with it. If one were to dip a bucket into the sea, he would still call the water in the bucket "sea water," not because it is the whole of the sea but because it is a part of the whole. It is a piece of the ocean, and hence, it can be described in terms of the whole ocean even though it is not literally the whole ocean itself.

In Isaiah 51, God interweaves the language of creation with the exodus.

> Wake up as in former times, as in ancient times. Did you not crush Rahab? Did you not mortally wound the sea monster? Did you not dry up the sea, the waters of the great deep? Did you not make a path through the depths of the sea, so that those who were delivered from bondage could cross over? (vv. 9b–10)

This is ancient Near Eastern language that describes creation, and yet, it is not the creation of the world in view but the exodus, where God dried up the sea so that enslaved Israel could cross over and be free of their oppression.

Isaiah furthers this picture by combining the macrocosmic picture of the new creation with the return of the exiled Jews (vv. 11–15).

> "I commission you as my spokesman; I cover you with the palm of my hand, to establish the sky and to found the earth, to say to Zion, 'You are my people.'" (v. 16)

The same type of macrocosmic language is used to refer to the promise given to Israel when they return to the land *if they are faithful* in Isaiah 65–66.

THE GENRE OF APOCALYPTIC   19

> Whoever pronounces a blessing in the earth will do so in the name of the faithful God; whoever makes an oath in the earth will do so in the name of the faithful God. For past problems will be forgotten; I will no longer think about them. For look, I am ready to create a new heavens and a new earth! The former ones will not be remembered; no one will think about them anymore. But be happy and rejoice forevermore over what I am about to create! For look, I am ready to create Jerusalem to be a source of joy, and her people to be a source of happiness. Jerusalem will bring me joy, and my people will bring me happiness. The sound of weeping or cries of sorrow will never be heard in her again. Never again will one of her infants live just a few days or an old man die before his time. Indeed, no one will die before the age of one hundred; anyone who fails to reach the age of one hundred will be considered cursed. They will build houses and live in them; they will plant vineyards and eat their fruit. No longer will they build a house only to have another live in it, or plant a vineyard only to have another eat its fruit, for my people will live as long as trees, and my chosen ones will enjoy to the fullest what they have produced. They will not work in vain, or give birth to children that will experience disaster. For the Lord will bless their children and their descendants. Before they even call out, I will respond; while they are still speaking, I will hear. A wolf and a lamb will graze together; a lion, like an ox, will eat straw, and a snake's food will be dirt. They will no longer injure or destroy on my entire royal mountain," says the Lord . . . They will bring back all your countrymen from all the nations as an offering to the Lord. They will bring them on horses, in chariots, in wagons, on mules, and on camels to my holy hill Jerusalem," says the Lord, "just as the Israelites bring offerings to the Lord's temple in ritually pure containers. And I will choose some of them as priests and Levites," says the Lord. "For just as the new heavens and the new earth I am about to make will remain standing before me," says the Lord, "so your descendants and your name will remain. From one month to the next and from one Sabbath to the next, all people will come to worship me," says the Lord. (65:16–25; 66:20–23)

All of this language is in the context of God punishing Israel with war but sparing a remnant who are exiled and then brought back from the exile (64:10–12; 65:6–15). Chapters 65–66 are God's promise of what He will do for the remnant of the exile. Rather than destroy them, He will give them another opportunity for Israel and Jerusalem to become a paradise, but this will occur only on condition of their future faithfulness. However, the Jews are not faithful when they return to the land (as the Book of Ezra-Nehemiah and Malachi suggest), so these prophetic promises, which are always contingent upon repentance and faithfulness, never come to fruition for Israel. Instead, the macrocosmic elements referenced in the text remain true for God's eschatological people, but the microcosmic fulfillment for Israel (e.g., long life well beyond 100 years, all the wealth of nations brought in, all Israel's enemies and apostates destroyed, etc.), which was to occur once God brought them back from the exile in 537 B.C., never came about.

Instead, creation/re-creation language is employed to present a microcosmic, socio-political event in the light of the larger purpose of God to create the world by removing all chaos/uncreated elements and filling it up with His covenant people. Macrocosmic language, therefore, is not some empty hyperbole, but is a real event that will occur when God has completed His creation. All other smaller events that are a part of this larger one in history, and indeed picture it, are placed within that framework.

This understanding is important for the interpretation of biblical creation/re-creation language, and this includes the biblical use of eschatological language since eschatology ultimately concerns itself with the completion of the whole creation process. What God begins in Genesis 1 and 2, He continues to its completion through Revelation 21 and 22. I have often argued that the account in Genesis 1 is, in fact, from the divine perspective (i.e., from heaven to earth) and presents the ordered world as void of any threat from disorder and chaos (i.e., non-creation), as God sees both the work toward and the completion of His creation all at once; but Genesis 2 through Revelation 22 is actually the second creation account from the human perspective (i.e., from earth to heaven) played out in time. It includes every event, from the beginning to the very completion of creation that accords with the divine perspective in Genesis 1. In that creation account, chaos/disorder have been completely overcome and the world is filled with God's covenant images. These images of God are righteous humanity, without any threat from chaos/disorder/death or chaotic agents that bring about those things, a world where God rests from and sits victorious over His work of creation.

To put it another way, as many scholars have noted, the physical cosmos in Genesis 1 is seen as God's temple, and the rest of the Bible describes how God orders/cleanses both His temple and His images within it from chaos/uncleanness. This means that not only is there a final point when this cleansing from chaos and chaotic agents is accomplished but that the individual events along the way are a part of the sanctifying process that leads to the final cleansing. To put it in soteriological terms, the world is given life, sanctified, and then glorified. To put it in biological terms, it is born, it grows, and it matures to adulthood. It is impossible to reduce the idea of creation, therefore, to a single event in the past or to a single event in the future, and hence, all events are creation and re-creation events. Apocalyptic speech merely draws upon this worldview when it speaks of major microcosmic events by combining them with the macrocosmic event t within this ancient, eschatological paradigm.

The Book of Daniel

In order to establish a correct interpretation of the Book of Daniel as an apocalyptic book, it is necessary to read the book carefully as one seeks to identify the antagonist in the book. The antagonist is the key to identifying the correct background to the book, and therefore, he is the key to identifying the time period and subject the book is addressing, which will subsequently aid the reader in his understanding of how apocalyptic literature speaks.

The Book of Daniel has the unfortunate position of being one of the most misinterpreted books in the Bible due to the context replacement fallacy. Often, interpreters will hear certain words and immediately associate those words with what is familiar. This is how the interpreter fabricates a context for a text that is not its actual context. For instance, most traditional readers interpret Daniel 9:24–27 and immediately assume that the words used in that context (e.g., Messiah, atonement, everlasting righteousness, desolation of the temple, etc.) refer to Christ and the temple in the first century A.D. They certainly *sound* like it to the modern Christian reader, who associates those words very specifically to Christ and the events that surround Him. The words are, then, assumed to refer to what is most familiar with the reader, which is the context of the first century A.D. This context is placed over the text as an improper contextual background that serves as an interpretive key to understanding the passage. What the reader does not realize, however, is that he has replaced the actual context in Daniel, which has little to do with the situations of the first century A.D., with a foreign one that relies wholly on first century referents. It is the Book of Daniel itself that provides the interpretive key that will correct this misinterpretation if the reader will allow his tradition of employing this linguistic fallacy to be critiqued.

The Historical Situation of Daniel

The message of Second Temple apocalyptic literature is often communicated through a highly symbolic environment. Images of mythical creatures, Old Testament and ancient Near Eastern structures and statues, the violence of war and weather, etc., all serve to communicate that message in a vivid display of wrath and redemption. However, the overall message is usually placed somewhere in the book in plain language. In other words, there is usually an interpretation to the overall point of the symbols in the book that then functions as the interpretive key to understanding all the symbols. Daniel is no exception to this. In fact, it is not only the individual symbolic pericopes that are accompanied by more straightforward interpretations (2:37–45; 4:19–27; 5:17–28; 7:15–28; 8:15–26), but there is a key given to the reader in order to identify the person and events the entire book is addressing in Chapter 11.

What this means is that the reader has information provided to him by the book itself that allows him to judge whether a suggested background to the text has been misapplied. According to the book itself, the author of Daniel is concerned about the time leading up to the persecutions of Antiochus IV, his desecration of the temple, his death, and the temple's restoration. This allows the reader to understand that the words in Chapter 9 have to do with this time period and that Antiochus IV is the ruler who will come and desolate the temple. The anointed leader often translated as "Messiah the Prince" actually refers to the office of the high priest, who took upon a governing role after the return from the exile and under the Seleucids, and is not referring to Christ at all.[4] The time decreed for the Jews to make atonement for their sins and to bring in a perpetual righteousness (i.e., a state of life that does not fluctuate between faithfulness to God and unfaithfulness to Him by throwing away their idolatry once and for all) is the extended exile about which Daniel was praying in vv. 1–19. In fact, this is what the text itself teaches. Verses 24–27 constitute the answer to Daniel's supplication that is brought to him by the angel Gabriel. The prayer concerns how long Israel will remain in a state of exile/oppression for their sin in light of the fact that Jeremiah said it would only last 70 years. The answer is that the exile has been extended (likely due to the principles laid out in Leviticus 26[5]),

---

4. God's establishment of the high priest as a ruler until the time of the Davidic king's arrival is addressed in Zechariah 3–4.

5. Collins, *Daniel* 352, notes that Leviticus 26 "threatens to punish the people sevenfold for their sin, and this could be taken to justify the extension of Jeremiah's prophecy." He also places the time period in the context of later Second Temple apocalyptic literature which describes a seventy weeks period as that referring to the exile.

and that the persecutions of Antiochus IV would mark its end. This means that the time period for all of that which happens previous to Antiochus IV refers to the anointed high priests that precede him, not to Jesus Christ who follows two hundred years later. The anointed priest, Onias III, who opposed the Hellenizing of the Jews, was killed under the reign of Antiochus IV by the rival, Hellenized high priest that he installed. This marked a season of persecution that saw Antiochus come into the temple and sacrifice a pig to Zeus on the altar, thus causing the temple to be desolate.[6]

Antiochus IV and the Defeat of the Seleucids as the End Event of the Extended Exile

The fact that the book addresses events surrounding Antiochus IV in the years 172–164 B.C. indicates that Chapter 9 is primarily about the persecution of Antiochus IV and not some other event in the future. The same Seleucid context also informs the interpretation of the rest of the book. Chapter 2 sees the removal of all other kingdoms from the earth after all the other empires are crushed and the Seleucid Empire falls at the coming of God's eternal kingdom. Chapter 7 sees the "son of man" (i.e., "human," as opposed to the demonic beasts representing the other kingdoms in the context) take possession of the domains of those kingdoms at the death of Antiochus IV. In other words, all the empires are crushed, and Israel rules the world empire instead (a theme common in prophetic literature). In Chapter 12, the resurrection of all humanity, both righteous and wicked, occurs on the heels of Antiochus' death. These are all macrocosmic events that are placed onto the microcosmic event and are not literally happening at that time. Chapter 8 makes it clear that the microcosmic victory in view is the re-consecration of the temple and the continuation of the daily sacrifices. Chapters 7 and 11 allude to the fall of the Seleucid control of Judah and the creation of the Hasmonean Dynasty. In other words, God's people and His religion have made it through the great tribulation of Antiochus IV; the exile is finally over. They have come out victorious and will rule the land autonomously for the next one hundred years. It is, therefore, both a picture as well as a contribution to the process that leads to the final victory of God's

---

6. "Verse 26 introduces a second anointed one and a second ruler. The interest of Daniel in the Antiochene crisis clarifies the identity of these individuals. Onias III is the anointed one. His murder in 171 B.C.E. marks the end of the sixty-two sevens and the beginning of the seventieth seven. The ruler and his people who destroy the city and its temple are Antiochus IV and his army. Both Jews and Seleucids added to the trouble during the sixty-two sevens with the result that the trouble continued and intensified during the seventieth seven." (Ulrich, *The Antiochene Crisis*, 121).

people when He once and for all will give all the kingdoms of the world over to His people, whenever that might be.

What this all means is that the "future/latter days" or "end" for Daniel is the end of the exilic punishment of Israel. It is marked by the end of Antiochus IV. The habit of those who do not read apocalyptic speech according to the uniqueness of its genre is to see only one event in Daniel and miss the fact that the macrocosmic end is being joined together by the author as a singular event with this religious and socio-political one. It is "at that time," (i.e., the time of Antiochus' death[7]) that the bodily resurrection is said to occur;[8] the righteous take over the earth and receive some sort of glorification, the Son of Man comes in the clouds to receive the kingdom from the Ancient of Days, and all other kingdoms, besides God's, are destroyed from the earth. If one fails to note the apocalyptic tendency to remove any remaining history between the two and join them together as though they are happening at the same time, then he will either need to say that Daniel is a failed prediction or he will need to allegorize everything as spiritual, which is a rather difficult task to do, especially in the predictions that there will be no other kingdoms left for another people on the earth and that all of the wicked dead are raised from the dust of the earth.

Instead, if one understands the mindset of the ancient reader, he will note that these are two different events that are brought together in order to suggest that the microcosmic event functions as a taste of the macrocosmic event. It is not literally happening at the same time, either physically or spiritually. It is simply a reminder that the smaller events are a part of, and hail, the larger one to come. The death of Antiochus IV and political freedom of the Jews from the Seleucid Empire is a salvation event that is likened to the exodus, the victories of David, and the supernatural victory over the Assyrian army in the time of Hezekiah in 1 Maccabees (4:8–9, 30; 7:41–42).[9] This event, and others like it, is part of the consummation, not because it is the final creation event but because it is a part of the larger eschatological fulfillment of the creation event. It, therefore, can be pushed

---

7. Collins (*Daniel* 390) notes the clear connection made by the phrase "at that time" to what precedes it. "This refers to the time of the king's invasion of Israel and his death, which is in "the time of the end" (11:40*) and is the time of the decisive heavenly intervention. Compare the use of the phrase in eschatological passages such as Jer 3:17*; 4:11* and the common eschatological marker in post-exilic prophecy, ביום ההוא."

8. Collins notes the nearly unanimous conclusion by scholars that "Daniel was referring to the actual resurrection of individuals from the dead, because of the explicit language of everlasting life. This is, in fact, the only generally accepted reference to resurrection in the Hebrew Bible" (*Daniel* 391–92).

9. John E. Goldingay refers to this as a partial realization of the ultimate program of salvation ("The Book of Daniel: Three Issues," *Themelios* 2 [1977] 47–48).

together with that final event as though it were a singular event with it. It is a mistake to assume that apocalyptic speech refers only to one event when, in fact, it often combines two events, the microcosmic and the macrocosmic, together as a singular phenomenon.

The Book of Enoch and the Influence of Its Apocalyptic Speech upon Second Temple Judaism and the New Testament

The Book of Enoch holds a special place in the heart of Second Temple eschatology. Not only has the book been found even among the separatist movement of the Qumran community, but its ideas, and even storyline, can be seen throughout other pieces of Second Temple literature. For instance, the story of the Watchers can be read about in the Book of Jubilees, another very influential work of the time. The motifs of the Book of Enoch are found throughout the Dead Sea Scrolls. Some scholars, such as J. J. Collins,[10] even believe that Enoch antedates parts of the Book of Daniel and that Daniel has likely been influenced by the work. It should be said that, at the very least, Enoch provides the basis for the primary eschatological vision found in Second Temple Judaism.

Likewise, the book has special importance for understanding New Testament eschatology. Ideas from the book can be seen all over the New Testament. Steven L. Bridge comments how "Luke's depiction of the end of time consistently betrays the influence of the previously discussed sources [i.e., *Testament of Moses, Testament of Judah, 1 Enoch*], especially *1 Enoch*."[11] Second Peter uses the concept of the imprisoned Watchers in 2:4-5, as well as the Enochian comparison between the flood in the past with the future melting of the world in fire in 3:6-7 and in vv. 10-13. Jude, likewise, not only uses the imprisoned angel concept (v. 6) but mentions the book specifically in the prophecy that the Lord will come with many of His holy ones (vv. 14-15). Similarly, the Book of Revelation takes from Enoch the idea of the angels' rebellion due to a single angel (12:4), the imprisoned angels in the abyss motif (9:11, 14-15; 13:1, 11), the resurrection of the righteous (20:4-6), and the new heavens and new earth being made new after they are devastated by God's judgment (21:1).[12]

10. *Daniel* 353.
11. Bridge, *Where the Eagles Are Gathered*, 115.
12. For a list of ideas presented by 1 Enoch that have influenced Second Temple Judaism, the New Testament, and even Patristic literature, see R. H. Charles, *The Apocrypha and Pseudepigrapha of the Old Testament in English* [London: Oxford University

The reason why this is of note is because the Book of Enoch stages two events as a singular event, the flood and the end of the world. The figure of Enoch is predicting the flood in the book. However, it becomes very clear that the author is presenting Enoch as not only predicting the end of his world in the flood but the end of the world, period.

The righteous elect will inherit the earth, but the wicked will be eliminated from the earth (5:6–7). The mountains will melt like max, the earth will quake (1:5–7), and all creation will be torn apart and destroyed; but the righteous will be protected from the destruction (v. 8). This is referred to as a coming of God with his many holy ones (v. 9). The event the book describes, however, is situated in the past flood event. The "microcosmic" event of the flood is not the final macrocosmic event at the end of the world, but these two events are intertwined in the text as one singular event so that the author continually moves in and out of both events in his description.

In 1:2, Enoch declares that his vision is not only for his contemporary generation (i.e., the generation of the flood), but for one that is remote.[13] The dual referent is the key to reading the book correctly as that which speaks of two events, the flood and the destruction of the world in the eschaton.

When speaking of this phenomenon, George W. E. Nickelsburg notes:

> Most obviously, this deliverance lies in the future, at the time of the judgment and thereafter. To begin with, the conflict in the *divine* realm will be resolved, as only it can be, through direct divine intervention. God and the holy ones will exterminate their malevolent counterparts—the rebel watchers, the evil

Press, 1913], 180–85.

13. The translation offered up by translations such as Charles (*The Apocrypha and Pseudepigrapha of the Old Testament* vol. [Oxford: Clarendon Press, 188], "I heard everything, and from them I understood as I saw, but not for this generation, but for a remove one which is for to come," or Matthew Black (*The Book of Enoch or 1 Enoch* [Leiden: Brill, 1985] 25), "not for this generation, but for a generation remote do I speak," ignores the context that includes visionary judgments upon both generations. The statement makes little sense in a context where Enoch is warning his generation about the judgment of God in the flood. However, the idea that Enoch is speaking to the distant generation alone is still a use of the macro through micro concept since this means the author's purpose is to speak about the macrocosmic event in the future while speaking about the microcosmic flood event in the past. The word διανοέομαι may refer to the idea that Enoch is not speaking to give understanding to his own generation but to the distant generation to come. The word πόρρω does not likely refer to a couple generations from Enoch since the word means "a far way off" or a better temporal rendering might be "a long time from now," and this corresponds to the cosmic catastrophic language that does not fit the deluge at all (e.g., fire melting mountains, the righteous inheriting the earth forever and the wicked forever removed from it, etc.). Regardless, the understanding of the text as saying that Enoch is not merely seeing a vision for "this generation only" is contextually mandated

spirits, and the angelic shepherds. Additionally, the wicked *human* perpetrators of sin and oppression will be judged, removed from this world, and destroyed. Equally important, the defiled and moribund earth will be cleansed and revived. Above all, the new state of affairs will be universal and permanent. All evil, sin, and impurity will be removed from the whole earth, and all the children of the whole earth will be righteous for all the generations of eternity (10:20–11:1; 91:16–17).[14]

Second Peter's use of the two catastrophes may be due to the fact that Enoch uses them both together, i.e., the destruction of the world in a flood as that which pictures the destruction of the world in fire to come. The point is simply that if Second Temple Jewish literature and the New Testament adopt motifs from 1 Enoch, it seems likely that the very literary device that is used in that text, the meshing of the microcosmic and macrocosmic events together as one, already common in prophetic and apocalyptic speech before Enoch, would be adopted by the apocalyptic speech in the New Testament as well.

The Book of Revelation

This dualistic referential understanding of apocalyptic speech can be seen in the Apocalypse of John as well. As I will argue, the Book of Revelation has its setting in the persecution of Domitian and argues that the churches need to remain faithful in their confession of Christ as Lord and in their works even in the face of that persecution. This entire first century situation, however, is framed in the imagery of the macrocosmic end. The coming of Christ, the resurrection of the dead, the new heavens and new earth, and the complete eradication of chaos and suffering from the earth takes place on the heels of the beast's defeat by the Son of Man, just like it does with the defeat of Antiochus IV in the Book of Daniel. Neither ruler is literally defeated by the Son in their deaths, as each dies in his respective bed, not in war.[15] Yet, both are said to be killed and burned or thrown alive into the lake of fire at the time of the coming of the Son of Man (Dan 7:11; Rev 19:11–25), the latter being thrown into the lake of fire by the Son of Man Himself.

The coming of Christ in the Apocalypse refers to Christ coming to His church in judgment, and the creation/judgment/enthronement event that Revelation is addressing directly is not the final one depicted throughout the book at all. The author seems to be arguing that Christ's coming to His

14. Nickelsburg, *1 Enoch I: A Commentary*, 41.
15. Epiphanes dies from an illness, and Domitian is likely poisoned.

church is a current judgment in time that is drawn from the final judgment in the end. The rewards He has to give to the various churches are a small portion of the rewards to come. Hence, He renders blessings of confirmation to the faithful in that they will receive the tree of life in Eden (2:7), eternal life (v. 10, 17), inheritance of the new Jerusalem (v. 2:17), the rule over all nations (v. 26; 3:21), honor in the presence of the Father and His angels (3:5), a permanent place in the new creation (v. 12); or He curses them and tells them that He will remove their lampstand, i.e., exile them from the invisible church, and therefore, from the new world to come (2:5), make war with them as He does the beast (v. 16), hand them over to suffering and death (vv. 22–23), and bring about their sudden destruction (3:3), mimicking that of the wicked city in Chapter 18. This is all said in the language of Christ's coming (*erchomai soi* "I am coming to you" [2:5, 16]; [*achris*] *hēxō* "[until] I have come" [v. 25]; *hēxō hōs kleptēs* "I will come like a thief" [3:3]; *erchomai tachu* "I am coming suddenly" [v. 11]; *eiseleusomai pros auton* "I will come into his presence" [v. 20]). All these instances of Christ "coming" have to do with His coming to render judgment upon the church. The fact that Christ is depicted as already walking among the lampstands (1:12; 2:1), i.e., the churches, and that He is already standing at the door and ready to come in (3:20), shows that the "coming" language cannot be what is literally happening here, as Christ is already present. Instead, it is the language of claiming what He owns, i.e., His kingship/kingdom. These are smaller/microcosmic claims that look forward to the larger/macrocosmic claim when He will come and take full possession of all things. Revelation addresses the smaller claim in light of the larger inheritance of the Son to be given in the future. The macrocosmic event is employed by the author to show what future outcome each professed believer in the visible church has presently chosen if he or she should choose to follow Christ or the beast through their confession, their works, or both. The point, of course, is that if one were to assume that the macrocosmic language is merely hyperbolic language in talking about microcosmic events, he would most certainly be mistaken. If the macrocosmic event is not true, then the microcosmic event is essentially meaningless, and the argument being made in the book is nonsensical. The former is employed precisely to give weight to the experience of the latter.

Microcosmic and Macrocosmic Language in Apocalyptic Speech

Scholars have noted this combination of macrocosmic and microcosmic language that is used as a literary device in apocalyptic speech for some time, albeit they attempt to describe it in diverse ways. When speaking of the speech used of local/sociopolitical/microcosmic events that are showered with universal/macrocosmic themes found within apocalyptic texts, David Aune notes that "though sometime mentioned individually and treated independently, are obviously interrelated and are therefore frequently found in combination."[16] What this means is that local events are often combined with the eschaton as a microcosmic picture of the macrocosmic event at the end.

The study of Edward Adams argues precisely this point.

> New Testament cosmic catastrophe language cannot be regarded as symbolism for socio-political change; writers who use this language have in view a 'real' catastrophe on a universal scale. It is plausible to interpret Mk 13.24–27 (+ par.) in terms of catastrophic events that lead to the end of the created cosmos. Other catastrophe passages, I will contend, anticipate more clearly the catastrophic end of the cosmos (as envisaged from an ancient cosmological perspective).[17]

In Adam's critique of N.T. Wright's view that texts like the Olivet Discourse in Mark 13 merely communicate socio-political change without reference to a larger cosmic event, he states:

> Wright's (and France's) view that 13.24–25 refers to the destruction of Jerusalem and its temple is related to a larger claim that the whole discourse (or a major part of it according to France) is entirely conditioned by the prophecy of the temple's demolition in v. 2 and does not look beyond this event. But I have argued against this claim. The question of v. 4 links the prophesied temple destruction to the climax of all history, and Mark's Jesus deals with both in the discourse that follows. The climactic event is his own eschatological coming, as God's agent of final deliverance (vv. 26–27) . . . Linguistically, Wright's 'destruction of Jerusalem' interpretation of vv. 24–25 is based on his contentions that the cosmic language we find in these verses was regularly used by Old Testament prophets to describe local socio-political upheavals and that subsequent Jewish writers, especially the apocalyptists, continued to use the language in this way. Wright may be right about the use of global/cosmic catastrophe language in Old Testament passages such as Isaiah 13 and 34, but the usage (as we saw in Chapter 1) is much debated, and in my view, it is best explained in terms of a strategy of particularization which *grounds the announcement of impending local judgement in the*

---

16. Aune, *Apocalypticism, Prophecy, and Magic in Early Christianity*, 16.
17. Adams, *The Stars Will Fall from Heaven*, 3.

> *genuine expectation of ultimate universal judgement by global or cosmic catastrophe*. Also, in later Old Testament prophetic oracles, such as Isaiah 24, global/cosmic disaster language has a more exclusively eschatological reference. Crucially, Wright is incorrect about the subsequent usage of catastrophe language in postbiblical Jewish apocalyptic and related sources. In none of the relevant post-biblical texts examined in Chapter 2 is the reference to the downfall of a city or nation. The evidence of the parallel material in Jewish apocalyptic and associated writings strongly counts against his reading of Mk 13.24–25. France, as we have previously noted, acknowledges that later Jewish apocalyptic writers employed this kind of language with a more 'end of the world' sense, and even recognizes that it sometimes refers to universal judgement in Old Testament prophecy, but insists that the more regular prophetic style of usage, for judgement against specific places, as in Isaiah 13,34, etc., is determinative for Mk 13.24–25. However, even if the originally intended meaning of the catastrophe language in Isaiah 13; 34, etc., could be established with absolute certainty, subsequent postbiblical Jewish usage of this kind of language (from the third century BCE to the end of the first century CE) has to be regarded as more important for interpreting Mk 13.24—25, and the fact remains that this evidence does not support a narrow socio-political reading of these verses.[18]

When commenting upon this phenomenon in Daniel, Ulrich notes that these individual socio-political events make up a larger, singular process of redemption.

> Because the same spirit of rebellion influences the human actors in each of these instances of hostility, what God says about evil and its solution on one occasion can paradigmatically apply to another. The reason is that God is progressively and organically working out one plan of redemption throughout the long course of history. The resolution of each apocalyptic imagining (to use Merrill Willis' term) contributes to the advancement of God's kingdom on earth and the telling of his metanarrative.[19]

J. J. Collins notes the prophet Isaiah's characterization of the judgment upon the northern kingdom as the macrocosmic event.

---

18 Adams, *The Stars Will Fall*, 155–56. Emphasis mine.
19. Ulrich, *The Antiochene Crisis*, 130.

The expectation of an end is also found in the prophets, however, with reference to a more specific, decisive event: the day of judgment. When the prophet Amos proclaimed that "the end has come upon my people Israel" (Amos 8:2) he spoke of the end of Israel as an independent kingdom, not of the end of the world. He also spoke of this event as "the day of the Lord," which would be darkness and not light (Amos 5:18-20). Other prophets expanded this occasion into a day of cosmic judgment. So, we read in Isaiah 13: The day of the Lord comes, cruel, with wrath and fierce anger, to make the earth a desolation and to destroy its sinners from it. For the stars of heaven and their constellations will not give their light; the sun will be dark at its rising and the moon will not shed its light. . . Therefore, I will make the heavens tremble and the earth will be shaken out of its place at the wrath of the Lord of hosts, in the day of his fierce anger. (Isa 13:9, 10, 13).[20]

Likewise, he notes the fact that the Book of 1 Enoch records the end of the world in terms of numerous ends that lead up to the final end.

The Apocalypse of Weeks (1 Enoch 93:1–10 + 91:11–17) is a revelation in the name of Enoch, written about the time of the Maccabean revolt. Here, as in Daniel, history is divided into "weeks," presumably weeks of years. At the end of the seventh week, "the chosen righteous from the eternal plant of righteousness will be chosen," but history does not come to an end. In the eighth week a sword is given to the righteous, to execute judgment. In the ninth, "the righteous judgment will be revealed to the whole world . . . and the world will be written down for destruction." Finally in the tenth week there will be a great judgment, the old heaven will be taken away and a new heaven revealed. Thereafter there will be many weeks without number." Even though this apocalypse envisages an end of this world, the "end" is not exactly a fixed point. Rather, we have an eschatological scenario in which there is a series of "ends" as the old order passes away and is replaced by the new.[21]

In other words, there is a progression of "ends" that culminate in a final end, but each can be described as the "end" because they are all a part of the final end to come. They picture it, are a part of it, and even produce it.

20. Collins, "The Expectation of the End in the Dead Sea Scrolls" in Evans and Flint (eds.), *Eschatology*, 76.

21. Collins, "The Expectation of the End in the Dead Sea Scrolls" in Evans and Flint (eds.), *Eschatology*, 78–79.

Hence, every microcosmic event that occurs in history is one and the same event as that of the final macrocosmic event, even if they do not occur at the same time in history.

Chapter 3

Three Arguments that Clarify the Timing of Biblical Eschatology

The idea that there is just one *parousia* leads to the common misunderstanding within preterist interpretation that if a text refers to the *parousia*, or "coming," of Christ, it must refer to the same event as that spoken of in the Olivet Discourse. However, if both microcosmic and macrocosmic events are often combined into one event, all of which is described as Christ's coming in the clouds (with some variation in the particulars), then it becomes obvious that the texts that speak of Christ coming cannot all be assumed to refer to the same event. Indeed, many of these texts refer to different historical events, but they all are joined to the final coming of Christ when described in apocalyptic speech. This means that while given texts may refer to distinct microcosmic events, they may all be using the same macrocosmic language to describe those events. Because of this, it is simply fallacious to reduce all texts to a singular event, as is done when preterists assume the Olivet Discourse as the context for every New Testament eschatological text outside the Synoptics.

There are three overwhelmingly persuasive pieces of evidence for the idea that these texts speak of many comings that lead up to the final coming of Christ.

1. The Contextual References Indicate More than One Event

The first piece of evidence, as previously discussed, is that when each context is allowed to speak for itself, without employing the exegetical fallacies of context replacement and illegitimate referential transference, the events described in each passage emerge as very clearly different from one another. Preterists are inclined to replace every context with that of the Olivet Discourse, and therefore, every text must somehow refer to the destruction of Jerusalem; but as discussed before, this ignores the unique referents provided by each context in its own right.

Daniel is about the persecution of Antiochus Epiphanes and the ultimate victory over him (Daniel 11–12). The Olivet Discourse is about the destruction of Jerusalem (Matt 24; Mark 13; Luke 21). One of the promises in the Synoptics is about the Mount of Transfiguration (Matt 17:1–11; Mark 9:2–8; Luke 9:28–36). Another statement refers to an ongoing coming in the clouds (Matt 26:64; Luke 22:69). Revelation is about Christ coming to the church to render judgment as to whether they had integrated themselves into the pagan practices of Rome due to Domitian's persecution or had remained unstained by them (Rev 2–3). There are also texts that convey the macrocosmic idea alone (e.g., 1 Corinthians 15; 1 Thessalonians 4–5; 2 Thessalonians 1–2; 2 Peter 3), and thus, they do not fit any historical situation. These would, then, only refer to the macrocosmic fulfillment of Christ's coming. Hence, the above microcosmic examples are all different historical events that provide different referents in terms of the time and nature of the events. They cannot all be meshed together simply because they refer to the macrocosmic event in their descriptions unless one simply ignores the context of each passage. Hence, the reader must conclude that there is more than one "coming," and each text must be examined in its own context in order to determine to what event, out of the many possibilities, the author is referring.

2. A Continual Work to Secure the Kingdom Given to Him by the Ancient of Days

The second piece of evidence is that the original text, Daniel 7,[1] which refers to the Son of Man coming in the clouds and taking hold of His kingdom,

---

1. Daniel 7 is the origin of the Son of Man concept in the New Testament. Other Old Testament texts do not even come close to the obvious parallels between Daniel 7 and the New Testament, nor is there any further messianic Son of Man terminology in Second Temple Judaism that would parallel the New Testament. As T. W. Manson concluded, "We have no good reason to suppose that he [Jesus] was aware of any other Son

presents this terminology as a way of conveying the idea of God's royal conferment upon the Son of Man, and in that text, part of that reception of the kingdom is fulfilled at the time of Antiochus IV.[2] It is fulfilled in various ways in the New Testament, per the argument above, and this means that there is more than one fulfillment of it. In other words, the reception takes place through a process and over a number of years and not within the time frame of a single event.

Daniel 7 provides for the reader the understanding of the nature of the "coming" of the Son of Man. In vv. 9–10, a scene exists where the Ancient of Days is sitting on His throne as ruler over the cosmos in all His glory as the Judge of the nations.

> While I was watching, thrones were set up, and the Ancient of Days took his seat. His attire was white like snow; the hair of his head was like lamb's wool. His throne was ablaze with fire and its wheels were all aflame. A river of fire was streaming forth and proceeding from his presence. Many thousands were ministering to him; Many tens of thousands stood ready to serve him. The court convened and the books were opened.

Throughout the book, God is depicted as having all authority over heaven and earth. He assigns empires to whomever He wishes. Since He has the ability to assign kingdoms, the author is arguing that He will assign the

---

of Man than the Danielic" ("The Son of Man in Daniel, Enoch and the Gospels," 143).

2. Although the terminology used contrasts the symbols of the wild beasts (i.e., the demonic) as pagan nations with one like a "son of man" (i.e., a human being) representing the people of the holy ones, it should be noted that, in Daniel, the nations often take upon the characteristics of their individual kings (cf. Nebuchadnezzar for Babylon and Antiochus IV for the Seleucids). Seyoon Kim implies that to choose one or the other exclusively would be a false dichotomy. "This means that the figure כבר אנש in Dan 7.13 is to be understood not as a human figure but rather as a heavenly, divine figure. In the interpretation of the vision in the same chapter of Dan, he seems to be identified with the "saints of the Most High" (vs. 18,22,27). However, just as in the interpretation of the four beasts there is an oscillation between the individual understanding as kings (v. 17) and the collective understanding as kingdoms (vs. 23 ff.), so there may well be such an oscillation also in the interpretation of the figure כבר אנש. If so, just as the four beasts are both the symbols and the representatives of four empires, so the figure כבר אנש is both the symbol and the representative (or the head) of the "saints of the Most High". Since C. H. W. Brekelmans has demonstrated against M. Noth and his followers that in the apocryphal and pseudepigraphal literature and in the Qumran literature ם קדישי is used both for angels and for the people of God (cf. also Ps 34.10; Dt 33.3), the "saints of the Most High" in Dan 7, as the context demands, seems to refer to the eschatological people of God. M. Black, therefore, goes so far as to say that "what Daniel was contemplating was nothing less than the apotheosis of Israel in the Endtime" (*The 'Son of Man' as the Son of God* [Tübingen: J. C. B. Mohr 1983] 18–19.

entire kingdom of the whole earth to the Son of Man. This idea is made clear in Daniel Chapter 2 and revisited again in Chapter 7.

> You were watching as a stone was cut out, but not by human hands. It struck the statue on its iron and clay feet, breaking them in pieces. Then the iron, clay, bronze, silver, and gold were broken in pieces without distinction and became like chaff from the summer threshing floors that the wind carries away. Not a trace of them could be found. But the stone that struck the statue became a large mountain that filled the entire earth. (2:34–35)
> In the days of those kings the God of heaven will raise up an everlasting kingdom that will not be destroyed and there will be no kingdom left for another people. It will break in pieces and bring about the demise of all these kingdoms. But it will stand forever. You saw that a stone was cut from a mountain, but not by human hands; it smashed the iron, bronze, clay, silver, and gold into pieces. The great God has made known to the king what will occur in the future. The dream is certain, and its interpretation is reliable." (vv. 44–45)

> Then I kept on watching because of the arrogant words of the horn that was speaking. I was watching until the beast was killed and its body destroyed and thrown into the flaming fire. As for the rest of the beasts, their ruling authority had already been removed, though they had been permitted to go on living for a time and a season (7:11–12).

> Then the kingdom, authority, and greatness of the kingdoms under all of heaven will be delivered to the people of the holy ones of the Most High. His kingdom is an eternal kingdom; all authorities will serve Him and obey Him.' (v. 27)

What this means is that all the kingdoms of the earth will be given over to the people of the holy ones. There will not be any other kingdoms left upon the earth.[3] This transfer takes place via a singular figure referred to as

---

3. Literally, "The kingdoms belonging to another people group will not be left. It [i.e., the kingdom of God] will shatter and put to an end all of these kingdoms, but it will rise forever." Its rising forever is the imagery of the rock growing and taking over the earth *after* it has destroyed all other kingdoms. This prophecy is, therefore, not fulfilled until the entirety of the kingdoms of the world are destroyed by the coming of the kingdom of God, and it alone remains. This will all happen "in the days of those kings" [i.e., the Seleucids] not because it is actually happening then but because the microcosmic shattering of the Seleucid hold on Judah is a picture, and part of, the larger hold of the world on God's people that will be shattered in the macrocosmic event to come.

"the son of man," i.e., human, who represents God's people as a contrast to the demonic creatures that characterize the pagan empires.

> And coming with the clouds of heaven was one like a Son of Man. He went up to the Ancient of Days and was presented before Him. To him was given ruling authority, honor, and sovereignty. All peoples, nations, and language groups were serving him. His authority is eternal and will not pass away. His kingdom will not be destroyed.

This text makes it clear that the Son of Man's reception of the kingdom is described as "coming with the clouds of heaven." Notice, however, that it is not described as a coming to earth in order to receive the kingdom (either to defeat Antiochus or destroy Jerusalem, or even to possess the world) but instead as an ascension in the clouds to the throne of God to receive it. Yet, it is clear that the kingdom is taken away from these other kings and that it consists of all the nations under the heavens as there is no kingdom left for another people since they all have been destroyed.

This evidences that verses that use terminology such as, "the Son of Man coming with the clouds of heaven" refer to any event where the Son is laying claim to His kingdom.[4] The New Testament presents the Son of Man as the Messiah Jesus because He is the ultimate Israel, the king who represents and characterizes the kingdom. The work accomplished by the Son in the *historia salutis* is that He has obtained the kingdom from the Father, the Ancient of Days, in terms of an "already" inheritance. The Son's current work is in taking hold of that kingdom He has acquired through His judging of the nations and the salvation of the church in the continual activity of the *ordo salutis* as something that is "not yet" completed until the day of His final coming.

Therefore, as discussed above, the terminology of the Son of Man coming in the clouds can refer to the defeat of Antiochus IV, the mount of transfiguration which uses Daniel 7 in its description, the ascension of Christ to the Father, the destruction of Jerusalem, the ongoing gathering of His elect in the preaching of the gospel, the reclamation of Christians who previously had been giving their allegiance to the world and its practices,

---

4. One of the indications that Second Temple Jews also read apocalyptic texts this way can be attested by the use of the Book of Daniel by the War Scroll at Qumran. Although the book acknowledges that the Book of Daniel's subject is Antiochus IV, it *applies* what is said therein to a completely different event, i.e., the Qumran community's war with the surrounding nations, specifically the Kittim (i.e., the Romans) as *a* fulfillment. For the clear dependency of the War Scroll on the Book of Daniel, see David Flusser, *Judaism of the Second Temple Period*, Volume 1: *Qumran and Apocalypticism*, translated by Azzan Yadin (Grand Rapids, MI/Cambridge: Eerdmans, 2007) 140–58.

the exile of false believers from His kingdom (as in Rev 2–3), or the final end of the present order when Christ will receive the physical world as His kingdom in full. Since the terminology is about royal conferment, it simply can refer to any event where Christ takes a portion of His kingdom, whether in part or whole.

What this means is that one cannot merely push all the texts that use this language together as though they were referring to the same event when, in fact, they may all be referring to different events while using the same terminology. To put it in the terms we have been using throughout this book, the act of Christ taking possession of parts of His kingdom through microcosmic events is a part of the process of His taking possession of all of His kingdom in the macrocosmic event to come. Hence, there is more than one *parousia*, more than one "coming," because there are multiple instances of Christ taking hold of His inheritance on smaller scales before the larger one takes place. Therefore, Christ Himself indicates that there is more than one "coming," as we will see in the next argument.

3. Christ Says That There Is More than One Coming of the Son of Man

The third piece of Scriptural evidence is that Christ Himself indicates that there is more than one coming. Here we will examine the texts in the Gospels that indicate an "already, not yet" nature to the Son's reception of His kingdom, with the "already" being an ongoing process that does not come to completion until the physical coming of Christ at the end of this present order.

This "already, not yet" theme that runs throughout the New Testament exists due to the fact that, although the promises of the kingdom throughout the Old Testament are physical, when Christ finally comes into the world, He makes the argument that a spiritual cleansing must take place before anyone can enter the physically cleansed kingdom to come. This scheme can be seen in the Lord's words in John 5:24–29.

> I tell you the solemn truth, the one who hears my message and believes the one who sent me has eternal life and will not be condemned, but has crossed over from death to life. I tell you the solemn truth, a time is coming—and is now here—when the dead will hear the voice of the Son of God, and those who hear will live. For just as the Father has life in himself, thus he has granted the Son to have life in himself, and he has granted the Son authority to execute judgment because he is the Son of

Man . . . "Do not be amazed at this, because a time is coming when all who are in the tombs will hear his voice and will come out—the ones who have done what is good to the resurrection resulting in life, and the ones who have done what is evil to the resurrection resulting in condemnation.

Notice the "Son of Man" language in this text describes the Father granting authority to the Son. The authority is granted to give life to (i.e., regenerate) those who hear the voice of the Son. During His ministry, Christ speaks of this reality as both a future event *and* an event occurring ("a time is coming and now is. This is an *ongoing* authority that is being conferred upon the Son of Man by the Father (v. 30) to bring His elect to Him (6:37–45). In this way, this is another instance of the Son's reception of the kingdom.

However, Christ then says that a time is coming when He will resurrect all of the dead out of the tombs in the sense of Daniel 12:1. This is the act of Christ taking physical possession of His kingdom by restoring His elect to the physical world (i.e., the kingdom He is to inherit in Daniel) and exiling the wicked, with their very physical bodies, from that kingdom. Thus, a physical possession of the earthly kingdom that belongs to the Ancient of Days (i.e., the Father) is still in the future when He will resurrect the godly and remove the wicked from the earth. The Jews of Jesus' day believed the final resurrection to be the only step in the process of earthly renewal, and it was a time coming, not now. Instead, Christ is cleaning the inside of the proverbial cup first, but this by no means indicates that this event alone signifies the full reception of His kingdom. There remains an outside of the cup to be cleansed as well.

This same "already, not yet" scheme can be seen in the writings of Paul, who argues in Romans 6–8 that believers have been made alive with Christ in terms of their spirits (Rom 6:13; 7:22), but that their flesh/body of sin is still subject to desires that are contrary to God (6:12; 7:18, 23; also see Eph. 4:22). Instead, these believers groan with all creation for Christ to take full possession and reveal the sons of God in the redemption of their bodies. The very battle between the flesh and spirit occurs within the believer because he is "already" redeemed and adopted as God's son in terms of his spirit (Rom 8:15–17; also Gal. 4:5–6), but he is "not yet" redeemed and adopted as God's son in terms of his body (Rom 8:23). It is when the Spirit, who raised Jesus from the dead, gives life to the mortal bodies of believers (vv. 11, 23) that the whole physical creation will be given over to Christ as His kingdom, and the macrocosmic promise of an eternal earthly kingdom that wipes all other kingdoms out will come to fruition.

It is within this "already, not yet" scheme that one can see microcosmic events as part of the process of Christ taking possession of His kingdom bit by bit until all that needs to be spiritually cleansed is cleansed and the only thing that remains to be cleansed is that which is physical. Then Christ will fully take possession of the inheritance that has been given to Him by the Father, i.e., all things in heaven and earth. Nothing will remain in the created order that does not truly belong to Christ in every way.[5]

There are multiple instances of Christ taking possession of the kingdom, and each can be described as the Son of Man coming in the clouds of heaven. In fact, Christ indicates this in His statements to the priests in Matthew 26:64.

> Jesus said to him, "You have said it yourself. But I tell you, from now on you will see the Son of Man sitting at the right hand of the Power and coming on the clouds of heaven."

Preterists often make a big deal out of this passage as though it somehow supports their eschatology. They point out that Christ is talking to the group of priests (*hymin* pl. "you") and tells this group that they will see the Son of Man receiving His kingdom. This should be absolutely affirmed. The group standing there will, in fact, see Christ receiving His kingdom which, as discussed above. Preterists, however, assume that this is referring to the destruction of the temple in A.D. 70, only forty years after Christ spoke the words of Matthew 26:64, and therefore, believe it has no other fulfillment than that event.

The problem with the preterist interpretation is that the full statement never seems to be addressed. Jesus does not say that they will see the Son of Man taking possession of the kingdom forty years from when he is speaking. Although the phrase "you shall see" is ambiguous in Mark 14:62 as to when and how many times this will take place, Matthew and Luke clarify this ambiguity. In Matthew, Jesus actually says, "from now on," you will see the Son of Man taking possession of the kingdom. The phrase *ap' arti* means "from this moment on into the future," "from this very point in time on forward," "from now on." Luke uses the phrase *apo nyn* "from now on"

---

5. One might object that unbelievers in hell do not truly belong to Christ and are never cleansed, and yet, are a part of the created order. However, this is not actually true. They are removed from the created order. Hell itself is described in a variety of metaphors that depict a place of chaos. It is "outside," a place of "darkness," "the abyss," a place that is always on "fire," and even described as a "lake of fire." Hell is created for the devil and his angels as a place of chaos that does not participate in the created order. Indeed, it is uncreated and disordered. That is the very nature of the place. Hence, whatever it is, it does not reside as a part of what is considered the created order of Christ's kingdom.

(22:69).⁶ From that very moment, as Christ is being delivered up to His death to claim His people from the nations and draw them to Himself and into the future as Christ continues to acquire His kingdom by gathering the elect (think the Book of Acts after His ascension), this group of priests will continually see Him taking possession of His kingdom. They will see the Son of Man acquiring His kingdom from the Ancient of Days, and this is an ongoing process that is happening *ap' arti* "from that very point on."

This is not a statement that affirms a single *parousia* in the first century but one that describes an ongoing process of fulfillment, each event having the possibility of taking upon itself the language of Christ's reception of His kingdom.

Jesus, earlier in His ministry, also indicated that there would be more than one time where He would receive and be exalted in His kingdom. In Luke 17, he informs the disciples that the "day of the Lord" is broken into many days.

> Then he said to the disciples, "The days are coming when you will desire to see *one of the days of the Son of Man*, and you will not see it. Then people will say to you, 'Look, there he is!' or 'Look, here he is!' Do not go out or chase after them. For just like the lightning flashes and lights up the sky from one side to the other, so will the Son of Man be in his day. (vv. 22–24; emphasis added)

There are numerous things to be said about this passage. First of all, the reader must take note that the disciples are told that they will long to see "*one of the days* of the Son of Man." This very clearly implies that there is more than one day characterized by the Son of Man's *parousia* imagery. Second to this, it is very clear that this particular day that the disciples will long to see is, in fact, the final *parousia* as explained in v. 24, where this final day is referred to in the singular. That day will see the Son of Man come suddenly (as lightning flashes from east to west), and this refers to His physical coming where He is revealed to the world (vv. 26–30).

Finally, however, the reader must take note that the day the disciples long to see, the final day that characterizes the full possession of the kingdom by the Son of Man in His physical reveal, *will not be seen by the disciples*! Hence, not only does there exist more than one day of the Son of Man, the final and ultimate day, the *parousia* of *parousias*, is not seen by any of the

---

6. ἀπὸ τοῦ νῦν δὲ ἔσται ὁ υἱὸς τοῦ ἀνθρώπου καθήμενος ἐκ δεξιῶν τῆς δυνάμεως τοῦ θεοῦ "From now on the Son of man will be sitting at the right hand of the power of God," i.e., the Father will be giving over to the Son His own authority to take hold of His inheritance from that moment forward.

disciples which means that this cannot refer to the destruction of Jerusalem in A.D. 70. It also indicates that it did not happen in the first century at all since the last disciple, John, lived all the way to the close of the first century.

These three pieces of evidence decisively show that there is more than one "coming" event in the New Testament, and indeed, throughout the time of Christ's ingathering of His elect into the kingdom. Craig Koester sums up this idea in his commentary on the Book of Revelation when discussing the petition at the end of the Apocalypse.

> Jesus concludes his witness by saying for the third time, "I am coming soon" (Rev 22:20a; cf. 22:7, 12), which invites the response: "Amen. Come, Lord Jesus!" (22:20b). The petition encompasses several dimensions of meaning. First, it is addressed directly to Christ, which presupposes that Christ is already present among the readers. They can speak to him because he now walks among them (1:12–20; 2:1). Second, the petition has an eschatological aspect, asking Christ to come in a final way to defeat evil and bring the redeemed deathless life (22:12–14; Aune; Satake). Third, the petition is flexible enough to include "comings" that are less than final. Christ spoke of coming to specific congregations for provisional disciplinary action (2:5, 16; 3:3). By extension, Christ could "come" in gracious ways that are less than ultimate. The Aramaic petition for Christ's coming was used this way in some eucharistic services (*Did.* 10:6; Blount; Giesen). To say "come, Lord Jesus" addresses the Christ who is present with language that is eschatological but open to other meanings (Beale; Smalley).[7]

The Habakkuk commentary found in the Dead Sea Scrolls (1QpHab), conveys the idea that the Jews at Qumran thought of God's judgment of the wicked and movement toward setting up His eternal kingdom upon the earth as a series of "ends" that would culminate in a final end.

> For there is yet a vision concerning the appointed time. It testifies to the end time (קץ), and it will not deceive. The interpretation of it is that *the last end time* (האחרון קץ) will be prolonged, and it will be greater than anything of which the prophets spoke, for the mysteries of God are awesome. If it tarries, wait for it, for it will surely come, and it will not be late. The interpretation of it concerns the men of truth, those who observe the Law, whose hands do not grow slack in the service of the truth, when the *last end time* is drawn out for them, for all of God's *end times* will

---

7. Koester, *Revelation*, 858.

come according to *their* fixed order. (IQpHab 7:6–13; emphasis added)

What seems foreign to the ancient reader, therefore, is that there would be only a single event that could be described as God bringing in His eternal kingdom. This modern assumption has unfortunately replaced the ancient assumption of many of the Second Temple and biblical authors that see the kingdom ushered in through a series of microcosmic events, only culminating in a climactic macrocosmic event that would transfer once and for all the entirety of the physical cosmos over to God's people through His Messiah. In other words, in the Second Temple Jewish mind, the creation of the world that God is making is a process of many creation events, not a singular one, that lead up to its completion.

The Olivet Discourse

This brings us to the interpretation of the Olivet Discourse. The preterist will often note that the Olivet Discourse talks about the coming of Christ in the clouds, cosmic destruction, the judgment of mankind, etc., at the time of the destruction of Jerusalem, which takes place in A.D. 70. Since Christ states in Matthew 24:34 that all He communicated in the discourse will come to pass within the generation to which he is speaking, the full preterist concludes that it must be referencing the sole fulfillment of the Son of Man coming in the clouds, cosmic destruction, the judgment of all mankind, etc., events which the he believes must have taken place simultaneously; therefore, this cosmic imagery either must function as a type of hyperbolic expression, or it must be radically reinterpreted in other ways to fit that paradigm.

There are two governing assumptions that must be made in order to draw this conclusion from the text. The first assumption is that if a text places the macrocosmic event as occurring at the same time of the microcosmic event, then these events must literally be happening concurrently. The second assumption is that there is only one coming of the Son of Man in the clouds, and therefore, if this is all taking place at the same time as the destruction of Jerusalem, it is the macrocosmic event itself. There is no macrocosmic event to follow. Hence, both the microcosmic event of the destruction of Jerusalem and the macrocosmic event of God raising the dead, judging all mankind, Christ coming back, etc., literally must be the same event.

We have already challenged both assumptions as being clearly false. Apocalyptic speech does not assume only one coming of the Son of Man, and it does not assume that joining the macrocosmic event to the microcosmic event means that they are literally happening at the same time. When one reads the Olivet Discourse in light of this, the idea that the macrocosmic coming of the Son, i.e., the ultimate reception of His kingdom from the Father, must take place at the same time as the microcosmic event being referenced in the discourse is a false inference.

Another factor to consider is that the coming is not actually the destruction of Jerusalem and the temple. The coming of the Son of Man in both Daniel and the Olivet Discourse occurs *after* the great tribulation that is characterized by the destruction of Jerusalem and the temple. In Daniel, it is at the time that Antiochus IV dies and the Seleucids lose power over Judea. In other words, it is not the tribulation period but after it that the Son of Man (i.e., Israel and its Messiah) "comes" (i.e., receives the authority of the kingdom). The same can be said in the Book of Revelation, where it is only after the tribulation caused by the beast and the destruction of Rome that the Son of Man comes to claim His kingdom. Likewise, each instance of the Olivet Discourse states that the Son of Man comes after the tribulation, not during it (Mark 13:24–26; Matt 24:29–30). Mark states that the Son will come in the clouds *en ekeinais tais hēmerais meta tēn thlipsin ekeinēn* "in those days, after that tribulation" (v. 24), the signs in the skies will take place and *tote* "then," "at that time," they will see the Son of Man coming in the clouds with great power and glory (v. 26). Matthew states that it will be *eutheōs de meta tēn thlipsin tōn hēmerōn ekeinōn* "immediately after the tribulation of those days" that the signs in the skies will appear (v. 29:29) and *tote* "then," "at that time" they will see the Son of Man coming upon the clouds of heaven with great power and glory (v. 30). Luke is more ambiguous in terms of the timeframe, merely stating at the end of his description of the city's destruction that there will be signs in the heavens and *tote* "at that time," or "then," referring to when the signs in the skies would take place (vv. 25–26), they will see the Son of Man coming in the clouds with great power and glory (v. 27). The placement, even by Luke, indicates that this is something that comes in the end, after the destruction has already taken place, and the parallel between the other two accounts confirms this.

What this means is that the coming of the Son of Man is not parallel to the destruction of Jerusalem and the temple that is described as the time of trouble/the tribulation. The one event is not the other. The event of the Son's coming is *after* the event of the city's and the temple's destruction.[8] If,

---

8. This understanding destroys the common attempt to use Josephus' description that there were signs in the skies while Jerusalem was being sieged by the Romans to cohere to what Jesus says here. Jesus is not talking about something that happens during the tribulation of the city and the temple's destruction but, as in other texts,

therefore, the coming is not the destruction of Jerusalem, what is it? I would argue that the reason why the coming of the Son of Man in the Book of Daniel, the resurrection, the reception of all of the kingdoms of the earth, etc., parallel, not the destruction wreaked by Antiochus IV, but instead his death, is because it is the description of the macrocosmic victory of those things that is tacked onto the microcosmic event of his demise. I would argue that the description of the macrocosmic event in the Olivet discourse is being tacked onto the microcosmic one (i.e., the destruction of Jerusalem), just as the coming of the Son of Man, the resurrection, reception of all the kingdoms of the earth, etc., in the Book of Daniel do not parallel the destruction wreaked by Antiochus IV but instead occur at or after his death. I would also argue, therefore, that all of those things are placed on the heels of the tribulation in the Olivet Discourse not because they refer to the tribulation and destruction of Jerusalem but because they represent the macrocosmic event that is placed onto the end of the microcosmic in the same way as the Book of Daniel.

This means, therefore, that the coming of the Son of Man in the Olivet Discourse is not the destruction of Jerusalem. It is placed immediately on the heels of that time to display the microcosmic event as a part of the macrocosmic event to come. This means that the Olivet Discourse is not *the* coming of Son of Man, but *a* type of coming of the Son of Man. The actual description of the Son's coming does not refer to something literally happening at that time, but instead language that describes the macrocosmic event is used to characterize the microcosmic victory of the Son over some of His enemies within the long process of obtaining His kingdom from them. The text cannot be used, therefore, to teach that the Second Coming of Christ was fulfilled in the destruction of Jerusalem as the two events are distinguished in the texts.

What is worse is that the average preterist will typically use the Olivet Discourse as the context for every other passage in the New Testament that uses the same language, drawing another false inference that if the same language is used then the same event is in view and displaying why context replacement is so deadly to the task of exegesis. It is often assumed that if the coming of the Son refers to the destruction of Jerusalem in the Olivet Discourse, then the coming of the Son must refer to that same event everywhere else it appears. If the stars fall, if the sun turns dark, or the moon turns to blood, etc., in one passage, it must refer to the same event in another. Of course, even Preterists must admit that the Bible uses this language for a variety of events. This exegetical fallacy is similar to the word study fallacy

---

something that occurs after it.

that confuses the unmarked meaning of a word with contextual reference. The same words can be used to refer to different things in different contexts precisely because words do not always refer to the same thing. Likewise, the language of royal reception/exaltation, i.e., the Son of Man's receiving of the kingdom, cannot be assumed to refer to the same event either.

Chapter 4

Three Arguments That Clarify the Nature of Biblical Eschatology

It is at this point that one must ask whether there really is any macrocosmic event at all. Perhaps, one might suggest, as the preterists do, that the macrocosmic language is merely hyperbolic and does not point to any major upheaval of the fallen world and installation of a new world in the future at all. The coming of the Son in the Olivet Discourse, therefore, does not refer to anything in the future. The question for the preterist then becomes whether the Olivet Discourse's description of the destruction of Jerusalem in A.D. 70 is the "macrocosmic" event itself or simply one of a number of microcosmic events with which the macrocosmic event is joined together.

This is partly answered in the discussion of Chapter 3 by understanding that the Synoptics distinguish the coming of the Son from the destruction of Jerusalem, so that the two must refer to different events. However, there are other ways to address this issue. As I have argued, the time indicator passages, as they are often called, cannot be the texts used to determine which type of event is being referenced simply because they either (A) refer to the destruction of Jerusalem and do not tell us whether it is the macrocosmic event or not, (B) refer to completely different events than the destruction of Jerusalem, or (C) are not time indicators as many Preterists have mistakenly thought (as I will argue). What this means is that it is the so-called nature passages that function as the key to understanding whether the events of A.D. 70 refer to the macrocosmic event or whether the destruction of

Jerusalem is another important microcosmic event that, in a smaller way, functioned as a taste of what is to come.

Hence, this is where a discussion of the nature of the resurrection, the nature of the gospel itself, the nature of Christ's return, the eternal state, etc., comes into play as vital in understanding whether A.D. 70 is the end or merely a precursor to it. Carefully studying what these "nature" texts say about these subjects will indicate to the interpreter what eschatology the Bible is truly teaching. Harden's statement that "time determines and defines nature of fulfillment"[1] is completely backward and evidences an oversimplification in this understanding of the passages. Time passages cannot limit the nature of the events since there is more than one event at play.

However, it is not merely in the nature passages that one is able to answer the question of when and how these events occur. It is also in the fact that the macrocosmic event is described independently of microcosmic events, so that it becomes clear that it is a standalone event itself.

A further contributing factor to this discussion is an understanding concerning what views were held by most Second Temple Jews at the time so one can understand what the contemporary audience would have understood by this language. If the most popular literature to be found in Second Temple Judaism holds a belief in a literal macrocosmic event that will remove the wicked from the face of the earth, cleanse God's creation, establish the righteous forever upon the earth via resurrection, and have the Davidic king rule forever upon the earth as his kingdom, then the meanings in the cultural context would dictate that the "unmarked meanings" of all this language, when used in the New Testament, should be assumed unless context makes it clear that it is being altered from its unmarked meaning.

Hence, we will turn now to discuss these three questions: (1) What do these nature statements mean in the popular literature of Second Temple Judaism? (2) What do the standalone passages that talk about the macrocosmic event contribute to the discussion? (3) What is the nature of the macrocosmic event and the elements that make it up?

The Macrocosmic Event in Second Temple Judaism as the Unmarked Meaning of Eschatological Speech

As discussed previously, words have unmarked meanings and when one uses these words, lacking within the context any indication that those meanings are being used of different referents, the unmarked meanings should be

---

1. Harden, *Overcoming*, 20.

assumed. For instance, if Second Temple Jewish people have a particular common understanding of what the resurrection is, what the new heavens and earth may be, where the Messiah will rule, etc., those referents should be assumed by the modern reader of their literature unless the context indicates that new referents are being supplied. I would argue that no such new referents are supplied for these things, and therefore, the New Testament, in the context of Second Temple Jewish literature, is relating the same principles as that literature does when it references those specific words and concepts. The following are just a few key ideas that have an almost uniform cultural understanding in regards to the nature of what is being referred to when these concepts are referenced.

All the Wicked and their Evil Will Be Eradicated from the Earth through a Violent Act of God

1QH 11:29–32 states that "the torrents of Belial shall reach to all sides of the world. In all their channels a consuming fire shall destroy . . . and shall consume the foundations of the earth and the expanse of dry land. The bases of the mountains shall blaze and the roots of the rocks shall turn to torrents of pitch. It shall consume as far as the great abyss. The torrents of Belial shall burst into Abaddon."

This is likely an affirmation of the teaching found in 1 Enoch, which describes the earth melting in fire.

> And the high mountains will be shaken,
> And the high hills will be made low,
> And will melt like wax in front of the flame
> And the earth will be completely torn apart,
> And everything that exists upon the earth will perish.
> And there will be a judgment of all mankind.

The Ages in Second Temple Judaism

As one reads through Second Temple literature, it becomes clear that a two-worlds view emerges as the primary paradigm through which that literature views all life. There is this world, or age/ages, which is/are characterized by poverty, sickness, oppression, corruption, and death, and there is the world, or age/ages to come, which is/are characterized by prosperity, physical health, power, incorruptibility, resurrection, and eternal life upon the earth. This world and the world to come is often described as multiple ages but can be described as a singular age that characterizes the fallen, wicked world versus the fully restored, completely righteous world to come (Matt 13:24–30, 36–43; Mark 3:28–30; 10:30; Luke 20:34–36; Eph 1:21; Col 2:14; Titus 2:11–13).

In this sense, the idea that there are two ages in Jewish thought is true. However, the contrast of ages is not between two ages where the presence of poverty, sickness, oppression, and death reside therein together but rather one age in which these things exist and one in which they do not.[2]

The Apocalypse of Abraham speaks of "this ungodly age to rule among the heathen and in thy seed; and until the end of the times it shall be as thou sawest" (29). This age is characterized by ungodliness where heathens rule until the end of the times.

4 Ezra 15.11 states that there are twelve divisions to what is called "the world-age."

The cloud and water vision in the Apocalypse of Baruch[3] also divides up the age. The present age is the age of ungodliness, where the rule of evil exists (cf. 1 Enoch xlviii. 7, which describes this world as the "the world of unrighteousness" and 4 Ezra iv. 29, which describes a corrupt world and corrupt nature even in believers until the end of this age.)

> If therefore that which has been sown is not reaped, and if the place where the evil has been sown does not pass away, the field where the good has been sown will not come. For a grain of evil seed was sown in Adam's heart from the beginning, and how much ungodliness it has produced until now, and will produce until the time of threshing comes! Consider now for yourself how much fruit of ungodliness a grain of evil seed has produced. When heads of grain without number are sown, how great a threshing floor they will fill!" Then I answered and said, "How long and when will these things be? Why are our years few and evil?" He answered me and said, "You do not hasten faster than the Most High, for your haste is for yourself, but the Highest hastens on behalf of many. Did not the souls of the righteous in their chambers ask about these matters, saying, 'How long are we to remain here? And when will come the harvest of our reward? And Jeremiel the archangel answered them and said, 'When the number of those like yourselves is completed; for he has weighed the age in the balance, and measured the times

---

2. When Paul refers to "this present evil age," he is referring to the age where the evil described above still thrives. ". . . Our Lord Jesus Christ, who gave himself for our sins to rescue us from this present evil age according to the will of our God and Father" (Gal 1:3–4).

3. liii.f

by measure, and numbered the times by number; and he will not move or arouse them until that measure is fulfilled.'" Then I answered and said, "O sovereign Lord, but all of us also are full of ungodliness. And it is perhaps on account of us that the time of threshing is delayed for the righteous — on account of the sins of those who dwell on earth" (4:29-39).

G. H. Box comments that Second Temple texts look toward the age of righteousness when all wickedness, including the wiping away of all evil inside each believer, as a coming age hastened by the Fall of Jerusalem that will end with the judgment of the world since there was no more light in the world preventing it.

> Ap. Bar. xx. 2 ("Therefore have I now taken away Sion in order that I may the more speedily visit the world in its season"). In the latter passage the fall of Jerusalem is regarded as hastening the End. Impatient longing for the End is characteristic of the Apocalyptists; see g. 4 Ezra iv. 33 ff.8 The coming Age is the "Age of the righteous" (for the expression cf. also chap. xvii. of our Book); it has been "prepared" for them (4 Ezra viii. 52), and they will inherit it (4 Ezra vii. 17). For the metaphor of growth in this connexion cf. 4 Ezra iv. 29, 35; the community of the righteous has already been "sown" (1 Enoch lxii. 8; cf. also 1 Enoch x. 16, "the plant of righteousness will appear"), but its full growth will only become visible after the judgement.[4]

Of course, from a Christian perspective, Zion was not destroyed, and the light remains in the world through the church. However, the point is that the age to come is after the judgment and removal of all chaos/evil in the world, including within believers themselves.

For instance, when Jesus speaks to the Sadducees about the age to come, He parallels that age with that of the physical resurrection where former husbands and wives receive back their bodies and, thus, create the problem of the one flesh union to which the Sadducees are objecting. Christ argues that there is no marriage in the age to come, so this does not create the problem the Sadducees are suggesting.

Luke 20:27-36 records Luke's version of the account.

> Some of the Sadducees, who say there is no resurrection, came to Jesus with a question. "Teacher," they said, "Moses wrote for us that if a man's brother dies and leaves a wife but no children, the man must marry the widow and raise up offspring for his brother. Now there were seven brothers. The first one married

---

4. Box, *The Apocalypse of Abraham*, 80.

a woman and died childless. The second and then the third married her, and in the same way the seven died, leaving no children. Finally, the woman died too. Now then, at the resurrection whose wife will she be, since the seven were married to her?" Jesus replied, "The people of this age marry and are given in marriage. But those who are considered worthy of taking part in the age to come and in the resurrection from the dead will neither marry nor be given in marriage, and they can no longer die; for they are like the angels. They are God's children, since they are children of the resurrection.

Notice that Jesus refers to "this age" in contrast to "the age to come" and refers to the time characterized as being "in the resurrection" as the age of the physical resurrection where those once married will be given their bodies back so as to create a potential problem if these people are still in a covenantal one flesh union in marriage. And what is done in this age as opposed to the age to come? People marry and are given in marriage. What is not done in the age to come? People marrying and being given in marriage. This avoids the objection the Sadducees have to a bodily resurrection from the dead. If bringing back the body brings back the one flesh union and marriage commitment thereof, then the brothers and woman in question would be committing adultery and incest according to Levitical law. However, if all unions are considered null and void in the resurrection because there is no such thing as marriage in that age, then the objection fails. Hence, the age to come is talking about the age where the physical bodies of people are brought back to life, and if marriage unions were still intact in that age to come, the resurrection would reconstitute the union. However, since that age is not the current age where marriage is still practiced, but rather the future age when marriage is no more, there is no possibility of adultery or incest taking place.

Likewise, the age is characterized as a time when the children of God will not be able to die, and instead, have become immortal like the angels. If death is no longer the experience of the children of God in the age to come, the age of the resurrection, then "the age to come" cannot describe this current age where death is still experienced, and the bodies of believers are still mortal.

This all means that the two ages here are not referencing an old covenant age and new covenant age, both existing in a world where marriage is still taking place, but instead exist as two contrasting ages where one is described by the things that are still done to this day, and one describes a state that has not yet come to be.

The Eternal, Earthly Reign of the Davidic King upon His Throne

The key to the restoration of the world was the return of the Davidic throne to Jerusalem. Through it, the seed of David would reign over all the other nations, end chaos in the world, and bring everlasting order to the created cosmos. Hence, the Second Temple expectation of the Messiah was an expectation of peace, not merely beyond, but within the physical creation.

It should be understood, therefore, that all of the biblical and postbiblical texts that talk about the Messiah ruling over the nations are referencing an earthly imperial power. In other words, the Messiah will be the emperor upon the earth. God already rules, and has ruled, over the nations from heaven, i.e., the invisible realm, but the promise given to David's seed is that he will rule over the nations from his throne, which is the earthly throne of Israel. His rule will be eternally from David's throne in Jerusalem/Zion, not from heaven. To say that Jesus merely rules from heaven over the nations is to miss the point of this union between heaven and earth that is promised in the Davidic covenant.[5] In essence, this misunderstanding implies that David's heir is not needed since God already rules over the world from heaven and has from the very beginning of time. In actuality, the point is that He will also rule over the earth from an earthly throne via His Messiah, thus bringing heaven and earth together.[6] The Messiah's current rule (Acts 2:34–35) is temporary while He establishes His kingdom through the preaching of the gospel and through His judgment of the world (1 Cor 15:24–26; Heb 1:13; Rev 6; 8–9).

Hence, when the Septuagint (LXX) of Isaiah 11:10 translates the text as, "And there shall be in that day the root of Jesse, even he who arises to rule over nations," a text applied to Jesus by Paul (Rom 15:12), it refers to His inheritance of David's earthly throne in fulfillment of the promise given to him. Jesus will rule the nations with an iron rod (Rev 12:5), i.e., an imperishable rule, as opposed to other earthly kings who will only rule on earth

---

5. One of the many passages that display this idea is 1 Chronicles 17:10–14 where the house of David and the house of God are united as one kingdom. The throne of David is the throne of God upon the earth. The seed of David, therefore, rules over the nations as the king who represents God upon the earth. Also cf. Ps 122; 132; Isa 9:6–7; 16:4–5; Luke 1:31–35.

6. Isa 11; 16:4–5; Jer. 23:3–8; 30:8–9; 33:15; Amos 9:11; Micah 5:1–9; Zech 13:1–3. These texts argue that it is all of the wicked who are removed from the land when the Davidic king rules upon the earth over the other nations and restores the rightful order to creation. There is no indication that He rules from heaven but instead restores the throne and dominion of David upon the earth.

for a time. Broyles argues that the exiles expected that God would keep His promises and give them a king upon the earthly throne to take David's place.

> The final collection and editing of the book of Psalms, or the Psalter, was done in the postexilic period when Judah had no Davidic monarchy under the Persian Empire. Why then were these royal psalms retained? It is doubtful the editors kept them simply as historical artifacts in a collection of liturgical and meditative songs and prayers. The most likely explanation is that they retained value because even before the Common Era they bore the hope of a new David. This transfer of referent — from the past Davidic kings to a future Davidic "Messiah" — was probably engendered by the Hebrew prophets. Prophecies contained in Isaiah (9:6-7; 11:1-5), Micah (5:2-5a), Jeremiah (23:5-6), Ezekiel (34:23-24; 37:24-28), and Zechariah (9:9-10) took up the language of the royal psalms and of the Davidic court and promised a new David, in view of the repeated failures of David's sons.[7]

David C. Mitchell argues that the "LXX, when faced with a choice between cultic or eschatological interpretation, adopts the latter, suggesting its translators interpreted Psalms eschatologically."[8] Hence, it was believed that many of the Psalms that speak about the messianic king are ultimately references not to David but to the Messiah to come. This is an important point as the messianic king in the Psalms is given the nations as his inheritance and rules from the Davidic throne upon the earth. He is the greatest among the kings of the earth (89:27; 18:43, 49), whose power will be over the sea and the rivers (89:25; 72:8). He will sit upon the throne of David, a throne which is established in the physical city of Jerusalem/Zion forever (132:13-18), by subduing all his enemies and crushing all other thrones and kingdoms that exist in the entire world (18:43-45; 72:9-11; 110:6).

The first century Jewish historian Josephus relates a common view among Jews of his day that an oracle promised that "one from their country would become ruler of the world" (The Jewish War, 6.312-313; cf. 3.400-402). God already rules the world from heaven, but what Jews meant by this was that one would come from them who would rule the whole world from a throne upon the earth. There would be no rival power left upon the earth; the Messiah would be emperor.[9]

---

7. Broyles, "The Redeeming King, 24.
8. Mitchell, *The Message of the Psalter,* 19.
9. Oddly enough, the ever-sycophantic Josephus applies this to Vespasian.

The Righteous Will Inherit the Earth

Jews understood that, when their king returned, the righteous would rule with him over the physical world. David Moffitt concludes that the age to which the Second Temple Jew was looking was "a reference to an eschatological age in which those who were faithful to the covenant would obtain not only the land, but the whole world."[10] (87)

> A survey of this literature will also show that some Jews explicitly linked their hope in a coming realm/age with the promise of receiving Israel's inheritance. As such, they did not appear to envision a spiritual/material dichotomy. Rather, the fundamental hope expressed in these texts is that of the inheritance of a renewed, incorruptible world."[11]

This elevation of Adam's sons will correspond with some kind of renewal described with images that suggest an Edenic state that encompasses the entire world.[12]

The Qumran Scrolls bear this out as well.

> And [the sons of righteous]ness shall shine *to all the furthest regions of the world*, they shall go on shining, up to the furthest reaches of the times of darkness; and in the time of God, his exalted greatness will shine for all the et[ernal] times, for peace and blessing, glory and joy, and length of days for all the sons of light." (1QM 8–9a; emphasis added)

The idea that the righteous will inherit the earth, not the wicked, is a stock view in the Bible and Second Temple Judaism. It is "the congregation of his chosen ones who carry out his will" (4QpPsa 2:5) who Ps 37:9 says will inherit the land/earth (cf. 4QpPsa 2:4). 4QpPsa 2:7b–8 interprets Psalm 37:10 as bringing to an end "all the wickedness at the end of the forty years, for they will be completed and upon the earth no [wic]ked person will be found." The very next lines (2:9–12) clarify the meaning of the promise in Ps 37:11 that the poor will possess the land and enjoy peace by claiming, "Its interpretation concerns the congregation of the poor who will endure the period of the tribulation and will be rescued from all the snares of Belial. Afterwards, all who shall po[sse]ss the land will enjoy and grow fat with everything enjoy[able to] the flesh."

---

10. Moffitt, *Atonement and the Logic of Resurrection*, 87.
11. Moffitt, *Atonement and the Logic of Resurrection*, 82.
12. Moffitt, *Atonement and the Logic of Resurrection*, 87.

Moffitt also argues that the phrase "all the inheritance of Adam" found in Qumran literature refers to the entire earth.[13]

> "The period of the wilderness wandering can be used as an eschatological metaphor for the penultimate age. The "last days" can be described in terms of the testing during the time of wandering that sorted out those who would go into the land. Significantly too, enduring the time of testing is identified with doing the will of God. Those who do God's will receive the inheritance of the eschatological promised land."[14]

> God descends to live with His people upon the earth for eternity (Jubilees 1:26).
> [T]he time of the new creation when the heavens, the earth, and all their creatures will be renewed like the powers of the sky and like all the creatures of the earth, until the time when the temple of the Lord will be created in Jerusalem on Mt. Zion. All the luminaries will be renewed for (the purposes of) healing, health, and blessing for all the elect ones of Israel and so that it may remain this way from that time throughout all the days of the earth. (1:29)
> First, at the center of this vision of the future lies the restoration of the people of Israel to the land God promised to them. A day is coming after their expulsion from the land of promise in which they will be regathered. At that time God will purify the people and create for them a holy spirit such that they will never again forsake the commandments. Along with this restoration and purification, God will descend and dwell permanently among his people in an eternal sanctuary. Second, this restoration is by no means limited only to the promised land of Canaan. In fact, the future redemption of Israel will correspond to a complete renewal of the world. The first creation and all of its creatures will be in some way transformed in accordance with the powers of heaven and the whole nature of the earth (1:29). The imagery is difficult to interpret but given the promise of the creation of a holy spirit for God's people in 1:23, it seems likely that the renewal of creation in accord with the powers of heaven entails some new unity between God and the created realm. The promise that God will descend and dwell with his people eternally in an enduring sanctuary coheres well with this assumption. The renewal of all things appears to be one in

---

13. Moffitt, *Atonement and the Logic of Resurrection*, 88–89.
14. Moffitt, *Atonement and the Logic of Resurrection*, 90.

which the created realm becomes like the heavenly realms— a fit place for the eternal, pure, and holy God to dwell."[15]

Jubilees makes this explicit.

> I am the Lord who created heaven and earth. I will increase your numbers and multiply you very much. Kings will come from you, and they will rule wherever mankind has set foot. I will give your descendants all of the land that is beneath the sky. They will rule over all the nations just as they wish. Afterwards, they will gain the entire earth, and they will possess it forever." (Jub 32:18–19)

4Q475, also known as *4QRenewed Earth*, is a fragmented text, but there is enough there to get the picture of what is presented of the new earth.

> [. . .] . . . in their midst, and he will tell them all [. . .] [. . . al]l the world, and there will be no more guilty deeds on the earth and not [. . .] [. . . destr]oyer, and every adversary; and all the world will be like Eden, and all [. . .] [. . . and] the earth will be at peace for ever, and . . . [. . .] . . . [. . .] [. . .] beloved son, and he will let him inherit it all, and [. . .]"

In 1 Enoch, the eternal state is an earthly existence.

> But for the elect there shall be light and joy and peace,
> And they shall inherit the earth.
> And then there shall be bestowed upon the elect wisdom,
> And they shall all live and never again sin,
> Either through ungodliness or through pride:
> But they who are wise shall be humble.
> And they shall not again transgress,
> Nor shall they sin all the days of their life,
> Nor shall they die of the divine anger or wrath,
> But they shall complete the number of the days of their life.
> And their lives shall be increased in peace,
> And the years of their joy shall be multiplied,
> In eternal gladness and peace,
> All the days of their life." (5:6–9)

---

15. Moffitt, *Atonement and the Logic of Resurrection*, 93.

The End of All Evil upon the Earth

What makes up the age to come is not merely inner peace or some sort of mystical spirituality but a complete (physical and non-physical) transformation of the cosmos and those who dwell within it. Anyone who was not transformed would be excluded from it. This means that all evil will be abolished from the earth in the coming age.

In 1QS 4:18, it states: "God, in the mysteries of his knowledge and in the wisdom of his glory, has determined an end to the existence of injustice and on the occasion of his visitation he will obliterate it forever" (1QS 4:18–19). 1 Q4M states that God "has gathered the assembly of the nations for destruction with no remnant." Likewise, 4Q475 speaks of a time when "there will be no more guilty deeds upon the earth" and indicates that the destroyer and adversary will no longer cause turmoil in it.

In 1 Enoch, the picture of eternity is one where the wicked have been completely removed from the earth.

> And he [i.e., the Son of Man] sat on his glorious throne,
> And total judgment was given to the Son of Man,
> And he caused the sinners to pass away and be destroyed from off the face of the earth,
> And those who led the world astray,
> They will be bound with chains,
> And according to their degrees of corruption they will be imprisoned,
> And all their works will vanish from the face of the earth.
> And from that time forward there will be nothing corruptible,
> For that Son of Man has appeared,
> And has seated himself on his glorious throne,
> And all evil will pass away before his face . . . (69:27–29)

George Ladd states that the passages in Enoch relate a restoration of physical creation that removes the chaotic elements and agents from therein.

> These passages anticipate the day of judgment which will restore the divinely intended order to the world. Sinners will be destroyed while the righteous enter into larger blessings, which are described in terms both of human happiness and spiritual well-being. The setting of this happy scene is the *earth*, where men will thereafter round out the full number of their days in perfect enjoyment of the blessings of God. This is a picture of Eden restored.[16]

---

16. Ladd, *The Kingdom of God in 1 Enoch*, 34.

Resurrection and the Inheritance of the Earth

Obviously, if the people of God are going to inherit the physical world, they must return physically to do so. Hence, Second Jewish literature has much to say about the physical, bodily resurrection as the hope of Israel.

N. T. Wright summarizes Cavallin's study of passages that have been translated in the Old Greek version in a manner that teaches about the resurrection.

> ... he notes the striking way in which the LXX has reversed the sense of Job 14.14; instead of a blank denial of a future life ('if a man die, shall he live again?'), the LXX declares boldly, 'If a man dies, he shall live' (*ean apothane anthropos, zesetai*). In the same way, the deeply obscure passage Job 19.26a ('after my skin has been thus destroyed') has been turned around: God 'will resurrect my skin' (*anastesai to derma mou*). Finally, the LXX adds a postscript to the book. After 42.17, where Job dies, an old man and full of days, it adds (42.17a LXX): 'It is written of him that he will rise again with those whom the Lord will raise' (*gegraptai de auton palin anastesesthai meth' hon ho kyrios anistesin*). Clearly, whoever drafted the translation of LXX Job had no doubt both of the bodily resurrection and of the propriety of making sure the biblical text affirmed it ... In Zephaniah 3.8, YHWH instructs his people to wait for him, for the day when he arises as a witness, gathering the nations for judgment. In the LXX this comes out as the summons to wait 'for the day of my resurrection (*eis hemeran anastaseos mou*) for witness'... All the indications are that those who translated the Septuagint, and those who read it thereafter (i.e., most Jews, in both Palestine and the Diaspora), would have understood the key Old Testament passages in terms of a more definite 'resurrection' sense than the Hebrew would necessarily warrant, and might very likely have heard overtones of 'resurrection' in many places where the Hebrew would not have suggested it."[17]

In Fragment 2 of 4Q245, also known as 4Qpseudo-Daniel, a likely interpretation of Daniel 12, in way of application to Qumran history, is offered that explains that this period will see an extermination of wickedness. Peter W. Flint relates this idea and states that "the extermination of wickedness is clearly an eschatological theme."

> The biblical book of Daniel refers to two books that may be of relevance. Dan 12:1 promises that "at that time your people shall

---

17. Wright, *The Resurrection of the Son of God*, 149–50.

be delivered, everyone who is found written in the book." This is the "Book of Life," which contains the names of those destined for deliverance at the resurrection. Dan 10:21 mentions a second kind of book: "the Book of Truth," whose contents are disclosed to Daniel by the angel Gabriel. These contents turn out to be a survey of Hellenistic history, culminating in the death of Antiochus Epiphanes and the resurrection of the dead. This provides a more promising analogy for the book in 4Q245, insofar as the list of priests and kings in lines 5–13 also constitutes a survey of history.[18]

Although Flint himself does not see the resurrection in the descriptions of those who "then will arise" and "will return," as do other commentators, it is difficult to imagine that these statements simply concern walking in the way of truth when the timing seems to parallel Daniel 11–12, as Flint suggests, and it is at that time when wickedness is exterminated. Furthermore, the very hope of Daniel is Israel's possession of the earth that is currently ruled by other nations. This promise would mean little to those dying at the hands of Antiochus IV unless there was a promise to bring back those who have died so that they might partake in the promise.

This idea is exactly what we see in the literature contemporary to Daniel. 2 Maccabees 7 tells the story of the torture and death of a woman and her seven sons under Antiochus IV. They were told to eat pork in violation of the law because Antiochus was attempting to wipe away their Jewish identity and devotion to YHWH, forcing them to become Zeus-worshiping Greeks instead. The text tells us that they refused and were tortured in the most brutal of ways and that they were willing to undergo this tribulation because of their hope that God would restore their lives and their bodies. Hence, of the second brother the text states, "With his last breath he said: 'You accursed wretch, you are depriving us of this present life, but the King of the universe will raise us up to live again forever, because we are dying for his laws'" (v. 9).

The text continues to evidence that this is a bodily resurrection to which the above statement refers by noting that the very body parts lost by the third brother will be restored.

After him the third suffered their cruel sport. He put forth his tongue at once when told to do so, and bravely stretched out his hands, as he spoke these noble words: "It was from Heaven that I received these; for the sake of his laws I disregard them; from him I hope to receive them again" (vv. 10–11).

---

18. Flint, *Eschatology, Messianism, and the Dead Sea Scrolls*, 52–53.

Likewise, the fourth brother states, "It is my choice to die at the hands of mortals with the hope that God will restore me to life; but for you, there will be no resurrection to life" (v. 14).

The mother herself encourages her sons to be faithful even in the face of such horrible deaths by reminding them that the God who made them is able to give them life again.

> "I do not know how you came to be in my womb; it was not I who gave you breath and life, nor was it I who arranged the elements from which you have been made. Therefore, since it is the Creator of the universe who shaped the beginning of humankind and brought about the origin of everything, He, in his mercy, will give you back both breath and life, because you now disregard yourselves for the sake of his law." (vv. 22–23)

Again, when finally speaking to her youngest son, she said,

> "I beg you, child, to look at the heavens and the earth and see all that is in them; then you will know that God did not make them out of existing things. In the same way humankind came into existence. Do not be afraid of this executioner, but be worthy of your brothers and accept death, so that in the time of mercy I may receive you again with your brothers." (vv. 28–29)

In 12:43–46, Judas Maccabeus takes up an offering to purchase sacrifices for fallen soldiers who had sinned. He did this because "he had the resurrection in mind; for if he were not expecting the fallen to rise again, it would have been superfluous and foolish to pray for the dead."

In 14:37–46, one of the elders in Jerusalem who is mortally wounded by Nicanor, throws his entrails into the crowd and calls "upon the Lord of life and of the spirit to give these back to him again" (v. 46).

Hence, resurrection is understood to be that of the very body and its parts that have died. In 2 Baruch 49–50, the nature of the resurrected body is described as the same body that died and was placed into the ground; and yet, it will be transformed and have the glory of the angels (51:5, 10), and of the resurrected it states that "time shall no longer age them" (v. 9).

> Nevertheless, I will again ask from you, O Mighty One, yea, I will ask the One who made all things. "In what shape will those live who live in Your day? Or how will the splendor of those who (are) after that time continue? Will they then resume this form of the present, and put on these entrammelling members, which are now involved in evils, and in which evils are consummated,

or will you perchance change these things which have been in the world as well as the world?"

And He answered and said unto me: "Hear, Baruch, this word, and write in the remembrance of your heart all that you shall learn. For the earth shall then assuredly restore the dead. It shall make no change in their form, but in the same form it has received them, so shall it restore them, and as I delivered them unto it, so also shall it raise them. For then it will be necessary to show the living that the dead have come to life again, and that those who had departed have returned. And it shall come to pass, when they have each in turn recognized those whom they presently know, then judgment shall grow strong, and those things which before were spoken of shall come about.

> And it shall come to pass, when that appointed day has gone by, that then shall the state of those who are condemned be afterwards changed, and the glory of those who are justified will be changed. For the state of those who now act wickedly shall become worse than it is, as they shall suffer torment. Also, the glory of those who have now been justified in My law, who have had understanding in their life, and who have planted in their heart the root of wisdom, then their splendor shall be glorified in changes, and the form of their face shall be turned into the light of their beauty, that they may be able to acquire and receive the world which does not die, which is then promised to them. For over this above all shall those who come then lament, that they rejected My law, and stopped their ears that they might not hear wisdom or receive understanding. 5 When therefore they see those, over whom they are now exalted, (but) who shall then be exalted and glorified more than they, they shall respectively be transformed, the latter into the splendor of angels, and the former will yet waste away all the more in astonishment at their appearances and in the beholding of the forms. For they shall first behold and afterwards depart to be tormented." (49:1–51:6)

It is clear, therefore, that such texts communicate the most popular idea concerning the resurrection: it is a bodily resurrection that transforms the mortal body into an immortal body that suits those who will inherit the physical world.

In the Apocalypse of Moses, Michael calms a weeping Seth by encouraging him with the resurrection.

> Seth, man of God, do not exhaust yourself with prayers and supplications concerning the tree which flows with oil to anoint

> your father Adam. For it does not belong to you now, but it will in the end of the times. Then shall *all flesh* be raised up from Adam till that great day, all that belongs to the holy people. Then the delights of paradise will be given to them and God will be in their midst. And they will no longer sin in His presence, for the evil mind will be taken from them and there will be given them a heart that understands good and obeys God only. (13:2–5)

1 Enoch envisions the physical return of the elect from the dead to dwell upon the earth forever.

> And in those days the earth will also give back that which has been entrusted to it,
> And the grave also will give back that which it has received,
> And the netherworld will give back that which it owes.
> For the Elect One will rise
> And he shall choose the righteous and holy from among them:
> For the day will have come that they should be saved
> And the Elect One shall in those days sit on My throne,
> And His mouth shall pour forth all the secrets of wisdom and counsel
> For the Lord of spirits has given to Him and glorified Him.
> And in those days the mountains will leap like rams,
> And the hills also will skip like lambs satisfied with milk,
> And the face of the angels in heaven will be lighted up with joy
> And the earth will rejoice,
> And the righteous will dwell upon it,
> And the elect will walk thereon. (51:1–5)

The Psalm of Solomon declares that "the ruin of the sinner is forever, and he shall not be remembered, when the righteous is visited. This is the portion of sinners forever. But they that fear the Lord shall rise to life eternal, and their life (shall be) in the light of the Lord, and shall come to an end no more." (13–16)

When referring to the eschatological expectations at Qumran, Moffitt argues that it is the remaining wickedness in the spirit of the righteous, and not their bodies, that will be removed in their purification so that their humanity will be reestablished.

> The refinement of the upright will involve their purification so that the portion of the wicked spirit that even they possess will be ripped out of the 'innermost part' of their flesh and their humanity will be reconstituted. (4:20–22a)[19]

---

19. Moffit, *Atonement*, 86

4Q385 2:5–10 is a literalized reworking of Ezekiel 37:4–10 that reads as follows:

> [And He said:] "Son of man, prophesy over the bones and speak and let them be j[oi]ned bone to its bone and joint [to its joint." And it wals so. And He said a second time: "Prophesy and let arteries come upon them and let skin cover them [from above." And it was so.] And He said: "Prophesy once again over the four winds of heaven and let them blow breath [into the slain." And it was so,] and a large crowd of people came [to li]fe and blessed the Lord Sebaoth wh[o] [had given them life. vacat And] I said: "O Lord! When shall these things come to be?" And the Lord said to m[e: "Until] (10) [after da]ys a tree shall bend and shall stand erect[ ].

Second Temple interpretation tended to make the national analogies in Scripture, like that of Ezekiel 37, into literal prophecies concerning the individual. This was due to the fact that God had promised Israel the earth in the Hebrew Bible. If the patriarchs and all their offspring are dead, however, the thinking was that they will never truly inherit the land God promised to them.

Likewise, the punishment of God throughout the Scripture is physical exile/physical death. Adam and Eve are removed from the garden on the day that they die (i.e., they go out from the created land to the chaotic and uncreated/uncultivated land). Cain must go out farther from his parents as a punishment, moving further into the realm of death. The wicked are removed from the earth in the flood. The unclean must go outside the camp, i.e., a symbol of the created order where God resides on earth with His people. Those who rebel against God's law must be removed from the camp via physical death. The Canaanites are removed from the land either via death or by being driven out. Israel is removed from the land in death and exile (typological examples of being removed from the physical, created order of the garden).[20] This is the penalty Jesus takes upon Himself. The wages of sin is death, so Jesus dies, not spiritually, which would be a heresy, but physically upon the cross. Hence, Paul states that "He condemned sin in the flesh, in order that the righteous penalty of the law might be fully met in us." Peter, likewise, declares, "and He Himself bore our sins in His body

---

20. This pattern of exile is true of the New Testament as well. In church discipline, the evil man is removed from among the congregation if excommunicated (Matt 18; 1 Cor 5). The wicked are removed from Jerusalem and exiled once again in the Roman siege of Jerusalem (Matt 24:39–41). Finally, all who follow the beast in Revelation will be removed from the earth, i.e., outside creation, at the final coming of Christ and restoration of all things (Rev 19–22).

on the cross, so that we might die to sin and live to righteousness; for by His wounds you were healed" (1 Pet 2:24). The punishment Christ endured is not spiritual. It is a physical removal from the created order, exiled from the world God made.[21]

Hence, if God were to permanently remove the patriarchs and their children from the land, it would be a condemnation of them, not a fulfillment of the promise. They would be receiving the same punishment that all the wicked receive, i.e., physical removal from God's created order.

Because of this, many in the Second Temple period saw the national resurrection passages as having significance for the individual as well. If God is to restore His people to the land, He will restore not just a collective body, but the individual bodies that make up the collective as well. Since Abraham and his children are promised the land, it must be given to them. God can, and does, give them more by causing them to inherit the whole earth (Matt 5:5; Rev 5:9–10). The context of Ezekiel 37, even though referring to a time after the exile, may indicate an eschatological resurrection that is far more literal than many scholars give it credit for. In the same passage, an Edenic paradise is created wherein the righteous dwell, and this language is likely a case of the microcosmic/macrocosmic element coming into play more than simple hyperbole.

---

21. What this means is that the spiritual problem man has, i.e., he is not reconciled to a holy God, is due to the fact that man is under sin (both Adam's and his own as a result) and has not paid the penalty for that sin, which is the physical removal from the created order, nor has he obtained the righteousness of God to dwell with Him for eternity through perfect obedience. Since God will dwell with His people within the created order, that is the new heavens and new earth that come together as an eternal created order, the wicked cannot dwell there. Hence, the spiritual problem of man is that he is under sin and has no way of reconciling to God in order to stay in, or even go back to, the created order. Christ's life and physical death on the cross accomplishes all of this. He has paid the punishment of being removed from the created order for all those who belong to Him, and He has also obtained the necessary perfection needed to dwell with God for eternity through His perfect obedience. Hence, once He dies, He can go immediately back into the created order through the resurrection. Such is not the case for the wicked outside of Him, who neither are covered by His taking upon Himself the penalty of the law, i.e., physical death, nor have they obtained the necessary perfection to return and dwell with God in His new creation once they have died. Hence, they must go out of the created order, cannot dwell in the realm of God, and must go to an unordered, uncreated, chaotic realm that has been prepared for the devil and his angels, that we call "hell." Hence, Christ does not need to pay for hell by going to hell or experiencing hell on the cross. The penalty is not hell, which is the result of man being neither reconciled to God nor in perfect harmony with His holiness. The penalty of the law, therefore, is the physical removal of the individual from the land of the living via physical death. If those who are "saved" never reenter the physical cosmos, they were never saved at all.

Therefore, even though there are a couple of exceptions (e.g., Hellenistic Jews, like the Sadducees or Philo, influenced by Greek ideas of naturalism and Platonic dualism), the vast majority of Jewish thought looked forward to the hope of a physical resurrection in a renewed creation, where the wicked, not the righteous, were removed from the created order.

Hence, the LXX scriptures that were often used by the apostles and Jewish believers and exclusively used by the Gentile believers, much of the apocryphal and pseudepigraphical writings that were heavily read by the apostles and their audience, and the Qumran community, which shared many similar ideas taught by the New Testament, provide the context for us to understand what would become the unmarked meaning of these terms and phrases for this religious body of believers. This does not automatically mean that the New Testament adopts the unmarked meaning of these terms, but it does mean that if there is no further context given to distinguish a new meaning from the unmarked meaning of the culture, the unmarked meaning is to be assumed.

This evidences that the unmarked meaning of the term "resurrection," especially in the context of ultimate salvation, is to be understood to mean a physical, bodily resurrection. The destruction and subsequent restoration of heaven and earth would have referred to the unmarked meaning of God's renewal of the physical cosmos. The eternal reign of David's seed upon the earth would have been understood as the physical reign of the Messiah upon the renewed earth. These phrases and allusions would have meant something very literal to the original audience. Although one can argue that they were wrong, what he or she must do is show that the contexts in which these ideas are presented in the New Testament make explicit breaks from the culturally accepted, unmarked meanings that these ideas conveyed to a Second Temple audience. Therefore, he would have to prove that what these ideas meant to the apostles and their first century audience is the opposite of what they meant to everyone else in that culture.

One of the problems with preterism is that it assumes that the context of the New Testament is the Old Testament as it is being objectively interpreted by *the individual preterist*. The context of the New Testament, however, is *Second Temple Judaism's* interpretations of the Old Testament as the apostles applied the teaching of Jesus in that context. Therefore, one cannot simply jump over Second Temple Jewish literature and go straight to the Old Testament as though *his* reading of the Old Testament will lead him to a right understanding of the New Testament context and what the apostles and their readers assumed. This is not to say that all Second Temple interpretations are standard without variation; but it is to say that within the larger worldview of the types of Judaism from which Christianity adopts its language, the unmarked meaning of these ideas should be assumed unless the individual contexts of the New Testament make it explicitly clear that they are being altered to refer to very different things. This means that the primary question to ask when one attempts to identify the cultural context of the New Testament is not what the imagery of resurrection, new heavens and earth, etc., mean in their original Old Testament context but rather what they meant to the audience that lived during the Second Temple Period, i.e., during the time of the New Testament.[22]

Hence, the New Testament believer is not told that he will live in some ethereal existence in heaven but rather that he will "inherit the earth" (Matt 5:5) and "rule upon the earth" (Rev 5:10). Indeed, the picture of Revelation 21 is that God's dwelling comes down out of heaven and situates itself upon the earth once all chaos (e.g., death, sorrow, pain) has been removed from the physical order, as they have passed away. The wicked are then confined to the lake of fire beyond the created order. The preterist can assign "spiritual" meanings to each of these, but the real question is whether the original readers would have done the same. It seems rather clear that they would not have adopted the assumptions of the modern preterist about these phrases unless prompted by the literary contexts themselves to change their referents to mean the opposite of what they literally meant in the larger cultural context.

Instead, when the language of a new heaven and new earth appear in the New Testament, it is without any clear indication that the meanings have been changed from what they normally meant in the Second Temple context. The only added element in the New Testament is not a rejection of the literal fulfillment of these things but that, in light of the concept of the "already-not yet" theology of the New Testament, each has been, and is being, fulfilled spiritually first before the physical fulfillment is brought about in the end. Likewise, when the inheritance of the earth, or the throne of David appear in the New Testament, they seem to retain the same meaning as that found within the literature surveyed above. Finally, when it comes to the literature on resurrection, the New Testament evidences that it means exactly what the literature above means. Paul himself even tells the Pharisees that he holds the same hope of the resurrection that they do, and he does not indicate that he means something different by it than they do. Likewise, it is clear that the Sadducees take issue with the physical resurrection that Christ is teaching in Matthew 22:24–32. If He were teaching a spiritual resurrection, or a resurrection of a completely different body, their challenge to him would make

---

22. It is quite ironic that Preterists will often charge others to read the New Testament in terms of how its original audience would have understood it ("audience relevance"), and yet, it is the preterist who continually reads in accordance with his or her eschatological paradigm and not that of the original audience.

absolutely no sense; but in the context of the Second Temple Jewish idea of physical resurrection, it becomes a clever objection.

In summary, therefore, to understand the most popular eschatological views in the cultural context is to get inside the head of the religious audience of the New Testament world that would have read and understood these concepts in very literal ways. To allegorize them, ironically, as some Preterists do, is to read them in the light of a different worldview (e.g., a pagan/gnostic one). If anything, the Second Temple literature in Judea evidences a far more literal, rather than spiritual or allegorical, approach to these concepts, and there is no attempt made by the New Testament authors to differentiate their understanding of these ideas from those within the larger culture other than to say that Jesus and His work is at the center of it all and that there is a spiritual fulfillment that precedes the physical (i.e., a cleansing of the inside of the cup before one cleanses the outside). What this means is that the unmarked meaning of these words and their concepts should be assumed when the New Testament uses the same terminology unless the context clearly indicates otherwise.

The Macrocosmic Event in the New Testament Standalone Passages

Another reason the Olivet Discourse is not the final *parousia* is due to the fact that the macrocosmic event is spoken of independently of the destruction of Jerusalem. Aside from the fact that the resurrection is mentioned in numerous places without any mention of a microcosmic event in the context (e.g., John 5:28–29; Rom 8:11–30; 1 Cor 15; Phil 3:20–21; 1 Thes 4), there is also mention in many passages of the coming of Christ in the clouds, the end of this fallen world and the wicked, the Son's reception of the kingdom from the Father, etc., without any microcosmic event in view. These texts were presumably meant in their contexts to be taken as elements of the macrocosmic event in the future as there is no microcosmic event in view that would allow the interpreter to conclude that the language of the macrocosmic event was merely hyperbolic, an exaggerated description of some socio-political event in the context, without any anchor in a larger macrocosmic event to come. Instead, the existence of these standalone passages indicates that the events described are self-referential rather than referencing some other event in the context. Hence, utilizing good hermeneutics by only taking from a text what the text itself offers to the reader, and not reading into it another context in order to replace the one offered, will serve the interpreter well in that he will be able to hear what the text, in its own right, is saying.

1 Corinthians 15

As discussed before, the passages that describe the nature of macrocosmic events become very important due to the fact that if they relate the nature of the final event in such a way as to indicate it could not have possibly happened yet, then limiting the event by a "time text" to a singular microcosmic event is faulty.

The nature of the resurrection of the dead becomes a crucial issue since if the resurrection has not yet occurred, then the second coming in the macrocosmic/ultimate sense has not occurred yet either. Many passages in the New Testament speak of the resurrection of the body, and hence, it becomes important to carefully read and exegete them, absent of any of the exegetical or logical fallacies mentioned previously.

In 1 Corinthians 15, Paul lays out a very clear understanding of the resurrection of the body based on the federal headship idea of what I would call *accidit alteri contingat* "what happens to the one happens to the other." Christians are united to Christ, and therefore, they are one with Christ. They, and their bodies, are His very body (Rom 6:5, 8:11; 1 Cor 6:15; 12:12–14; Eph 4:1–16). Through unification with Christ, Christians inherit all of Christ's rewards. His Father sits Him upon His throne and so the Christian united to Him will sit upon His throne (Rev 3:21); He was granted authority over the nations to rule them with a rod of iron, so He will grant Christians united to Him authority to rule over the nations with a rod of iron (Rev 2:26). Likewise, His resurrection is a reward for His faithfulness to the Father. Hence, that reward is given to His saints as well (Rom 8:11; Phil 3:20–21). Paul relates this idea most clearly in 1 Corinthians 15.

> But now Christ has been raised from the dead, the firstfruits of those who have fallen asleep. For since death came through a man, the resurrection of the dead also came through a man. For just as in Adam all die, so also in Christ all will be made alive. But each in his own order: Christ, the firstfruits; then when Christ comes, those who belong to him. Then comes the end, when he hands over the kingdom to God the Father, when he has brought to an end all rule and all authority and power. For he must rule until he has put all his enemies under his feet. The last enemy to be eliminated is death. For he has put everything in subjection under his feet. But when it says "everything" has been put in subjection, it is clear that this does not include the One who put everything in subjection to him. And when all things are subjected to him, then the Son himself will be subjected to

the One who subjected everything to him, so that God may be all in all. (vv. 20–28)

Paul informs the Corinthians here that Christ is the "firstfruits" which represent the larger crop. As such, He is raised (bodily in the context) first. After Him, at His coming, those who belong to Him will also be raised (again, bodily in the context). The kingdom over which Christ reigns at the time Paul is writing, i.e., Paul's present day, will be handed over to the Father when the Son returns, and the resurrection of His people takes place. This means that Christ, while ruling from the Father's throne over the kingdom in Paul's day, is not on His permanent throne until He returns. The makeup of the kingdom over which He rules presently is not the makeup of the kingdom He is to rule forever, as the kingdom over which He rules here will be handed over to the Father. Jesus will relinquish the throne and vanquish His last enemy, i.e., physical death in the context, at the resurrection. However, it is only *achri* "until" (v. 25) He vanquishes this final foe that He remains upon the throne with the Father, reigning over the Father's kingdom, which is the kingdom of the invisible realm. Instead, the Son has been given the entire physical cosmos ("all heaven and earth" in Matthew 28 refers not to the invisible and visible realm, but to the physical cosmos as it does in Genesis 1) by the Father as a fulfillment to His promise to David that a descendent would sit upon his earthly throne forever. God the Father rules over both kingdoms, but He does so by dividing up the invisible realm and the visible realm between Himself and the Son. He will rule the invisible realm directly and the visible realm through the agency of the Son who will sit upon the Davidic throne.

This is an important point since the Son does not remain in heaven, i.e., the invisible realm, to reign forever. This means that the throne of David is temporarily a singular throne in heaven that belongs to the Father. The eternal, earthly throne that derives its authority from the heavenly, the visible that derives its authority from the invisible, will be a second throne that comes from the heavenly one, united by the unification of the Divine Persons who rule from them, but distinct in terms of their locations. Hence, Jesus will physically return, physically raise those who belong to His kingdom from the dead, and take hold of His physical inheritance, i.e., all sky and land/the entire physical cosmos.

Hence, as in the macrocosmic event seen in Daniel, every kingdom, and everything that belongs to those kingdoms (e.g., possessions, authority, dominions, etc.), is given over to the Son of Man, so all things are put in subjection to the Son, excepting the Father alone. Once the Son has subjected all things (including physical death), He will hand the invisible kingdom over to the Father and return to rule the physical world that He has conquered.

There is simply no microcosmic referent evident in this text. These events are said to occur once the Son has subjected all His enemies, all rule, indeed, all things in both the visible and invisible realms under His feet. He sits on the throne until that time. Physical death is said to be the last enemy to be conquered, so it is not conquered until the physical resurrection of those who belong to Him. This means that Christ does not hand the kingdom over to the Father until every Christian who will ever live is raised from the dead. This did not happen in A.D. 70 or within any other microcosmic event either. Hence, the apocalyptic description stands on its own without any microcosmic event attached to it.

Christ is, therefore, the firstfruits of the same kind of crop, not a different kind of crop. He is not physically raised to represent a bunch of people who are only spiritually raised. In Pauline theology, spiritual regeneration is the "already" aspect of the resurrection that occurs when every elect person believes (Rom 6:1–5; Eph 2:4–6). The resurrection Paul speaks of in this text is still to come from his vantage point. This means that it is not a reference to a spiritual resurrection but instead is to be understood as the same type of resurrection as Christ's physical, bodily resurrection, which is the subject Paul is addressing in the context.

The Greeks would have thought that the idea of physical resurrection was crude. Hence, many of the Corinthians were saying there is no physical resurrection. They believed in an afterlife of the spirit, and even one where the spirit entered a glorious state, but Paul here corrects them by saying that Christians believe that there is a physical resurrection of the body because Christ is physically raised. If Christ is not physically raised, then Christians are still in their sins (vv. 12–19), as He has not received the reward of salvation (eternal life within the physical, created order) that Christians thought He had.

Finally, the attempt to place all of this within the context of the destruction of Jerusalem in A.D. 70 fails by the fact that there is no mention of this event as the background nor does it fit the nature of the event. Instead, the fallacy of context replacement is necessary to completely change the referents, and therefore, the meaning of the statements in the passage. The actual passage, however, very clearly refers to a time when Christ will return to acquire His physical kingdom, and the physical bodies of believers will be resurrected to partake in that kingdom. As such, there is no microcosmic event to which this text refers, and therefore, the referent is the macrocosmic event itself.

There is nothing about Old Testament saints escaping from Hades, spiritual renewal, or completely different physical bodies being given out in heaven when people die. There is only a singular resurrection of the saints that occurs at the same time when Christ hands the kingdom over to the Father and all His enemies in both the physical and spiritual realm have been vanquished. Therefore, the event that 1 Corinthians 15 describes did not occur in A.D. 70 nor has it yet come about to this day.

1 Thessalonians 4–5, and 2 Thessalonians 1–2

Preterists have a very difficult time interpreting 1 and 2 Thessalonians. The text does not seem to coincide with any event in the first century, and as such, there is a bit of scramble in the attempt to find a referent to ideas like Christ returning, Christians meeting Christ in the air, the man of lawlessness who seats himself in the temple above every god, etc. The texts are as follows:

> Now we do not want you to be uninformed, brothers, about those who are asleep, so that you will not grieve like the rest who have no hope. For if we believe that Jesus died and rose again, so also we believe that God will bring with him those who have fallen asleep as Christians. For we tell you this by the word of the Lord, that we who are alive, who are left until the coming of the Lord, will surely not go ahead of those who have fallen asleep. For the Lord himself will come down from heaven with a shout of command, with the voice of the archangel, and with the trumpet of God, and the dead in Christ will rise first. Then we who are alive, who are left, will be suddenly caught up together with them in the clouds to meet the Lord in the air. And so we will always be with the Lord. Therefore encourage one another with these words. (4:13–18)

Note that this text references no microcosmic event in the context. Instead, Paul is encouraging the Thessalonians, who were in despair concerning their loved ones who had died, with the hope of the return of Christ and resurrection of the saints. The text informs us that Christ will return with the resurrected saints who have died, and those who are still alive will welcome their coming King, along with all the resurrected saints who come with Him, into their world. Hence, believers will always be with Christ. These descriptions make little sense when applied to the destruction of Jerusalem and the coming of the new covenant. Instead, without replacing the context or forcing the foreign context of the Olivet Discourse onto the account, it clearly refers to the macrocosmic event of the resurrection and reception of the physical world by the Messiah and His saints.

> Now, brothers and sisters, about times and dates we do not need to write to you, for you know very well that the day of the Lord will come like a thief in the night. While people are saying, "Peace and safety," destruction will come on them suddenly, as labor pains on a pregnant woman, and they will not escape. But you, brothers, are not in darkness so that this day should surprise you like a thief. You are all children of the light and children of the day. We do not belong to the night or to the darkness. So then, let us not be like others, who are asleep, but let us be awake and sober. For those who sleep, sleep at night, and those who get drunk, get drunk at night. But since we belong to the day, let us be sober, putting on faith and love as a breastplate, and the hope of salvation as a helmet. For God did not appoint us to suffer wrath but to receive salvation through our Lord Jesus Christ. He died for us so that, whether we are awake or asleep, we may live together with him. Therefore encourage one another and build each other up, just as in fact you are doing. (5:1-11)

Almost without fail, preterists will seek to interpret 1 Thessalonians 4-5 within the context of the Olivet Discourse. The reason why this is an essential move for them to make in order to harmonize this passage with a preterist understanding is because the passage itself gives no indication that it is about anything other than the macrocosmic event of the coming of Christ and the physical resurrection of the dead. There is no mention of a microcosmic, socio-political event, such as the destruction of Jerusalem, even hinted at in the passage. Instead, the language used of the macrocosmic event in Thessalonians is similar to that in the Olivet Discourse, leading the preterist to believe he is justified in supplying referents to Thessalonians from the Olivet Discourse as though the two texts were really just one text.

The problem, of course, is that this context replacement fallacy feeds off the faulty assumption that this is a case of Scripture interpreting Scripture rather than a case of a person twisting Scripture with other Scripture. One must interpret each text in its own context first and then compare and contrast what each says and does not say. In this case, the macrocosmic event is made clear by the lack of referent to anything microcosmic. There is an unspoken rule in exegesis that when a text does not limit itself with a specific referent, it is to be interpreted generically/universally. For instance, many seeking to interpret passages relating to the condemnation of homosexuality attempt to limit those texts to specific instances of homosexuality that describe relationships as promiscuous or abusive in some way. However, it is clear that these texts make no mention of such relationships because they condemn any relationship that can be described as homosexual. Those who try to limit these condemnations do so because they realize that by adding a limiting element to the text, they change what the text says. Hence, this type of context replacement exists to allow the interpreter to make the text harmonize with his preconceived ideas.

In the same way, Paul is not discussing Jerusalem in these passages. He is not talking about the changing of covenants or the destruction of the temple. He is not talking about a spiritual renewal at all. He is comforting the Thessalonians who had seen fellow Christians die and believed they had missed Christ's return and the salvation He brought when He came. Paul tells them that no Christian will miss it; the dead will, in fact, rise first and then be joined by the living to greet the coming King as He descends.

In no way would this have been understood as something happening on a spiritual plane, some speech about the new covenant taking over for the old, etc., as there is simply nothing in the context about such things. Instead, it is a generic, rather than a specific and limited, description of Christ's second coming and the resurrection of the dead that will take place at His coming. The burden of proof is upon those who would see it otherwise as they must look to the context that is there and not a supplied context, either fabricated whole cloth or taken from another text of the Bible.

Preterists, like Preston, attempt to supply the microcosmic context for the passage via context replacement by arguing the similarities between the macrocosmic language found here and that found in passages like Daniel or the Olivet Discourse. We have already explored the fallacious nature of this eisegetical methodology. However, it would be, perhaps, helpful to take a look at Preston's reasoning in order to assess precisely where his methodology has gone awry. Preston constructs his syllogism as follows:[23]

1. 1 Thessalonians 4:13–18 is about the resurrection.

2. The time of the resurrection is the time when the sting of death, sin, is removed (1 Corinthians 15:54–56).

3. Sin will be removed by the end of the seventieth week of Daniel 9:24.

4. The seventieth week of Daniel 9:24–27 deals with the end of the old covenant world of Israel in AD 70.

5. Therefore, the resurrection would occur by the end of the seventieth week of Daniel 9:24, i.e., by the time of the end of the old covenant world of Israel in AD 70.

---

23. Preston, *We Shall Meet Him in the Air*, 270–71.

The argument above is a good example of the type of interpretation found in preterist hermeneutics. Since 1 Thessalonians 4 is about the resurrection, and the resurrection occurs when sin is removed in 1 Corinthians 15, and Daniel supposedly says sin will be removed at the end of the old covenant world of Israel, and that supposedly happened in A.D. 70, then 1 Thessalonians refers to a resurrection that occurred in A.D. 70. Hence, even though no such context is supplied by 1 Thessalonians 4, Preston has supplied one for it by relating a series of highly interpreted texts that, when meshed together, make his argument "obvious." We might call this the "Six Degrees of Kevin Bacon Hermeneutic," where a series of only remotely related passages are linked together so they end up referencing the same thing.[24] A syllogism is then constructed out of them in order to make an argument supporting one's theological paradigm.

The problem, however, is that the essential link to A.D. 70 in Preston's argument is his interpretation of Daniel 9, and Daniel 9 is not about the end of the old covenant world of Israel but about the end of the exile marked by the death of Antiochus IV as the inquiry in Daniel's prayer in Chapter 9 makes clear. Daniel is asking how long the exile will last after reading Jeremiah, and Gabriel's reply pertains to this question, not to any other. The end of sin refers, not to the sin of all mankind in general, but to the sin of Israel for which atonement is being made in the extended exile. The end of sin in Daniel 9:24 does not, therefore, refer to the end of the old covenant world of Israel. Since it is not referring to this concept, nor is it referring to A.D. 70 since the end of the exile in Daniel occurs when Antiochus IV dies in 163 B.C., Preston's entire link between 1 Thessalonians and the context of A.D. 70 is dissolved, and the syllogism falls apart.

If he were to argue that the macrocosmic event of the resurrection occurs in both the Olivet Discourse and 1 Thessalonians 4, and therefore must be the same event, he is simply confused, as the presence of macrocosmic language itself does not reference any one specific microcosmic event by itself but rather numerous events depending upon the context. This is why joining texts in an effort to supply a new context to one of those texts is a purely eisegetical endeavor and usually leads to a faulty conclusion. Hence, there is simply no link between 1 Thessalonians 4 and any microcosmic event. The literary context is simply absent of such a referent, and without

---

24. Such fallacious interpretive methodologies conjure up the example of the fire engine cited in D. A. Carson's book, *Exegetical Fallacies*: "Why Are Fire Engines Red? They have four wheels and eight men; four plus eight is twelve; twelve inches make a ruler; a ruler is Queen Elizabeth; Queen Elizabeth sails the seven seas; the seven seas have fish; the fish have fins; the Finns hate the Russians; the Russians are red; fire engines are always rushin'; so they're red."

any language supporting a microcosmic context, the macrocosmic event should be taken at face value. In other words, if it is not being used to magnify another event, the author is magnifying it as an event within itself.

What this means is that Preston's observation that 1 Thessalonians 4 concerns the resurrection is, indeed, correct. However, since this is the macrocosmic event in view, not that of A.D. 70 or any other microcosmic event in the context, the resurrection is a part of the macrocosmic event in this text. Linking microcosmic events using the presence of language referring to the macrocosmic event is a faulty interpretive methodology, since the language of the macrocosmic event is applied to differing microcosmic events throughout the Old and New Testaments.[25] 1 Thessalonians 4–5 refers to the macrocosmic event itself and is a standalone passage that evidences the existence of the actual event in the future. The same can be said for 2 Thessalonians Chapters 1 and 2. The standalone context that is provided is ignored in the attempt to supply a first century referent to what Paul says. The man of lawlessness becomes Nero, or Titus, or Vespasian (although only Titus stands on the temple ruins and is not considered a god or emperor at the time nor is He destroyed by Christ at His coming), or the false teacher Cerinthus (even though Cerinthus did not exalt himself above every god and would have taught that one must follow the one true God of the Old Testament through law—the opposite of lawlessness—and was also not destroyed by Christ at His coming). Christ reigning fire on the enemies of Paul and the Thessalonians is interpreted as the destruction of the Jews via the destruction of Jerusalem even though the persecutors of the Thessalonians are their fellow Gentile countrymen (1 Thes 2:14–15), not the Jews who are persecuting Paul, along with other Gentiles, and therefore, the Gentile enemies of the Thessalonians are not destroyed in A.D. 70.

Finding first century references is a stretch, to say the least, because the text does not cooperate with the practice of context replacement without having to be twisted beyond recognition. Instead, the texts in Thessalonians are standalone passages that should be understood as having the macrocosmic activity they describe as the only referents supplied by the context. As such, there is simply no microcosmic event in view.

---

25. E.g., the destruction of Babylon (Isa 13:1–13), the destruction of Egypt (Isa 19:1), the judgment of northern Israel in the 8th century (Amos 5:18–20; 8:9), the destruction of Jerusalem in 587/586 B.C. (Jer 19:23–28; Ezek 32:7–8; Zeph 1:7–16), a judgment of famine in the post-exilic period (Joel 2:28), the destruction of Jerusalem in A.D. 70 (Mark 13 // Matt 24 // Luke 21), etc.

Preterist Interpretations

2 Thessalonians: The Destruction of Jerusalem as Christ Reigning Fire on the Enemies of the Thessalonians

Many Preterists will argue that Paul describes the destruction of Jerusalem in 2 Thessalonians 1 based on the idea that the enemies upon whom Christ will reign fire are the Jews, who were very clearly persecuting Christians in various places throughout the empire. The problem with this interpretation is that not only does the text nowhere mention this specific judgment of Jerusalem and the Jews,[26] but the enemies of the Thessalonians are specifically said to be fellow Thessalonian Gentiles. Paul makes this clear in contrasting his own countrymen with theirs in 1 Thessalonians 2:14–16.

> For you, brothers, became imitators of God's churches in Judea, which are in Christ Jesus: You suffered from your own people the same things those churches suffered from the Jews who killed the Lord Jesus and the prophets and also drove us out. They displease God and are hostile to everyone in their effort to keep us from speaking to the Gentiles so that they may be saved. In this way they always heap up their sins to the limit. The wrath of God has come upon them at last. (2:14–16)

Notice that the suffering and persecution of the Thessalonians is by the hand of their own countrymen (*hypo tōn idiōn symphyletōn* "by your own ethnicity"), not the Jews. It is Paul and the churches in Judea who are persecuted and suffer at the hands of the Jews. This becomes important for understanding the actual enemies of the Gentile Christians in Thessalonica.

Hence, when Paul argues in 2 Thessalonians 1:5–10 that those who are afflicting them in persecution will be repaid by God when the Lord Jesus is revealed from heaven and hands out punishment to those who do not know God and do not obey the gospel, he is talking about both the Gentiles in Thessalonica and the Jews who have persecuted Paul throughout the empire, not simply the Jews in Jerusalem. How exactly are the Thessalonian

---

26. Nowhere in these texts is there an indication of the common controversies Paul mentions when mentioning Jewish opponents in other epistles. As Ernest Best (*A Commentary on the First and Second Epistles to the Thessalonians* [BNTC; 2d ed. London: Continuum. 1977], 16–22) has noted, there are no references to any disputes about the law (such as those concerning foods, holy days, or circumcision); there is nothing in the text concerning a specific group of antagonists within the community (as opposed to it being the community of Gentiles itself that opposes them); and there is no call to unity as is usually the case when Paul is urging Jewish and Gentile believers to see one another as the new Israel.

pagans being punished by the destruction of Jerusalem? And where, again, exactly is that referent alluded to in the text?

> This is evidence of God's righteous judgment, to make you worthy of the kingdom of God, for which in fact you are suffering. For it is right for God to repay with affliction those who afflict you, and to you who are being afflicted to give rest together with us when the Lord Jesus is revealed from heaven with his mighty angels. *With flaming fire he will mete out punishment on those who do not know God* and do not obey the gospel of our Lord Jesus. They will undergo the penalty of eternal destruction, *away from the presence of the Lord and from the glory of his strength*, when he comes to be glorified among his saints and admired on that day among all who have believed—and you did in fact believe our testimony. (2 Thess. 1:5–10; emphasis added)

The text seems rather clear that the referent of those being judged are "all those who have afflicted you," bringing rest to both the Thessalonians who are being persecuted by Gentiles and Paul who is being persecuted by Jews, precisely, because the judgment is upon "those who do not know God and do not obey the gospel of the Lord Jesus" in general. In fact, how would the destruction of Jerusalem rain fire and destroy the pagans in Thessalonica so as to give relief to the Thessalonian Christians? How would it give relief to Paul from his persecutors if they are Jews who are scattered among the larger empire? This text only makes sense if one understands the destruction of the wicked from the earth is universal.

Another interesting interpretation of 2 Thessalonians 2:1–12 is that the "lawless one" here refers to a Jewish-gnostic heretic named Cerinthus. By gaining a following in the church, Preterists argue, Cerinthus had lifted himself up in the temple of God and led people astray. They read the following text in that light.

> Now regarding the arrival of our Lord Jesus Christ and our being gathered to be with him, we ask you, brothers, not to be easily shaken from your composure or disturbed by any kind of spirit or message or letter allegedly from us to the effect that the day of the Lord is already here. Let no one deceive you in any way. For that day will not arrive until apostasy comes and the man of lawlessness is revealed, the son of destruction. He opposes *and exalts himself above every* so-called *god* or object of worship, and as a result *he takes his seat* in God's temple, displaying himself as God. Surely you recall that I used to tell you these things while I was still with you. And so, you know what holds him back, so that he will be revealed in his own time. For the hidden power

of lawlessness is already at work. However, the one who holds him back will do so until he is taken out of the way, and then the lawless one will be revealed, whom the Lord will destroy by the breath of his mouth and wipe out by the manifestation of his arrival. The arrival of the lawless one will be by Satan's working with all kinds of miracles and signs and false wonders, and with every kind of evil deception directed against those who are perishing, because they found no place in their hearts for the truth so as to be saved. Consequently, God sends on them a deluding influence so that they will believe what is false. And so, all of them who have not believed the truth but have delighted in evil will be condemned. (emphasis added)

It is important to note that any identification of the man of lawlessness must meet all the criteria, not just some of it, including what is said about Christ destroying all of the wicked at His coming. The man of lawlessness must seat himself in the temple, perform all kinds of miraculous signs and wonders, lift himself up above every god and sacred object, display himself as God, and be destroyed by the coming of Christ.

The attempt made by Preterists to identify Cerinthus as "the lawless one" is made for two reasons: (1) He is an early heretic that can be identified as being significant in his influence of what will become a major heresy (even John's Epistles are said to be written to counter his teachings), and (2) the knowledge we have of what dates to assign to his life and his exact workings in the early church is so scarce he basically becomes a wax nose that one can form to fit the mold of the man of lawlessness.

The problems with this identification, however, are legion. First, from what we do know of Cerinthus, he believed the Jewish law was the means of salvation and all should follow it. This hardly made him a man of lawlessness, which usually described an antinomian or one opposed to the law, since the language was taken from Second Temple Judaism's memory of Antiochus IV who not only broke the law but was opposed to it. Second to this, Cerinthus did not do all kinds of miracles. Third, he did not exalt himself above every god and object of worship nor did he view himself as God. Instead, he worshiped and exalted the Supreme God and believed that God must be worshiped by everyone through their obedience to the law. The description given in the passage is instead taken from Antiochus IV, and if it is to be applied to anyone at all in the first century, it sounds much more like a Roman emperor than some heretic in the church who was simply one among many false teachers therein. To be clear, however, this description does not even fit a Roman emperor or Antiochus IV from whom the images are obtained. Neither Antiochus IV nor a Roman emperor performed miraculous signs (although this may refer to supernatural things that were thought to have occurred during the festivals of the imperial cult). Some argue that this references Titus' standing in the place where the sanctuary used to be after it was torn down by his troops, and therefore, is speaking about the destruction of Jerusalem in A.D. 70. However, there are numerous problems with this. Titus was not the emperor at that time and so would not have been viewed as a god (that would likely have been treason). His father seemed to think the imperial cult was a joke, and neither Vespasian nor Titus restored the imperial cult to its former glory and so did not lift themselves up above every god and sacred object. Except in certain parts of Asia Minor, the emperors before Domitian were not usually viewed as deities until they died, and none of them would have lifted themselves up over every god as they were viewed as gods themselves under Jupiter. The one exception might have been Domitian who may have seen himself as a manifestation of Jupiter himself, but Domitian was never in the literal temple in Jerusalem nor in the figurative temple of the church. The largest problem, of course, is that none of these people were destroyed at the coming of Christ in A.D. 70. In fact, Titus was victorious and gained more peace for his father's empire. Vespasian went on to live another eight years and died a natural death. Titus continued to live for another decade and was likely poisoned by Domitian. Domitian was likely poisoned by his wife fifteen years later. Cerinthus went on to teach his heresy until the end of the first century. None of these people were destroyed or even hindered in any way by the events in A.D. 70.

The truth of the matter is that the description of the lawless one in 2 Thessalonians does not really fit well with anyone in the first century, and since it is tied to the macrocosmic event of Christ's return, there must yet remain one to come who will fully fit the description.

2 Peter 3

Peter Leithart, a partial preterist, sets up a series of what he calls "knock-down punches" that supposedly prove that 2 Peter 3 is talking about the destruction of Jerusalem in A.D. 70. and not the end of the present wicked world. Of course, what is not included in any of the "evidence" he brings forth is an explicit context in 2 Peter 3 itself that relates the event to the destruction of Jerusalem or the old covenant world under the law. Observing the unmarked meaning of the words in this passage, as well as how the entire passage would have been read by a Second Temple audience, is enough to discard the idea that a microcosmic event is in view. To ignore the unmarked meaning is to commit the exegetical fallacy of context replacement.

Furthermore, the purpose of 2 Peter (i.e., to refute antinomians, not Judaizers) negates the idea that 2 Peter is concerned with an argument that does away with having to obey the Old Testament and instead argues against the idea that one can live in lawlessness as a Christian due to a series of bad theological arguments made by antinomian teachers who were characterized by their licentiousness, not their Jewish commitment to law-keeping. Frankly, if Peter's argument were against Judaism and the Old Covenant, his actual antinomian opponents in the book would have thanked him for it.

However, it is again helpful to explore some of the reasoning that Leithart puts forth to prove that these are Jewish believers. It will be sufficient to show the error in his exegesis at the foundation of this argument. Hence, his first and foundational argument is presented below.

Leithart's Ghost Punches

Summary of the First Argument: Since 1 Peter is linked to 2 Peter, and 1 Peter is all about seeing present events in view of the imminent return of Christ, 2 Peter has this same imminence to it.

Response 1: This argument is a *non sequitur* as all who are not preterists, partial or otherwise, can agree that the apostles had a sense of imminence. That the apostles treated Christ's return as imminent is not under dispute. The issue is whether they knew that Christ's return was imminent (i.e., to occur in their time) or whether they communicated it as imminent because the expectation of Christ's return was, and continues to be, an essential motivation for sanctification in the New Testament. We are told that the apostles do not know when Christ is returning and that His sudden and surprise return is the primary motivation for Christian sanctification. British scholar J. D. Kelly notes that "In the NT the approach of the End is regularly (e.g., Mt. xxiv. 45-xxv. 13; Mk. xiii. 33-37; Rom. xiii. 11-14; Phil iv.4-6; Heb. x. 23-31; Jas. v. 7-11; i Jn. ii. 18; Rev. xxii. 12) interpreted as a challenge to watchfulness and irreproachable behaviour."[27] Hence, of course, it would be spoken of as (and even believed to be) imminent by the apostles. This does not mean that the event actually was imminent from the apostles' perspectives unless one wants to argue that the apostles really did know when Christ would be returning and that Christ's indication to them that it was not for them to know was mistaken (Acts 1:6-7).

Leithart seems to assume a superficial view of inspiration in that it must somehow convey an omniscient knowledge of these things given to the apostles by God via inspiration, but this is nonsense. As humans,

27. Kelly, *Epistles of Peter and Jude*, 177.

the apostles can have all sorts of misunderstandings that are then used as a framework for communicating inerrant teaching to God's people. What God intends to teach is what is absolutely true. The language used to convey that truth is neither true nor false; it is just language. It is a mistake to assume that every detail or attitude conveyed through the limited knowledge of an author who is writing an inspired text somehow must be taken as accurately describing reality. This would mean that whenever an author evidences belief in a flat earth or geocentric model it must be taken as fact. There exists in the text both the truth God means to convey and the human means to convey it. One is inerrant, and one is neither errant nor inerrant since the elements of human thought constitute separate propositions to be explored absent the intended teaching in the scriptural context in which it is used as language. This is what I consider to be a far more robust understanding of inerrancy. If a biblical author, for instance, conveys the idea that the earth is flat, it does not mean that he knows the earth is flat via God's revelation and everyone must therefore believe that it is. Instead, one must look to the message the author conveys using the idea that the earth is flat, and it is that theological/ethical message, not the mistaken idea, that is inerrant. Leithart's form of inerrancy leads to liberalism and apostasy when one studies the mistakes of the biblical authors at length within that superficial mindset. It creates a further problem of inerrancy since the Bible teaches from the lips of Christ Himself that it has not been given to the apostles to know the times the Father has set in reference to the restoration. While on earth even the Son did not know. However, if Leithart is going to argue that they did come to know it, then it actually had been given to them to know those times, and Jesus' words were in error. All of this is completely unnecessary if one merely allows God to speak through humans without making them omniscient beings themselves or overriding their humanity in some sort of docetic, mechanical dictation view of inspiration.

Response 2: It is clear by the nature of the elements involved in their descriptions of the event that the apostles see as imminent that they are not talking about the destruction of the old :covenant or Jerusalem but about the termination of things like commerce and marriage (1 Cor 7:29–31), heresy and sin (1 John 2:17), all those persecuting Christians (2 Thes 1:6–8), etc. None of these come to an end in A.D. 70 for anyone but those in Jerusalem. Yet, these things are portrayed as having their imminent end for people outside of Jerusalem (e.g., the Corinthians in 1 Corinthians 7, the Thessalonians, etc.).

Response 3: In this argument, Leithart must find his imminent event not in the text, which exegesis would demand, but by arguing that the audience is Jewish and that those oppressing Christians in 1 Peter, which he seems to think are Jews, will be squashed at Christ's coming when He destroys Jerusalem. The problem with all of this, of course, is twofold: (1) He has to make Peter's audience Jewish Christians, and (2) he must make their oppressors the Jews who scattered them in the persecution of Christians in Jerusalem. Neither one of these ideas, however, is supported by the evidence gleaned from 1 and 2 Peter. Even Leithart admits that almost all scholars conclude that the audience of the books are Gentiles.[28] He wishes to discount the fact that most commentators understand the audience of both letters to be Gentile Christians who are being given the designation of the *diaspora* because of their being exiled in the wicked world, which Peter describes metaphorically as Babylon, an analogous designation never given to Jerusalem but almost exclusively to Rome in the first century. The letters clearly spell this out with the designations given to the audience as those who did not "know God," something Peter would have never said of Jews and their forefathers, and that they inherited a futile way of life (1 Pet 1:18), having practiced abominable idolatries (4:3), and have had a long practice of idolatry, orgies, debaucheries, etc., which describe the Jewish moral markers for Gentiles. They were once "not a people,"[29] but now in the church they are a people, God's Israel, who function as a kingdom of priests (2:10). These are all terminologies given to the Gentiles in the New Testament and taken both from the Prophets and from Jewish authors in the first century. The books also spell out to whom they are addressed through the issues and heresies which Peter addresses in the letters, none of which seem very Jewish but very much related to the culture at large: Gentile heresies (e.g., antinomian Gnosticism), Roman households (e.g., Peter uses the Roman *haustafel* as a literary structure), and Christian troubles with the Roman government.

Secondly, the oppressors in 1 Peter are clearly different forms of government, from household governments like slave masters and husbands to the Roman Empire set up under an emperor and magistrates. This is why Peter tells his audience to honor the emperor and submit to every rule and authority, including disobedient husbands and harsh masters (1:13—3:7). There is nothing that indicates a Jewish persecution in the book, and one

---

28. Leithart, *The Promise of His Appearing*, 15.

29. Leithart is committing an illegitimate referential transference fallacy here by assuming that if Hosea is talking about Israel with this phrase in its own context, then the New Testament must be as well. However, as argued before, referents are not transferred from one context to another unless the other context includes them itself. Hence, this methodology ignores the New Testament context in which the phrase has been appropriated to fit the Gentiles who have been made one with the Jews into a new people group (cf. Rom 9:24–26; Eph 2:11–20).

must wonder where the judgment of God upon Rome was in the first century if Peter believes that the destruction of their oppressors is so imminent.

The raison d'etre of ignoring all of this is an attempt to bend the context to the word *diaspora* in what must be described as an illegitimate referential transference, the common lexical fallacy that attempts to replace the contextual referents with referents from another context by linking them with a word that is used in both passages. As such, it is a subcategory of the exegetical fallacy I have designated as "context replacement." Without committing this fallacy, however, the necessary foundation for Leithart's argument concerning the context of 2 Peter fails and along with it the argument that 2 Peter 3 is about the destruction of Jerusalem.

In a way, his contention that all of the descriptions above can portray a Jewish audience is much like attempting to show that the Corinthians are all Jewish because Paul applies lots of Old Testament designations to them, refers to their former lifestyles as idolatrous, and references them as being at one time "Gentiles," implying that they are not Gentiles anymore and are instead Jews (1 Cor 12:2). Of course, everything taken in context makes it clear that all of this "Jewish" terminology is applied to Gentile Christians because they are, in fact, the Israel of God now. Hence, referring to Gentiles, who are mistreated in this world and not at home in it because they are Christians, as *diaspora* makes perfect sense.

Leithart quotes a few passages out of 1 Peter that, in his mind, "explicitly state that there is an event on his readers' immediate horizon."[30] However, none of these texts communicates any event that is about to occur at all. The statement that there is "a salvation prepared to be revealed in the last time" sounds imminent when one puts a preterist spin on it, but, as discussed in this book, the term "last" does not always mean final but more often "future" in temporal contexts. It is also indefinite and so should be translated, "a salvation prepared to be revealed at a future time." Of course, that sounds a lot less specific and could refer to any time in the future. The idea that it is ready to be revealed in that time is the idea that salvation has already been obtained by Christ, not that it is "about" to be revealed. This is simply spinning the words to indicate more than they do.

Leithart also falls into the linguistic fallacy of what I would call "limitation to the immediate audience." In other words, if an author talks about his audience in terms of future events, it must mean that the author believes that those future events will happen to his immediate audience within their lifetimes. The problem with this is that biblical authors often speak to their specific audience as though they are the people of the future to whom the

---

30. Leithart, *The Promise of His Appearing*, 13.

event will occur. The curses and prophecies concerning Israel's unfaithfulness are told to it in Deuteronomy, to the Israelites in the wilderness, as though the Babylonian Exile is something God is going to do to those Israelites who have participated in the wilderness journey. He speaks to them as though they are the ones both enduring the punishment and receiving the restoration from the exile because they are seen as a singular group with their descendants, not because they will actually be alive at the time of the exile, which is at the very least almost seven hundred years later.

> For instance, in Deuteronomy 30:3–7, God states:
> "God, your God, will restore everything you lost; he'll have compassion on you; he'll come back and pick up the pieces from all the places where you were scattered. No matter how far away you end up, God, your God, will get you out of there and bring you back to the land your ancestors once possessed. It will be yours again. He will give you a good life and make you more numerous than your ancestors. God, your God, will cut away the thick calluses on your heart and your children's hearts, freeing you to love God, your God, with your whole heart and soul and live, really live. God, your God, will put all these curses on your enemies who hated you and were out to get you.

This sounds like God will be restoring the audience under Moses from the exile and enacting the New Covenant over them. Yet, this is something that happens centuries later.

In fact, most vindication prophesies (and prophesies in general for that matter) given to the nation are given to the people as though God will accomplish what He has spoken to them in their lifetimes when, in fact, God does them in the lifetimes of their descendants. The Book of Isaiah is filled with these types of prophesies that speak to the immediate audience as though they are the future group that are seeing these things take place.

Imminence is almost always a characteristic of judgment texts as well, whether it truly is imminent or not. For instance, in Deuteronomy 32:34–36, God speaks of the calamity He will bring on the nations who attacked Israel during and after their exile as though it is about to happen. Yet, in the biblical timeline, God proclaims the judgment of the exile anywhere from seven hundred to almost a thousand years before this occurs.

> *"Is it not laid up in store with Me, sealed up in My treasuries? Vengeance is Mine, and retribution. In due time their foot will slip; for the day of their calamity is at hand, and the impending things are hastening upon them. For the LORD will vindicate His*

people, and will have compassion on His servants, when He sees that their strength is gone.

"*The day of their calamity is at hand*"? "*The impending things are rushing quickly/soon upon them*"? According to Leithart's argument, this must take place to the group in the wilderness or Scripture is wrong. Such a false inference is hardly warranted, however.

In fact, numerous prophesies of the future are given to Israel and spoken of as though those prophesies refer to the audience addressed by the prophetic books and have some sort of imminence about them but, in fact, are meant to refer to events occurring to people in the distant future. The fallacy of limitation to the immediate audience misunderstands the fact that predictive speech can, and often does, address an immediate audience as though they are the group who will experience the future event not because the future event is happening in their lifetimes but because they are one group with the audience of the future. The link between the two, therefore, is not that the timing is the same as the future group to which the text refers in the context but that their identity as a group is the same and, therefore, can be spoken of as though they are the future group. This language is widespread throughout the Bible.

In eschatological speech found in the New Testament, this is taken even further since the audience will, in fact, experience the macrocosmic event as God's people will be brought back in resurrection to witness the subjugation of God's (and their) enemies. But the use of predictive speech that is directed toward the audience is typical, and it is a way of making the timing of the future event ambiguous so that everyone in that particular group heeds the words from the time they are spoken to the very generation in which they are fulfilled. I would, of course, also argue that it is ambiguous because the authors are not given omniscience to know the people to whom these events will occur or the timing of these events at all. They are only given the revelation that they will, in fact, definitely occur. Since the direct audience in the author's day is one group with the future peoples to which these events will occur, they can be addressed as though these events will happen to them. It is like an author who writes to this generation of people, "If you keep polluting the earth with garbage, one day you will live in a landfill." The author does not mean to suggest that the people he is addressing will be the ones living in a landfill, but rather he has in mind a future time when his audience is dead, and their descendants live in a garbage-filled earth. Such language is intentional to motivate not only the immediate audience but also their descendants. Leithart has simply misunderstood predictive language here and as such has made a non-argument in the attempt to support his point.

Furthermore, Leithart seems to have misunderstood the reference in 2 Peter 1:16. The text makes it clear that Peter is referring to the *parousia* of the transfiguration, not the coming that refers to A.D. 70. Each of the Synoptics makes this clear by placing the event of the transfiguration immediately after the prediction that some of the disciples will see Him come in His glory "before they taste death." Authors often use narrative to make their argument through the thoughtful placement of passages so as to often link what comes before with what comes immediately after. This is not always the case, however, as context must determine interpretation. However, because all three Synoptic authors place the passages concerning the Parousia and the Mount of Transfiguration together in the same place, whereas they do not often do this with other statements and parallel passages, it becomes a significant argument that the authors all wish to link, in some way, what Jesus says about His Parousia to the transfiguration event.

Furthermore, Peter himself links them and, therefore, makes explicit that the event to which he is referring in 2 Peter 1:16 is the transfiguration. He does this by stating that he was an eyewitness of the *parousia* "royal inauguration/conferment" he proclaimed to them, "for we were eyewitnesses of His royal inauguration." And when did the Son of Man's coming up to the Ancient of Days to receive His royal kingship occur according to Peter? "When this voice was conveyed from heaven, we ourselves heard it, for we were with him on the holy mountain" (1:18). The entire passage links the *parousia* to which Peter is referring to the Mount of Transfiguration.

> For we did not follow cleverly concocted fables when we made known to you the authority and *parousia* of our Lord Jesus Christ; no, we were eyewitnesses of his royal conferment. For he received honor and glory from God the Father, when that voice was conveyed to him by the Majestic Glory: "This is my dear Son, in whom I am delighted." When this voice was conveyed from heaven, we ourselves heard it, for we were with him on the holy mountain. (1:16–18).

The *parousia* here clearly refers to the reception of the Son as king, harkening back to the imagery of the king being received into a city. In this case, Christ is being received as king by the Father and receiving His royal conferment from Him as per the "Son of Man" narrative in Daniel 7. In fact, the entire narrative of the prediction and transfiguration mimics the language of Daniel 7. The language of the "Son of Man," "coming," the ascension to the Father as the Son of Man in Daniel ascends to the Ancient of

Days, the majestic appearance of the Ancient of Days in Daniel is applied to the Son in the Gospels, the clouds, and the reception of the kingdom from the Father/Ancient of Days, is used in the Gospels and by Peter, and it is what Peter means by *parousia* in this passage, which he makes explicit.

Therefore, 2 Peter 1:16–18 is not parallel with 1 Peter 1:5 or any other eschatological predictions in 1 Peter because its events have already occurred at the time Peter is writing. The other texts to which Leithart refers, however, have an ambiguous future reference to them and in no way convey an immediate event that will definitely occur.

Furthermore, upon further investigation, Leithart's treatment of the eschatological statements in 1 Peter ignore what these words and phrases actually mean in their context. For instance, Leithart seems to understand the word *hetoimos* to mean "about to," but the word refers to something that is prepared and ready to go, not something that is necessarily occurring in the immediate future. The idea is that it could come at any time, not that it is coming soon. Both the United States and Russia have had nuclear weapons "ready to go" for years. Hopefully, this does not mean that they are about to be fired. In 2 Corinthians 9:5, the word refers to a gift that is prepared and ready to be picked up, but it in no way describes when it will be picked up. Leithart is attempting to place the idea of imminence in the word when imminence must be gained from the context instead.

Likewise, he seems to assume that the word *engizō*, a verb that is often translated as "is at hand" or "draws near" refers to something that is about to occur in the immediate future. Although this is a possible interpretation, since all of the apostles have the idea of imminence in their writings as discussed before, *engizō* more often conveys the idea of something that is made accessible, within arm's reach, to where one can reach out and grab it. In other words, it refers to something that is already here in one's presence, not something that is about to come. It is something that is accessible. As Kelly comments, "is at hand (*eggikeri*) is almost 'has arrived': cf. esp. Mk. i. 15; Rom. xiii. 12."[31] Hence, when Peter states that the *telos* of all things is *engizō* he is saying that the *telos* is accessible, within their presence, something attainable to them because it has already been within their reach.

With this understanding, one must ask, then what is the *telos*? In 4:17, he uses the word to refer to the outcome or goal of God's judgment upon the wicked in contrast to His judgment of believers. It seems to refer in 4:7 to one of two things, each conveying the same idea. Either it refers to the "end" as in the abolishment of the evil he mentions in the preceding verses and, hence, the judgment of the pagan world; he mentions the activity of

---

31. Kelly, *Epistles of Peter*, 177.

the Gentiles/pagans as something in which they once indulged but would be coming to an end. If this is the case, it could be an example of Peter conveying the imminent judgment of the world, as the apostles often do, but that would not support Leithart's view that this is a judgment just upon Jerusalem since all these oppressive institutions and their sins (sins characterizing pagans in the first century) are not limited to Jerusalem. In this regard, since the wicked world is coming to an end, believers are to pursue godliness instead of the practices of the world that is passing away. In other words, they are to seek godly maturity.

However, it seems to be more the case that Peter is talking about *telos* as a maturation of believers in line with their response to his exhortation for them to pursue godliness. The time is past for them to indulge in any of the sins of the pagans in which they once indulged themselves, and it is now time to become mature since the end goal of maturity (i.e., *telos* as "outcome") is accessible to them through God's discipline via the trials of the world, abusive authorities, and prayer. Thus, they are to discipline themselves in prayer, pursue love, hospitality, godly speech, etc. In other words, "end" does not mean that all things are coming to an end but rather that the outcome of all things (e.g., their trials, their pursuit of what is good, etc.) is within their reach. They are, therefore, to live accordingly. If we understand that false teachers among them have been arguing that humans cannot attain to godliness because of their fallen nature, this interpretation might make much more sense. Either way, however, this passage is not about Jerusalem or a switch in covenants but instead about believers pursuing maturity instead of indulging in the sins of the entire pagan world that is under the judgment of God.

What seems to trip people up when they read this passage is that they assume certain meanings of these words; they see that God is "ready" to judge the living and the dead (ironically, a merism referring to all people everywhere, living or dead, not just in Jerusalem) and then conclude that this is talking about the end of the world, or the end of Jerusalem in the case of the preterist. The idea that this has anything to do with just Jews in Jerusalem and/or the Old Covenant is simply ignoring the context and replacing it with another.

Finally, Leithart's first "knockdown argument" fails to show that either First or Second Peter are dealing with the fall of Jerusalem or a change of covenants. Instead, 1 Peter is about Christians becoming like Christ in the light of unjust persecution from various authorities (Roman authorities, masters, husbands, etc.), and 2 Peter is written against antinomian heretics, likely proto-gnostic, who argue against apostolic Christianity by emphasizing the human perspective (e.g., humans do not have the ability to resist temptation due to their evil natures, the apostolic gospel and Scripture is human opinion, the church is an institution run on human authority, it seems like a long time, from a human perspective, since Christ said He would return so He must not be literally returning). Neither of these books is addressing the issues of covenants or the waywardness of the Jews and the judgment of Jerusalem. All that must become a manufactured context taken from the Olivet Discourse for the Petrine Epistles to support any kind of preterist idea. In fact, such is the central fallacy of context replacement among Preterists in that they typically ignore the literary context that would clarify the words, phrases, and passages before them in order to replace them with the Olivet Discourse as their context so that they can then remold what is said into that image. However, this is nothing more than eisegesis, and Leithart has not succeeded in knocking anything down other than a responsible exegesis of the text.

This is an important point, as typically it has been the tendency of Preterists to supply the microcosmic element to the context of these passages, via illegitimate referential transference, in an effort to argue that they also are referring to the destruction of Jerusalem. However, this is simply the failure to employ linguistically sound methods in the interpretation of these texts. The first is to ignore what was argued in the last section, i.e., that the unmarked meaning of these concepts is not microcosmic and symbolic/spiritual, but macrocosmic and literal/physical. Without any signification in the context to suggest otherwise, they should be understood to mean what they normally mean to the ancient religious audience. Hence, to interpret them as referring to a microcosmic, socio-political event that is nowhere present in the context is to ignore the unmarked meaning of the language in the context. Likewise, it is an example of context replacement to ignore the purpose of what is said in these contexts in order to blend them together with foreign contexts or an idea gained from foreign contexts.

Essentially, Leithart is attempting to change the context of 2 Peter 3 by making the Jews the audience and then interpreting the passage as if the author is addressing Judaism and the old covenant, none of which logically follows or appears in the context.

Likewise, rather than provide biblical examples or anything contextual that would supply the necessary referents to support his argument, Marion Morris' explanation as to why the phrase "new heaven and new earth" refers to the new covenant is that the tranquil nature of God's glory in the new covenant "is certainly heaven for the sin-sick, repentant, disburdened, and spirit-filled soul, and is the second heaven for the Jew who turned from the

THREE ARGUMENTS THAT CLARIFY THE NATURE OF BIBLICAL ESCHATOLOGY 91

old to the new covenant."[32] In other words, the new heavens is simply a spiritual state that one enters into when he enters the new covenant. To argue that the new earth *is* the new covenant, he first argues that the heaven that is passing away cannot refer to the third heaven, i.e., the invisible realm where God dwells. Since Christ was not literally referring to the third heaven, "it is also possible that He did not have reference to the earth on which tower the 'everlasting hills.'"[33] He then argues that the state of the earth that the New Covenant will bring about in the postmillennial paradigm supports the idea that the new earth *is* the New Covenant.

The misunderstanding of the phrase "heaven and earth" as something that refers to the invisible and visible realms is common, but the phrase is most often taken from Genesis 1 where it refers not to invisible and visible but land and sky, i.e., the physical universe. Hence, his argument concerning the third heaven stands on a faulty premise. That Peter is employing the phrase to refer to the physical cosmos is clear from numerous contextual indicators in 2 Peter 3. For one, the heavens and earth that Peter refers to are made clear in vv. 5–7 where it says that "by the word of God heavens existed long ago and an earth was formed out of water and by means of water. Through these things the world existing at that time was destroyed when it was deluged with water. But by the same word the present heavens and earth have been reserved for fire, by being kept for the day of judgment and destruction of the ungodly."

What most preterists want to do is switch from a literal heavens and earth that existed in creation and the flood to a figurative heavens and earth that somehow represent the old covenant/old order of things and not the entire physical world as it existed in Peter's time (and, of course, in ours).

Furthermore, the contextual referents make it clear what heavens and earth are being talked about when the elements that belong to this heaven and earth are described.

> But the day of the Lord will come like a thief; when it comes, the heavens will disappear with a horrific noise, and the celestial bodies will melt away in a blaze, and the earth and every deed done on it will be laid bare. Since all these things are to melt away in this manner, what sort of people must you be, conducting your lives in holiness and godliness, while waiting for and hastening the coming of the day of God? Because of this day, the heavens will be burned up and dissolve, and the celestial bodies will melt away in a blaze! But, according to his promise, we are

---

32. Leithart, *The Promise of His Appearing*, 57.
33. Leithart, *The Promise of His Appearing*, 54

waiting for new heavens and a new earth, in which righteousness truly resides. (vv. 10–13)

The celestial bodies melting away refers to the celestial bodies in the sky, not in the invisible realm nor in the old covenant. Every deed is not laid bare in the judgment in A.D. 70 so that all the wicked are removed and only righteousness dwells in the new heavens and earth/physical cosmos. Now, this last statement may confuse some as Preterists can argue that righteousness resides because of the new covenant. The text does not make this connection, but neither does the phrase seem to be understood by Preterists. Peter is not arguing that righteousness does not reside in the present heavens and earth; he clearly just argued that it does in Chapter 1. Nor would he argue that it did not reside in the Old Testament as he notes that there are many righteous saints in the Old Testament in his first epistle. What he is arguing, taking this imagery and theology from 1 Enoch, is that the wicked will be completely removed from the earth, and so the new heavens and new earth will be characterized only as a place where righteousness dwells. In other words, evil will not dwell there. What this means is that this is not a spiritual existence or the new covenant world that still has unrighteousness dwelling in it because it has not yet seen its fulfillment of the removal of the wicked and all that is defiled.

Second to this, the tendency to blend together things that may be associated with a covenant in a particular text with the new covenant itself is fallacious. The idea that the phrase "heavens and earth" that is merely mentioned in the context of the covenant somehow turns into a reference for the covenant itself is a common one in preterist interpretation. Some use the statement in the Deuteronomic treaty to bolster this type of argument.

> "I call heaven and earth to witness against you this day, that you will soon utterly perish from off the land where you are going when you cross the Jordan to possess it; you will not prolong *your* days upon it, but will utterly be destroyed." (4:26)

> "I call heaven and earth as witness this day against you, that I have set before you life and death, blessing and cursing: therefore choose life, that both you and your descendants may live . . ." (30:19)

Notice that the former argument is a reference created purely out of speculation and a misunderstanding of the term "heaven" here. There is no concrete reference of the phrase "heaven and earth" referring to the covenant or temple in Jerusalem, and even if there were in some text, the referent would not be carried into a new context unless it formed the unmarked meaning. However, it is clear that the unmarked meaning in Second Temple Judaism refers to the literal, physical cosmos. It is that meaning, therefore, that must be assumed until new referents supplied by the context dictate otherwise.

The second argument that preterists use to identify a phrase with the covenant with which it is associated in some way constitutes a type of association fallacy or hasty generalization where the interpreter insists that because X is somehow associated with Y, X is to be identified with Y. By doing this, an illegitimate referential transference is created where the words carry this made-up reference to the thing with which they are loosely associated. This would be much like arguing that because a hammer is used to build a house, the word "hammer" is to be identified as a reference to a house. Hence, if a man says, "I need a new hammer," he is really referring to needing a new house. Another example is the idea that if Bob and Mary are witnesses to a will, it becomes possible that when the names "Bob and Mary" are mentioned they somehow refer to the will itself. This would only be possible if a secret language is made up between the parties who are communicating to one another as everyone else would assume the unmarked meaning of the names as referring to the two individuals and not to some will to which they bore witness.

This same fallacy is committed when the witnesses of the covenant are confused with the covenant itself. But "heaven and earth," even in Deuteronomy, refer to the physical cosmos that stands as a witness of the covenant, not to the covenant itself. What this would mean, if preterists were to insist that "heaven and earth" had passed away in A.D. 70, is that the old covenant would still remain. That is not good news for those believing that the old has transitioned into the new. The passing away of heaven and earth would only mean that there are no witnesses left that God used to make this covenant and that the old covenant still stands long after the witnesses are gone. In other words, there is nothing that supports the idea that when biblical authors and speakers say, "heaven and earth," they somehow mean "covenant."

Furthermore, this twisting of the phrase functions as context replacement for the actual context that indicates that Peter is talking about the physical cosmos. As said before, he does this by defining the phrase in his use of the creation and flood story, by naming elements in the heavens, and by arguing that God's withholding this judgment until a later time is to give Christians in Asia Minor a chance to repent so that they do not perish.

This latter argument is important because if heaven and earth refer to the new covenant, then this would surely allow for repentance all the more. These Christians are unlikely to perish if the new covenant is brought about in its fullness. On the other hand, if it refers to the destruction of the temple and Jerusalem, how would these Christians in Asia Minor be affected? They are not going to perish from something occurring many miles away. In what way is God delaying His judgment upon Jerusalem preventing their perishing?

It seems clear, instead, by the multiple referents as well as the source text of 1 Enoch from which Peter draws, that Peter is assuming the unmarked meaning of the phrase, as he desires his audience to do, and even supports that meaning by providing a few referents that indicate exactly what he means by the phrase. The attempt to make it say something else is just bad exegesis.

Instead, the context of 2 Peter 3 gives a clear picture of the macrocosmic event without reference to a microcosmic one.

> Know this first of all, that in the last days mockers will come with *their* mocking, following after their own lusts, and saying, "Where is the promise of His coming? For *ever* since the fathers fell asleep, all continues just as it was from the beginning of creation." For when they maintain this, it escapes their notice that by the word of God *the* heavens existed long ago and *the* earth was formed out of water and by water, through which the world at that time was destroyed, being flooded with water. But by His word the present heavens and earth are being reserved for fire, kept for the day of judgment and destruction of ungodly men. But do not let this one *fact* escape your notice, beloved, that with the Lord one day is like a thousand years, and a thousand years like one day. The Lord is not slow about His promise, as some count slowness, but is patient toward you, not wishing for any to perish but for all to come to repentance. But the day of the Lord will come like a thief, in which the heavens will pass away with a roar and the elements will be destroyed with intense heat, and the earth and its works will be burned up. Since all these things are to be destroyed in this way, what sort of people ought you to be in holy conduct and godliness, looking for and hastening the coming of the day of God, because of which the heavens will be destroyed by burning, and the elements will melt with intense heat! But according to His promise we are looking for new heavens and a new earth, in which righteousness dwells. Therefore, beloved, since you look for these things, be diligent to be found by Him in peace, spotless and blameless, and regard the patience of our Lord *as* salvation; just as also our beloved brother Paul, according to the wisdom given him, wrote to you . . . (vv. 3–15; emphasis added) ·

Second Peter 3 would have been one of the clearest descriptions of the macrocosmic event to a Second Temple audience. Historically, it has been clear to those who have read it since then that the unmarked meaning of the terms "heaven and earth" is shared by many, if not all, cultures. However, due to the need to blend all of the apocalyptic texts together by collapsing all of these events into a singular event, Preterists work hard to interpret the text as yet another description of the destruction of Jerusalem in A.D. 70 and the ending of the old covenant.

Since one of 2 Peter's reasons for Christ's "delay" is that God is being patient with them, not wishing any of them to perish but for all of them to come to repentance, it seems clear that this event would cause these people to perish if He came before they repented. It would make no sense to say this to a Gentile audience, or even a Jewish diaspora not in Jerusalem, if this text were about the destruction of Jerusalem or a changing of covenants, Preterists would have to argue that Peter is talking to Jews in Jerusalem. Others still try to argue that these are Jewish Christians scattered abroad, but of course, this still does not answer the question as to why they, who have not repented of their adherence to the false, antinomian teachings mentioned within the letter, will perish if Christ returns too soon.

The Nature References

The nature references, that is those texts that describe the nature of the final *parousia* event, become important in that if they describe things that did not happen in A.D. 70, then one is left to conclude that they have not yet occurred; this means that they refer to a future time when they will occur.

The Resurrection of the Body

A word should be said about a more popular preterist view that interprets the "body" in resurrection passages as a reference to the church, i.e., the corporate body. Some Preterists argue that the "body" in resurrection texts is actually the corporate body of the Church, as in "the body of Christ" metaphor that Paul uses in 1 Corinthians 12:12–27 and Ephesians 2:15, 3:6, and 4:4, 12. Hence, it is claimed that when passages like Romans 8 or Philippians 3 or 1 Corinthians 15 use the word "body," the texts are merely continuing this metaphor.

The exegesis of these texts, however, refutes this idea. The resurrection is based contextually in Christ's resurrection, which is of a physical nature not a spiritual one. Christ isn't spiritually raised from the dead, and His resurrection corresponds to ours in terms of a transformation of this earthly, mortal body into a spiritual, immortal body. The attempt to insert the church or Old Testament saints as the referent in these texts is a case of illegitimate referential transference where "body" is thought to mean "collective group" when, in fact, it carries no such meaning. That understanding comes from contextual referents in other passages, and they cannot be transferred to other contexts as though they were optional meanings of the word.

What Preterists seem to do here is ignore that even the collective use of the word "body" is an argument that believer's will receive their bodies back. The "body of Christ" terminology in other passages that reference the church is not an analogy but a result of how Christ saves us via federal headship. The possessions of an individual are a part of that individual, one with him and his very body. Hence, when the church is called the "body of Christ," it refers to the fact that believers are one with Christ and will receive what Christ receives. What He obtains for Himself, He obtains for us. If Christ obtains the kingdom, we obtain the kingdom. If Christ obtains all things, we obtain all things. If Christ is saved, we are saved. If Christ dies, we die. If Christ is raised bodily, we are raised bodily.

This is not a mere analogy because it is arguing that we are literally a part of Christ's body since He is our federal head. Since all of Him, His complete self, is saved and believers are a part of Him, and believers are a part of him, the whole believer, body and soul, belongs to Him and is saved through Him. Hence, Paul argues that it is "in Him" that we have obtained the inheritance of all things (Eph 1:3–14).

Likewise, this means that everything that belongs to the believer is saved with him because he, and all that belongs to him, are one; and since the believer is united to Christ, so are all things that belong to him, including his physical body.

Romans 6–8

Paul argues in Romans 6 that since Christ was raised the spirits of believers during his own day have been given life and are able to walk in that new life. This is stated because Paul is arguing that resurrection has two phases to it: one where the spirit is given life in regeneration and another where the life that has already been given to the spirit is now given to the physical body. In fact, that is Paul's *entire* understanding of salvation when one considers the whole of Romans 1–8 and does not take Chapter 6 out of context. But the argument Paul makes in this and other passages, such as in Romans 8,

1 Corinthians 15, 2 Corinthians 4–5, Philippians 3:20–21, etc., is not an analogy between the physical and the spiritual in these contexts (i.e., Christ was raised physically, but we'll only be raised spiritually) but rather a correspondence between what Christ receives and what we, as those who are unified as one in Him, will receive as a result of that unification. Hence, the resurrection of the body to come cannot be construed as an analogy or metaphor of something that is happening to the spirit in Paul's future.

The "analogy" between the bodily resurrection and the spirit merely exists because Paul makes the same "already/not yet" distinction that Christ makes between regeneration and resurrection. His argument is essentially that of Christ's in the Gospel of John that says that whoever will partake in the resurrection tomorrow must first partake of regeneration today (see John 5:25–29). There is no resurrection (a regeneration and transformation of the body), then, without first being regenerated (a coming to life of the spirit), and this is why the analogy of resurrection can be used to represent the spiritual enlivening. However, the NT is also careful to never call the spiritual "resurrection" a resurrection (*anastasis*). Instead, other types of resurrection language are used for regeneration (e.g., "we may walk in newness of life [Rom 6:4], "made us alive together in Christ" [Eph 2:4; Col 2:13], "raised together with Him" [Col 2:12], although note that these passages reflect what is positionally done for us, not necessarily what has been fully realized by us), but these spiritual texts display only that Paul is using language that trades on the analogous imagery of our future bodily resurrection and is not referencing the entire nature of the thing itself. However, even in these contexts, one notices that the referent is the individual, not the corporate body.

Furthermore, the attempt to argue that because plural pronouns are used in these texts the apostles must be using the word "body" in a collective sense has no force to it because the apostle addressing the group as a plural does not prove one way or the other that he is speaking of what will occur corporately. In fact, such language most often addresses the individuals within a collective not the collective as a singular entity, which would actually be addressed more frequently with the pronominal "it." If anything, then, the use of the plural "we" or "you" would indicate that individuals within the group are being addressed and not the group as a whole entity (cf. Israel or the Church being referred to as a singular masculine or feminine pronoun, singular demonstrative, or with a 3rd masculine singular verbal form). Hence, if the plural pronouns lean in any direction, it is in the direction of taking these statements as directed to the individuals of the corporate group, not to the collective as a singular entity.

There are a few further problems with this view that make it an eisegetical error rather than an exegetically valid interpretation.

1. It is linguistically fallacious to transfer a contextual referent from one passage to another. Nowhere in the contexts of texts like 1 Cor 15, Phil 3, or Rom 8 does Paul use the body of Christ metaphor as the collective church. The context of these passages is the individual. The idea of the "body" being used corporately must be read into the text from elsewhere, which is the very nature of eisegesis not exegesis.

2. The Body of Christ is never referred to as "our body" but "Christ's Body" or just "the Body" in reference to Christ's Body. Yet, in these texts, the body being raised is ours, not Christ's. This is obvious in the context. "The Body of Christ" or "Christ's Body" can refer to His actual physical body or the church in certain contexts due to His federal headship of the church, but the term "our body," "your bodies," etc., isn't the metaphor that Paul uses elsewhere and would make no sense as a referent to the church since we are not the federal head of Christ's church.

3. In Romans 8:11, the term is "your mortal *bodies*," a plural which not only is never used to refer to the singular body of Christ but would not be as Christ does not have multiple "bodies"; rather, we are told in the analogy of Ephesians 4:4 that there is, in fact, only one "body" when it comes to the Body of Christ. Instead, the context of Romans 6–8, which lays out the already spiritual and not-yet physical redemption in the timeline of a believer's salvation, makes it clear that Paul is referring to the redemption of our actual physical bodies.

4. The body that is raised is also called things like "mortal/dead," "corruptible," "perishing," "without honor," etc. Yet, this cannot be true of Christ's Church which has been brought to life, purified, eternal, seated in the heavenly places with Christ in exaltation, etc.

5. The "Body of Christ" analogy also trades on the idea that we are one with Christ right now. We were joined to Him when we believed. Hence, what is true of Christ right now is also true of His body right now. Since this is the case, the resurrection could not be a future event of the collective spiritual body since what is true of Christ now is already true of the spiritual collective body of Christ. What is not a realized experience of those in the body of Christ is the future bodily resurrection, even though Christ has already been raised in His own physical body. It is, instead, our bodies that have not entered into the redemption of Christ and, therefore, have not been redeemed yet.

Hence, we await this hope as a promise from God verified by the fact that He has given spiritual life to His Church through Christ already. Preterism requires a future resurrection from the time that Paul wrote these things since Paul himself speaks of the resurrection as a future event (the aspect of expectation), but the spiritual work of bringing to life the one new man, the body of Christ, through the Spirit has already occurred at the time Paul writes (John 3:3, 6; 5:25; Rom 6:3–5, 13; 2 Cor 5:17; Eph 2:4–5; Col 2:13; 3:1–2; Titus 3:5; 1 Pet 1:3, 23; 2 Pet 1:22–23; 1 John 3:14; 5:4, 18). There is nothing left, therefore, to raise but the individual bodies of believers (John 5:28–29; Rom 8:11, 23; Phil 3:20–21).

6. From a historical redemptive view, if Christ does not redeem our bodies, then everything that was lost would not be redeemed as redemption holds the idea of buying back something in order to restore it. This is where the gnostic tendencies within preterism come into play. In gnostic thought, the human is a spirit in a body, a crude shell, not an ensouled body as Genesis 2 tells us (the body God makes in Genesis 2 is referred to as a man before He even breathes into it [2:7]). What we have in preterism is a loose end, where a person's body, which I would argue is a huge part of what makes up that person, is lost and never saved. The body God made and called a "man" is never redeemed. Hence, only part of a person is saved, not the whole human being. The goal of God's salvific plan to redeem and restore the humans He made is never realized as He must now throw away a huge part of what makes them up and either leave them bodiless or replace that body with a completely new one. This would be replacement, not redemption. Humans, creatures made up of ensouled bodies, as the Bible defines them, therefore, are never really saved. This is why full preterism must believe in an unbiblical view of humanity and an alternate plan of redemption in order to say that God saves people. The error may be related somewhat to the failure to distinguish between *ordo* and *historia salutis*. If we understand that Christ is fulfilling a redemptive history of humanity, body and soul, that was lost and then restored in terms of the *historia salutis* in his death and resurrection, then we understand that this is what has been, and will be, applied to us in terms of the *ordo salutis*, i.e., a complete restoration of our humanity as it exists in the ensouled body. This is why in Romans 8:10–25 even the physical creation groans/longs for the physical redemption of God's children so that it will be restored as well. Note that when the word *ktisis* that appears in vv. 19–22 is used both in Romans and throughout

the New Testament, it is used to refer to the physical created cosmos. It does not speak of the current state of a believer as a creation. I would even include in this conclusion, as an example, the later second century interpolated ending of Mark where the disciples are to proclaim the gospel to all creation, since the physical creation is connected to the humans who dwell upon it. Thus, the entire physical world under redeemed humanity will be redeemed, not merely because they have been spiritually redeemed but physically redeemed by Jesus' death and resurrection. This is the salvation to which Hebrews 9:28 refers. The first coming was to accomplish the *historia salutis*, the second to complete the *ordo salutis*, the final and complete application of the finished work of Christ to all the redeemed creation. Hence, the application of the work of Christ on the cross was applied immediately to all believers spiritually as the "already," but the full application to the bodies of believers and physical creation is yet to come as the "not yet."

7. If resurrection is merely a corporate spiritual event, and the body is to be discarded, why is the work in sanctification most often linked to the body? God sanctifies His people when they are saved (1 Cor 1:2; 6:11). This refers to the regeneration of the spirit/conscience when it has been cleansed and set apart for God to walk in newness of life. This is why the Corinthians can be addressed as "sanctified ones" and those who were "washed" and "cleansed," yet they are in need of sanctification of the body as that which is immature and corrupt. Sanctification is still needed of the body because it too will enter life. If it is not going to enter into life, and the spirit is already sanctified, what exactly is the point of sanctifying the body? The proto-gnostics were correct to conclude that if the body is just going to be discarded in the end, then one ought to just eat and drink for tomorrow we die. Paul agrees with this assessment in 1 Cor 15:32 if the body will not actually be raised. Instead, however, since he states that our bodies are parts of the very body of Christ, again via federal headship, and will be saved therefore with him, we ought to refrain from joining them to sexually immoral persons (1 Cor 6:15).

8. The idea that the salvation won on the cross is a spiritual event misses the fact that Christ is physically dying to pay for a physical punishment that the law prescribes (Rom 6:23; 8:3–4; Gal 3:13; 1 Pet 2:24). The physical salvation of His body in resurrection is an overturning of the physical punishment of the law for mankind. He has both paid the physical price by being put to death via the penalty of the law, and He has paid the perfect obedience needed to inherit God's creation and,

thus, is brought back physically. This redemption is what is applied to believers. They will not be cast out of the physical creation forever; Christ's sacrifice and resurrection will be applied to them, and both He and they will return physically to their glorified cosmos.

I realize there may be avenues out of this particular conundrum for certain preterists, but I offer it up merely as something to be considered since the idea that one needs to sanctify his body is consistent with a view toward a redemption of the body but not necessarily with a non-redemptive view of the body.

In any case, I wish to now summarize the argument in Romans 1–8 in order to show that, contextually speaking, it is simply implausible to take the body referred to in Romans 8 as the corporate body of the Church.

Chapters 1–3: All men, both Jew and Gentile, are corrupt and under the judgment of God.

Chapters 3–4: Hence, faith has always been necessary for sinners to be forgiven, and the works of the law cannot justify anyone, Jew or Gentile.

Chapter 5: Our sin problem, however, must be dealt with, so Paul begins a discussion concerning its roots in Adam and the fact that the law does nothing but condemn those with a fallen nature. The need is for a new nature found in Christ.

Chapter 6: God takes us out of Adam when we have faith in Christ, unites us to Christ as our federal head instead, puts the old man spiritually to death, and gives life to our spirit, the inward man, so that a change of nature occurs through faith.

Chapters 6–7: However, even though the spirit has been given new life, the body is still unredeemed and carries the old man with it. Therefore, a war breaks out between the desire of the flesh, evidenced in one's body, which desires to be enslaved to sin, and the desire of the spirit to be enslaved to righteousness. In fact, in 6:12–14, Paul identifies the phrase, "your mortal body" (v. 12), with "your body parts" (v. 13) and, finally, with "you" (v. 14).

Chapter 7: Paul explains that the law only increases the problem because it expresses a desire for righteousness that is foreign, external, and adversarial to the nature of the flesh, causing Paul to enter into despair and to cry out in v. 24, saying, "Who will save me from this body of death?" ("body of death/mortality," which is a variation of saying, "mortal body"). He states that even though the law is good (vv. 12–13, 16), there is nothing good in him, that is, in his flesh/body (v. 18). The governing principle in his inner man is that the law is good and he delights in it, but the governing principle, as Paul says, *en tois melesin mou* "in the parts of my body" is one of rebellion (vv. 22–23).

Chapter 8: The answer to this dilemma is not that one day the body will be discarded but that Christ has already saved us in an "already, not yet" framework so that we can seek to live and take victorious refuge in the spirit He has regenerated while we eagerly await, along with the rest of creation, the redemption of our body in glorification (a process described as the goal of God's predestining us, a divinely set destiny from which nothing can separate us; and thus, we may take comfort and hope in that). So, the answer to the desires of the flesh is to live in the regenerated spirit with the expectation that one day God will change the nature of the flesh to be in harmony with the law of God in the same way that He changed the nature of the spirit/the inner man to be.

Chapters 9–11: Hence, this is what a true Israelite is, whether of a Jewish or Gentile ethnicity: all must come by faith, and those seeking to come by this redemption via works do so because God has not granted to them, via election, the ability to believe.

Chapters 12–15: Paul now explains what living out the Torah in the new life of the spirit by faith as true Israel looks like for the Christian community.

Now, this is the context for the word "body" in Romans 6–8, explained as the Roman Christians themselves, who have bodies that are inclined to desire sin, would have understood it. This is the context for the phrase, "your mortal bodies" (v. 11), and "our body" (v. 23), in Chapter 8. Denying this is nothing short of ignoring the context and committing numerous exegetical fallacies, all in the effort to save a doctrinal position that misunderstands even the central texts (i.e., the Olivet Discourse texts within the Synoptics) with which this text is being reinterpreted in order to harmonize it with that misunderstanding. Any attempt to put foreign meanings on the words that speculation, not the context itself, supplies is eisegesis that changes what God has said through Paul into what the eisegete's preconceived theological paradigm wants it to say.

1 Corinthians 6:13–15

The salvation of the Christian is made possible because of a concept we refer to as "federal headship." Although the concept is often lost on us today due to an enlightenment-oriented, radical individualism, the ancient world saw the heads of households as representative of the entire household. Whatever the head of a household owned, whatever was a part of his household, was considered part of him, a part of his very body. The metaphor "the body of Christ," often used of the church, is likely connected to this idea. Since we are of Christ's household via faith, we are united to Him as our federal head, the Lord of the household. Hence, as He has obtained the reward of salvation through obedience for Himself, all that He owns is saved with Him. We, as His possessions, the members of His household, are of His very body and are, therefore, saved with Him not because we acquired this salvation for ourselves individually but because He has acquired it for Himself through His obedience (Phil 2) and, therefore, also for us. This means that all that we are belongs to Him and is to be sanctified and redeemed in Him.

This concept becomes particularly important in understanding the gospel as whatever is considered a part of Christ's body must also receive the salvation of Christ. If anything that belongs to Christ is not saved, then Christ has not been fully saved and has not received salvation as His reward. According to the Bible, all believers in Him are His reward, along with the physical creation given to Adam and his descendants.

What makes this important for our discussion is that our physical bodies are also said to be parts of Christ's body. In 1 Corinthians 6, Paul argues that our physical bodies should not be joined to prostitutes because our physical bodies are actually *melē Christou* "Christ's body part" (v. 15). He states, therefore, that the physical body belongs, not to sexually immoral behavior, but to Christ (v. 13) and reminds the Corinthians that God will resurrect us as He resurrected the Lord (v. 14). Again, the resurrection here is clearly in the context of the physical body. The idea is that since Christ, our federal head, owns all of us, body and spirit, then all of us, body and spirit, will be saved with Him. Since He owns all of us, including our bodies, they therefore belong to Him and are part of His body. They, therefore, are to be sanctified by abstaining from sexual immorality since this would be to join Christ's very body to a sexually immoral person (v. 15). Because of this unique placement of our bodies in Christ, they belong to God and are considered sacred temples of the Holy Spirit. Hence, they are to be treated as such since they too one day will be redeemed.

Notice as well the statement concerning resurrection here. Paul uses a double *kai* construction to pair two things to a single event. He does this first in v. 13 where he argues that "God will make both of them [the stomach and food] unnecessary." The same thing, being rendered "unnecessary," is happening to both things. Likewise, the same construction is used to refer to what God does to Christ in resurrecting both Him and the believer in Him. God physically raised Christ in His body, and Paul argues that the Corinthians will also be raised physically in their bodies. The syntactical construction merely conveys the federal headship idea which Paul wishes to communicate: whatever happens to Christ must also happen to those in Christ. If He is raised physically, then they must also be. Hence, since the bodies of believers belong to Christ and are to be raised with Him, they ought not be used for sexual immorality.

1 Corinthians 15

In 1 Corinthians 15, Paul argues that there is a resurrection of the physical bodies of believers and grounds his argument in the fact that Christ has been raised physically in His body as well. This apparently is answering the claim of some group in Corinth that was arguing that there is no resurrection (v. 12).

Hence, he links Christ's resurrection to the general resurrection by using it as the prototype for the general resurrection. He refers to Christ's resurrection as the *aparchē* "first fruits." The first fruits were a portion of the larger crop which was representative of the whole. Hence, Paul here is stating that Christ's resurrection is representative of the larger resurrection. What happened to Him is representative of what will happen to believers who have fallen asleep. As I said before, the metaphor for falling asleep in Scripture (*koimaomai*) refers to the body, and it is the body that is in view here as the ancients believed that the spirit was alive in another realm. It was the return of a person to his or her physical body that was difficult for a dualist-Hellenistic culture to grasp (cf. Acts 17:18 with 1 Cor 1:23; a god who dies in flesh and is raised in flesh is simply unfathomable to the Greeks). Because of this, many in the Corinthian church that was heavily influenced by these Greek ideas were saying that there was no physical resurrection, yet they were still considered Christians by the Corinthian believers due to their belief that Christ saves the soul in some way. Since the Greek concept of Hades was an afterlife that was somewhat dark and grungy, these particular believers must have believed that salvation comprised of Christ saving souls to a paradisal afterlife rather than directing the soul to Hades. Therefore, their understanding was one of salvation within the spirit realm rather than a physical restoration to the created world.

Instead, however, Paul counters this idea by saying that Christ was risen in His body and was witnessed by all His disciples, including himself. Hence, when Paul uses the word *anastasis* "resurrection," it is incumbent upon us to realize that he is referring to the physical resurrection of the body since that is what he is referring to when he speaks of Christ's resurrection. Indeed, the physical body is clearly his subject in the pericope (v. 35). When the term "resurrection" is used here, it is used to refer to the physical body of the individual. There is no referent to a spirit, and to say that the resurrection is simply God giving some other body is to say that the body of the believer, a very body part of Christ, is not actually raised at all. Hence, Paul is speaking about the resurrection of the earthly body in the same way that he is speaking about the resurrection of Christ's earthly body.

Therefore, he can describe its death as "sleeping." Again, the ancients did not believe in soul sleep—a modern idea—but rather that the spirit was awake in the spiritual world. What went dormant was the body. It is the body, therefore, that must be woken up if the whole person is to be raised.

This raising, therefore, follows an order: *Ekastas de en tō idiō tagmata; aparchē Christos, epeita hoi tou Christou en tē parousia autou* "But each in its own order: Christ as first fruits, then those who belong to Christ at His *parousia*." So, Christ was raised in His own physical body first, then those who belong to Christ will be raised in their own physical bodies at His *parousia*. This is the flow of Paul's argument using the words according to the way in which they would have been understood by Paul and his audience in this context.

When Paul discusses the last enemy that must be put into subjection (a "not yet" event for Paul with an "already" sense to it that occurred at the cross), he is speaking about the death in this realm that ended the life of the person in his or her body here on earth. It is this death that must be abolished in order for all things to be complete.

Notice that the end comes after this takes place and includes the abolishing of all other rule and authority on the earth (v. 24), a theology extremely familiar to anyone who has studied Second Temple Judaism, starting with the statement in Daniel that there will be no other kingdoms left besides the kingdom of God (2:44). God's Kingdom completely abolishes the others. They do not reign along with Him. There are no co-regents in that eschatological view. Again, there is a sense in which the kingdom has come and a sense in which the kingdom is not yet, but what is clear is that all other kingdoms will end when the kingdom of God comes upon the earth in its fullest measure. That is the picture Paul has in mind as a Second Temple Jew. All the wicked will be removed from the earth, their kingdoms will be abolished, and the righteous will reign upon the earth forever. And how will the righteous reign? In their resurrected bodies. As Christ received back what He lost in death, so also those who belong to Christ will receive what they lost in death.

But there is further evidence here that when Paul speaks of resurrection, he is speaking of the resurrection of the same body that the believer has on earth. In describing what the resurrected body will be like, Paul assumes that it is this body that is transformed to its best existence rather than a new body that replaces this one.

In verse 29, Paul discusses a group who is baptizing for the dead.

> Otherwise, what are those who baptize on behalf of the dead doing if the dead are not actually raised? Why are they being baptized on their behalf?

Now, Paul's statement is difficult here, but I am going to assume that this group, if comprised of the same people who are saying that there is no resurrection, is practicing baptism in order to save those who have died. These people seem to be practicing water baptism for those who have died in order to save spirits, since they don't believe in a bodily resurrection. Paul seems to be asking, "Why would anyone baptize their physical bodies in order to save spirits if physical bodies are not resurrected?" Baptism signifies a salvation of the whole self. It is not an insignificant point, then, to see many preterists, who hold Gnostic assumptions in their anthropology and soteriology, believe that water baptism is not something taught in the New Testament but only a baptism of the Spirit into Christ.

Paul argues that if the dead are not raised, then one may use the body as he wishes. It is to be discarded anyway. He says that one might as well "eat and drink, for tomorrow we die" (v. 32). The modern reader often thinks of death as annihilation but death in the ancient world is removal from the physical world and the entrance into a spirit world. Again, if we read this in the understanding of Paul's world, instead of in the context of our own, then "death" does not mean we are annihilated but that our bodies are not raised, and we, therefore, have no obligation to purify them and live a holy life in them. After all, they are just shells as the Gnostics would argue. The spirit and the body are not intermingled as a whole. Hence, one might as well do whatever he wants with his body until he dies since there is no redemption of the body a believer is defiling anyway.

In any case, the real argument that Paul is making concerning the resurrection of the whole person is found in the next few statements he makes concerning its nature. The first thing to notice is that he argues that the body that is to be raised is the same body that is buried. It is raised transformed but the same body that went into the grave, nonetheless. Paul states that "what you sow does not come to life unless it dies" (v. 36). Notice, what comes to life is what dies, not something other than what dies. Also notable is the imagery of the seed that is sown; a seed is the entity from which the living plant springs, not some other entity. One does not sow a seed in one place and then a plant springs up in another. The life is produced from the dead seed in Paul's analogy, not apart from it. Furthermore, the imagery of the seed as that which is buried corresponds to the body, not the spirit of a man.

In vv. 37–38, Paul tells us that what is sown in farming is not the form that will come to be, but a bare seed or grain of wheat or something of that nature. He, then, proceeds to tell us that "God gives it a form just as He desires, and to each of the seeds a form of their own."

To what does the *autō* "it" refer in this text? It does not refer to "him," as though this were saying that God gives a believer a body as He wishes, since there is no "him" in the context. Instead, the antecedent seems to be either *gumnon kokkon* "the naked seed" or the *sitou* "wheat grain," both of which are masculine and singular in agreement with the pronoun. Hence, the verse should be translated, "God gives *it* a body as He desires." God gives what? The seed that is sown. The seed that goes in the ground is an analogy of the body that goes into the grave. These are attributes that God is giving to it in the resurrection. It cannot, therefore, be a different body that is given any more than a plant is a different entity than the seed which bore it. As the seed is transformed into a plant, so the mortal body is transformed into an immortal one.

In case this fact eludes anyone, the next clause is clear: *kai ekastō tōn spermatōn idiom sōma* "and to each of the seeds its own body." Hence, He is giving a body/form to each of the seeds that are sown in the ground. That makes the above analysis pretty solid. Paul is talking about what God is giving to the body that goes in the ground. God is not finished with it at death. He is taking it and giving it greater attributes in order to make it the best body possible, an immortal body fit for the kingdom of God.

Paul proceeds to argue that it is possible for the body to take on other attributes because there are different kinds of bodies (that of animals and fish and heavenly bodies), and hence, the body can be given different attributes. It does not have to keep the same attributes it had before, so God has options to choose different attributes for it if He so desires; and indeed, this is the case in the resurrection as God gives immortal qualities to it. But it is the same body, nonetheless. Hence, he tells us:

> *speiretai en phthora, egeiretai en aphtharsia*
> *speiretai en atimia, egeiretai en doxē speiretai sōma psychikon,*
> *egeiretai sōma pneumatikon*

Notice:

>]*It* is sown as perishable. *It* is raised imperishable. *It* is sown as dishonorable. *It* is raised in glory.
> *It* is sown as weakness. *It* is raised in power.
> *It* is sown as a natural body. *It* is raised a spiritual body.

The "it" here is in the third person singular verbs which can be male, female, or neuter. There is no "he" or "she" in the passage and the subject is the *sōma*. Hence, in the context, the neuter pronominal "it" refers to the same subject, i.e., the body. The body is the "it" that is sown and the "it" that is raised. This is clear also from the fact that what is sown is what is being raised up. The imagery of the seed pervades this text. The seed is planted/buried and from "it" is brought a living plant that has been produced from the seed, not apart from it. A farmer does not plant a seed and then expect that a shoot will come up disconnected from the seed. Instead, in Paul's analogy, the seed is transformed into a plant.

Hence, it is the same body that is sown as a perishable, dishonorable, weak, natural body that is raised up as an imperishable, honorable, strong, spiritual body. The whole person has been redeemed because the body has been redeemed, not just his spirit.

It should be noted here that Paul does not use the term "spiritual" to refer to that which is non-physical but rather to refer to that which is redeemed and has its trajectory aimed toward the worship of God. This is why the Corinthians in their physical bodies at the time Paul writes to them can be spiritual. It has nothing to do with being non-material. The spiritual body is the redeemed, glorified body and, according to this context, refers to the raised physical body. Paul, then, continues to argue that Jesus was heavenly but Adam earthy. "We have borne the image of the earthly, so we will also bear the image of the heavenly." He, then, continues to make his analogy of our bodies with that of Jesus. Notice that when Jesus is being referred to as the heavenly, it does not denote that Christ has a different body than the one which was raised, but rather refers to His resurrected body. As Jesus is a heavenly man with His earthly body, so believers will be like Him and be heavenly men with their heavenly bodies, their transformed and glorified bodies that were sown in death and weakness.

Then Paul tells the Corinthians that the natural man, Adam, came first and then the spiritual man, Jesus Christ. As all believers are in the natural man and bear his likeness, they must undergo death or transformation in order to bear the image of the spiritual/heavenly man, Jesus (vv. 45–49). That Adam preceded Christ, and all are in him, is the reason why believers still carry his perishable, weak, dishonored body with them. However, they will receive attributes in the resurrection that bear the image of the heavenly man, Jesus Christ, and His resurrected body. A mortal body cannot inherit the kingdom of God, but a body raised up and given immortal attributes can. Hence, Jesus, in His immortal body of literal flesh and blood reigns in the kingdom, but "flesh and blood" as Paul uses it here is clearly identified as the mortal body that is sown, not the raised immortal body. The phrase, "flesh and blood," cannot be taken literally lest Christ be incapable of inheriting the kingdom of God because He has his very own physical body (cf. Luke 24:37–39). This is further evidenced in v. 50b which clarifies that the body of "flesh and blood" describes the mortal, corruptible, and perishable attributes of the non-glorified body in contrast to the immortal, incorruptible, imperishable attributes of the body once it is glorified and made like Christ's.

Finally, Paul tells us that it is, in fact, *this mortal body* that will be raised up when he reveals that not all of them will fall asleep, i.e., die. Instead, some of them will be transformed immediately thus showing that it is this body that is transformed, not some other body received in place of this one.

He states in vv. 51–52 that he and those who have not yet died at Christ's coming will be altered (*allagēsomtha*). In the context, this clearly refers to the body. It is the body that will be altered, not discarded in order to receive a different one. This will happen in contrast to dying: *ou koimēthēsometha* "we will not all sleep."

Instead, this perishable body (both the adjective and *touto* are singular and neuter and refer to *sōma*, which is the continuing subject of the pericope) must put on the imperishable and this mortal body (again, both the demonstrative and adjective are neuter singular referring to *sōma*) put on the immortal.

Paul ends by showing the Corinthians that death will be swallowed up, i.e., the victory of Christ in subjecting death underneath His feet, to which he alluded before, will only come about when this physical resurrection of the body occurs. When the body is glorified in resurrection, then death truly, in every sense, will have been defeated.

Hence, Paul's argument is that victory has "not yet" fully come about but that Christ's bodily resurrection as first fruits that looks forward to the resurrection of believers is the "already" that assures believers that the "not yet" will, in fact, occur. Hence, contrary to what some were saying at Corinth, there is, indeed, a resurrection of the body.

Preterist Rebuttals

One of the ways that Preterists have attempted to sidestep these problems is by assigning to the word *sōma* one of its referential meanings gained from other contexts, specifically that of the collective body of Christ, i.e., the church. Hence, some Preterists will argue that this is not the raising of the individual believer's physical body, but of the Body of Christ. The raising is then given various meanings that range from a literal raising out of Hades to a spiritual resurrection that takes place in the spiritual new heavens and new earth that is established in A.D. 70.

This fallacious methodology of illegitimate referential transference that I have noted before is a fundamental problem of eisegesis in that the individual does not understand that the reference of a word gained from another context is not available to him to use in any text he sees fit. The interpretation is simply linguistically naïve because it thinks that any use of a word in one passage is a possible meaning that can be plugged into another passage, regardless of the absence of the contextual references that allow the word to be used in such a way.

Instead, as discussed before, most words have what is called an "unmarked meaning." The unmarked meaning is the most common meaning given to a word by the speakers of that language. So, for instance, if one were to ask me what the meaning of the word "dog" is, I would answer that it refers to an animal, specifically a canine. That is the unmarked meaning. It is what the common culture would understand if one said the word, "dog," without any further context provided that might nuance the word further.

However, if one says, "I want to watch *Dog the Bounty Hunter* tonight," a further context that this is a show that refers to a human being is provided so that the unmarked meaning is no longer the assumed meaning. Likewise, if one says, "You dirty dog," when the "you" refers to a human being, the word "dog" obviously no longer carries the assumption of the unmarked meaning, even though the unmarked meaning is assumed in terms of its base meaning (i.e., the person is being likened to a cunning dog). In contexts where "dog" refers to worthless human beings ("You're a bunch of dogs"), or friends ("What up, dog?"), or a human that is unattractive ("She's a dog"), the context, not the mere presence of the word, provides the possible referent.

In this way, merely reading a list from a lexicon can be deceiving as a lexicon is simply listing how various *contexts* use the word together with other referents in the context, not the possible unmarked meanings of the word that can carry over to other contexts. The unmarked meaning of "dog" describes a four-footed creature called a canine. Various contexts may use the word analogically or in other various ways that play off of the unmarked meaning, or it may depart from the unmarked meaning entirely, but the word does not supply those references as possible meanings itself.

This is an important point of exegesis, as a principle emerges where if a context gives little to no indication that the word is being nuanced figuratively or otherwise, either by explicit referent or by providing enough context that it would be absurd to read the word literally in that context, then the unmarked meaning of a word must be assumed to be the meaning intended by the author. Nothing else can be substituted for it simply because the word does not convey anything else but the unmarked meaning by itself.

When one comes to the word *sōma*, therefore, in 1 Corinthians 15, it is important to note that the context begins with Christ's physical resurrection as the first fruits representing the crop to follow. Hence, Paul is speaking of the physical resurrection of one's body in the context.

But even if we did not have this indicator, there is nothing in the context to indicate a specialized use of the word. Instead, the reader is to assume the unmarked meaning of *sōma* as an individual's physical form/body unless otherwise nuanced by the context. Merely pointing out that other contexts nuance the word to refer to the church collectively, i.e., in an analogy Paul makes of Christ's body, does nothing for the case that such a nuance is being used in this context as the unmarked meaning must be assumed until otherwise proven untenable by the contextual referents themselves. If no referents exist and the literal meaning is not absurd (e.g., when Jesus talks about Himself as being bread or something of that nature), then, in the case of Paul's use of *sōma* here, the unmarked meaning of an individual's physical body or physical form/nature must be assumed by the reader.

Further indication of this assumption by both Paul, as the author, and what he wants his Corinthian readers to assume, is when Paul describes the body as mortal, corrupt, perishable, etc., which are descriptions that are never given to the church collectively as the elect and eternal bride of Christ.

Further indication of this assumption is found when Paul distinguishes the bodies of those who have died with those who have not yet died but will be transformed. If *sōma* referred to the church collective, why would Paul now split it into two groups: one dead and one alive? And why is the resurrection for one different than resurrection for the other? Some Preterists attempt to split it between old and new covenant believers, but why does Paul refer to "we" when he says that "we will not all sleep"? The "we" in the context is himself and the Corinthian believers, and the verb is future-referring, speaking of deaths that will occur in the future, not those that have occurred in the past.

Instead, if one merely follows the logical rules of communication, the unmarked meaning should be assumed here, and this means that the two groups are broken up because Paul is talking about individual bodies of believers, some dead and some alive, that are to be given a new immortal and imperishable nature. Only then will death, physical death, the last enemy to be conquered, finally be destroyed as a result of the work that Christ accomplished in His physical death and physical resurrection.

The same linguistic principles apply to the word *anastasis* "resurrection." Many Preterists attempt to force a spiritual meaning onto the word from other contexts (e.g., a regeneration of the spirit) or simply supply a meaning that is never given to the word at all (e.g., some sort of jailbreak from Hades). Yet again, one must first assume the unmarked meaning until the context would have the word refer to something otherwise. The most common meaning of the term, and the one from which other spiritual meanings can be seen to branch, is that of the physical resurrection of the body.

Rather than being dislodged by contextual referents in 1 Corinthians 15, the word is affirmed to carry its unmarked meaning throughout the text. First, as said before, the text begins with Christ's physical resurrection, where Christ is seen by His disciples. Paul immediately proceeds into a diatribe that if there is no resurrection then Christ Himself has not been raised either. Here, we see that Paul's rebuttal of the Corinthian claim that "there is no resurrection" refers to the physical resurrection of the body as that is the only resurrection referenced in the text thus far.

There is simply no mention of a spiritual resurrection with which the Corinthians would have taken no issue at all (and to place it into the text is another example of context replacement), nor is there mention of anything about a release from some netherworld prison. Instead, the entire argument centers around whether one's physical body will be brought back to life and in what way it is possible for a corrupt, mortal body to inherit an eternal kingdom. Paul addresses this by arguing that it does so by taking upon itself a new, immortal, and incorruptible nature in the resurrection.

The attempt to make words mean something other than what their unmarked meanings indicate in contexts that do not indicate otherwise is simply linguistically unjustifiable; and to do so in a context that not only does not supply referents that would indicate nuanced meanings to the words but one that does supply indications that affirm the unmarked meaning can only be considered one of the most egregious examples of eisegesis

2 Corinthians 5

Some Preterists argue that Paul refers to a spiritual resurrection in 2 Corinthians 5 or that he references covenants here. The text states as follows.

> For we know that if our earthly house, which is the tent, we have a building from God, an eternal house not made with human hands in the heavens. For, indeed, because of this, we groan, longing to put on our permanent house, which is of heaven. Indeed, if having put it on, we will not be found naked. For while

> we are in the tent we groan, being burdened, because we do not desire to be uncovered, but clothed over in order that what is mortal might be swallowed up by life. (5:1–4).

However, in the context, Paul is contrasting temporary dwellings with permanent ones in terms of the mortal versus immortal state of the body. This is made clear in that he uses the same terminology as that in 1 Corinthians which indicates that what is mortal, i.e., the temporary tent/body which believers currently experience, will be swallowed up by life, clothed over, etc. In other words, this is not contrasting clothing and nakedness in terms of the body but rather in terms of mortality. The body in its immortal state is clothed. The body in its mortal state is naked. What is seen now is the body in its mortality which is likened to a tent, a temporary dwelling, as opposed to what God has reserved for the future.

In his Analytical Greek Lexicon, Friberg translates the verb "to be (further) clothed with, put on (in addition)." Louw and Nida, in their Greek-English Lexicon of the New Testament, translate it as "to put a garment on over existing clothing—to put on over, to put on an additional garment." Thayer translates it as to "put on over" and BDAG, likewise, "to put on (in addition)." The word references the body in the context as the object that is being clothed once it has been torn down in its mortality, the same idea Paul previously noted to the Corinthians in his first epistle, providing an additional supporting context congruent with this one.

> For this perishable body must put on imperishability, and this mortal body must put on immortality. But when this perishable body will have put on imperishability, and this mortal body will have *put on* immortality, then will come about the saying that is written, "Death is swallowed up in victory. (1 Cor 15:53–54; emphasis added)

Notice the parallels in language between this text and that of 2 Corinthians 5:3–4 in terms of the body being clothed over with immortality, i.e., an eternal nature, as well as the language concerning swallowing up what is mortal. The language becomes even closer when one realizes that the words translated as *thanatos* "death" and *thnētos* "mortal" are actually cognates in the Greek, both of which convey the idea that death and the body of death are synonymous and refer to what is being swallowed up by victory and life. In other words, "death" refers to the death of the body, and hence, what is being swallowed up is the death of the body so that it lives again in life and victory.

For indeed in this dwelling we groan, longing *ependusasthai* "to be additionally clothed with"/"to put on an outer garment of" our dwelling from heaven, inasmuch as we, having put it on, will not be found naked. For indeed while we are in this tent, we groan, being burdened, because we do not want to be unclothed but to be clothed, so that the mortal dwelling will be swallowed up by life.

That which is being clothed over, or "additionally clothed," in each case is the mortal body. In fact, in each text, Paul refers to "this mortal" as a reference to the body/temporary dwelling. Christians long to be clothed over with a more permanent dwelling from heaven, which Paul seems to be using as terminology not for the location of this body but for immortality, that which is immortal and eternal versus temporary, which is his entire point in the context of both the immediate passage and the letter as a whole. We know this because in each text, *thnēton* "mortal" is neuter and refers back to *sōma* "body," which is also neuter, in 1 Corinthians 15. In 2 Corinthians 5, it refers back to *skēnous* "tent/temporary dwelling," which very clearly references the mortal body in the context.

What is being given, then, is not a new body in either context but rather a new nature to the existing body. It is being clothed with immortality, i.e., that which is eternal and not yet seen, as what is seen is only this current mortal body. The imagery of being naked does not refer to some naked spirit as those who fail to read the analogy in the context often suppose. Instead, it is *mortality* itself that is being described as nakedness, vulnerable to chaos and death. This body must take upon a new nature to become immortal, and this nature, like an additional clothing, becomes a protection from chaos and physical death.

But what of the time reference in verse 1 where Paul says, "when our earthly dwelling is torn down . . ."? The translation "when" is a rather unfortunate rendering and has led to a bit of confusion on the matter. The conditional particle *ean* can mean "when," but it is more commonly translated "if," a translation far better suited to this context as Paul does not believe that all people will die (1 Cor 15:51–52). The Greek conditional *ean* "if" is far more ambiguous in terms of providing a time reference (again, context provides that reference, not the word) and merely posits a hypothetical that could take place at any time. The sentence, "If we are robbed today, God will restore what was stolen in eternity" does not mean that God will replace it immediately as though the text said, "When we are robbed . . ." "When" tends to denote a time frame, such as "at the time of," but this is not at all required by the conditional particle and clearly would contradict what Paul is teaching here. In fact, it would make no sense even in a preterist paradigm as Paul states this long before the supposed resurrection in A.D. 70. Yet, if Paul means "when," i.e., "at the time of" the destruction of the earthly tent, the new body is given, then this means that people are being resurrected into their eternal dwellings before the preterist timeline concerning the resurrection that is to take place in A.D. 70.

Instead, Pauline teaching indicates that the mortal body will be resurrected as an immortal body, and hence, all Paul is really saying here is that we know that if our mortal body dies, God has reserved for us something we do not currently see, i.e., the future resurrection where our bodies will be clothed with immortality. These are not two different bodies but a singular body that has now taken upon itself (i.e., "has been clothed over with") an immortal nature that can no longer suffer or be destroyed. Hence, Paul urges the Corinthians to look toward what they do not see, i.e., the immortal resurrected body, rather than to focus on what they do see, i.e., the frailty of the mortal body which is easily torn down.

Philippians 3:20–21

The clear text of Philippians 3:20–21 states:

> For our citizenship is in heaven, from which also we eagerly wait for a Savior, the Lord Jesus Christ; who will transform our crude body into conformity with His glorious body, by the exertion of the power that He has even to subject all things to Himself.

There are a few things of note here. There is a transformation of the body of our humble state into *summorphon tō sōmati tēs doxes autou* "a physical nature that shares in His glorified body." In other words, the nature of the believer's body will match the glorified nature of His body. Jesus Christ can do this because He has the power to subject all things to Himself and that includes even the wayward body. It is important to pay careful attention to the wording. The text does not generically say that He will conform "us" to Christ but rather he will transform our crude "body" to conform with Christ's glorious "body." It is the body being transformed, not the inward spirit or the Christian absent of his body.

Notice, as in Romans 8, Paul states that "we eagerly await" this transformation because Christians are still at war with their unredeemed bodies. This war experienced by the believer in his body is in contrast to those who indulge in the flesh and whose appetite is their god (v. 19). Here, the contrast is between the bodies we have now (the crude body) and the transformed body to come which shares in the glory of Christ's body. Again, the language here is concerning "our crude body," not the Body of Christ, which is the church. The church is never referred to as "our body" but rather Christ's Body. And if there is a distinction to be drawn out between the crude body and Christ's body, what is it? A spiritual one where we who have already been made like Christ in our spirits will be made like Christ in our spirits and so we eagerly await what we already completely have?

It makes no sense to take this as anything other than a reference to the physical bodies of believers, which rather than be discarded will be transformed. Hence, it is "our" body, and this body is in a lowly state that must be glorified in the future as it will be transformed into conformity with His glorified body as an act of Christ causing all things, including all physical things, to submit to Him as Lord.

The unmarked meaning of the term *sōma*, absent of any further contextual indicator that would give it another reference, refers to the literal, physical form/body of something or someone. The term is not referencing the body of Christ here but "our" body that is to be changed to be like Christ's body.

What I find interesting is that preterists, like Kelly Birks, admitted that passages like Philippians 3:21 seem to teach a resurrection of the earthly body that is transformed into a glorious body like Christ's physical body but then backtrack to argue that such is impossible because we know that the resurrection is tied to the *parousia*; and based on the Olivet Discourse placing both at the time of the destruction of the temple, it must be that the resurrection is something different than what is happening to this body since we all know that the bodies of Christians have not, in fact, been physically resurrected. Birks states:

> You look at this text carefully, and what you've got here is a statement of fact. You've got a resurrection stated as fact. In this case, it has to do with transformation. He says that Jesus will transform the body of our humble state into conformity with the body of His glory. *Metaschimatizo* . . . It's simple. It just means to transform the form of a thing. It doesn't say how it's going to happen. Does this say how it's going to happen? He will transform the body. Doesn't say how. How's He going to do it? How does that take place? . . . Now, if this is all the Bible had to say on this subject, if this is all we had, Philippians 3:21, if this is all we had on this subject, then I would have to say, "Yeah, this body, this physical body is going to go through its transformation, but we have more. We are required to compare Scripture with Scripture in order to elucidate the meaning of any doctrine in

order to get the full picture of it. You can't just cherry-pick here and there . . . If the nature of the believer's resurrection body is these carbon-based bodies that get raised, then the *parousia* never happened, the AD 70 *parousia* never happened."[34]

The driving force of this hermeneutic can be seen in what Birks says next.

> Now a bunch of you out there might be going, "Well, that's right, that's what I've been sayin' all along." Yeah, but see, here's the problem with that: If that's the case, then the Bible's a lie. The Bible's wrong. Jesus was wrong. The apostles were wrong. Because you not only cannot produce any Scripture that has the Second Coming happening anywhere else outside of the first century, you can't produce a Scripture that says anything but that the *parousia* would happen within the first century because that's all that's being taught . . . so if you're holding onto a point of view that says that the resurrection, the nature of the resurrection body, is this carbon-based earthly body, basically you're tossing the Bible into the toilet.[35]

This statement nicely sums up the overarching assumption that has hedged in the preterist argument he is making whereby he *must* reinterpret the nature of the resurrection and all other passages to meet a preterist criteria at all costs. He has set up a false dichotomy that either preterism is true, or the Bible is false. Since he believes the Bible is true, preterism must be true. Hence, even though these texts seem to teach a physical resurrection of the believer's body, they must be understood in some other way.

At this point, therefore, he has shown his hand. He is forcing interpretations onto the text in order to maintain what he thinks would otherwise be a cause to reject the Bible as God's Word. Hence, we are not getting exegesis here, but eisegesis demanded by the false dichotomy that has been created by misinterpreting the Olivet Discourse in Matthew as though Matthew 24 was attempting to place the *parousia* at the time of the destruction of the temple in A.D. 70.

As discussed before, there are a couple problems with this view.

1. Scripture interpreting Scripture does not mean one ignores the various contexts of individual texts and replaces them with the contexts of other scriptures. It means one is to interpret everything in its own context first and only afterward compare what it teaches to other passages

---

34. Kelly Birks, SCS 9:104:37–50
35. Kelly Birks, SCS 9:104:51–105:20, 106:30–42

in order to come to a more nuanced picture of the whole truth. That is not what Birks is doing when he ignores the context of one passage in an effort to argue that the Olivet Discourse must tell us what a passage, word, etc., in another context means. This is the very fallacy of context replacement.

2. The driving force of the hermeneutic is the premise that because the resurrection and *parousia* are spoken of as one event with the destruction of the temple in A.D. 70, this somehow means these events happened at that same time. This premise is completely false. The microcosmic event is seen as a smaller bubble distinct from the larger bubble, a drop of water from the ocean, of the macrocosmic event and so spoken of as though they are one single event not because they happen at the same time but because the smaller is viewed as linked in some way to the larger and can, therefore, be spoken of together.

In any case, Birks' is a faulty hermeneutic that ignores the numerous linguistic and logical elements needed to interpret a text accurately. Some examples of this are that his hermeneutic ignores the objects of verbs, the contextual referents of words, relies upon the importation of foreign contexts in an illegitimate transference of contextual referents, uses false dichotomies, strawmen, credulity of the interpreter, and a Gnostic presupposition of what constitutes a human being, e.g., one's true self is his spirit, etc.) all to maintain a harmonious narrative between two seemingly conflicting elements of data that, if read in light of the literary devices used by the Second Temple apocalyptic genre, would not be viewed as conflicting elements in the first place. Preterism seems merely to be a case of false inference that has snowballed into a massive conglomeration of texts that are now interpreted eisegetically to support the original false inference made from misinterpreting the nature of the Olivet Discourse. The false dichotomies, which Birks makes above, that unless the final *parousia* happened in A.D. 70 then no *parousia* happened in A.D. 70 or that either Philippians conforms to Matthew 24, or the Bible contradicts itself and is false show the weakness of this approach. This is not an exegetically honest system but one that must maintain a particular theology at all costs lest the Bible be denied as God's Word and Jesus be made a liar. Hence, this is the grid through which all of these resurrection texts must be pulled even though they seem to be saying something vastly different from the preterist interpretation, something even Birks recognizes but back-pedals to rationalize that it must mean something else since the *parousia* is a one-time event and must have happened only in A.D. 70. This conclusion, however, is due not to responsible exegesis but a non sequitur drawn from a particular view of the Olivet Discourse which assumes that the *parousia* is a singular event and must occur uniquely in, and simultaneously with, the destruction of the temple in A.D. 70 due to the fact that they are depicted as occurring together.

John 5:25–29

The terminology of resurrection is taken from words that mean to "rise up." These terms were often used of one rising in the morning after sleeping. The verb *egeirō* and noun *anastasis* both depict a rising or standing up. This imagery then lends itself to the body that dies and is referred to as sleeping. Whatever sleeps rises in the morning. It is the body, not the person as a soul/spirit, that sleeps, and it is the body, not the person as a soul/spirit, therefore, that rises to the new day. This imagery of sleeping is taken from Daniel 12:2 where those who are dead are said to be sleeping in the dust of the ground. They awaken either to eternal glory or eternal shame. Again, what is "sleeping" in the ground is what is awakened, and this refers to the body.

There are a plethora of passages that indicate that resurrection is of the same body that goes into the grave. For instance, in John 5:25–29, Jesus expresses His concept of the resurrection.

> "Truly, truly, I say to you, an hour is coming and now is, when the dead will hear the voice of the Son of God, and those who hear will live." (v. 25).

From this, we can see how one could interpret resurrection as merely a spiritual reality. Indeed, the fact that Jesus says that the time is now likely refers to a present spiritual reality; and in the larger context of the Gospel of John, this refers to regeneration. Hence, the "already" aspect of resurrection reality is likely present in the text. The question, however, is whether the resurrection only consists of the "already" spiritual aspect or if this is a present reality which looks forward to a future one. That question is answered in the verses that follow.

> "For just as the Father has life in Himself, even so He gave to the Son also to have life in Himself; and He gave Him authority to execute judgment, because He is [the] Son of Man. "Do not marvel at this; for an hour is coming, in which all who are in the tombs will hear His voice, and will come forth; those who did the good [deeds] to a resurrection of life, those who committed the evil [deeds] to a resurrection of judgment." (vv. 26–29)

Here, Jesus expresses the idea that the reason why resurrection is a present reality is because the Son has authority to give life, referencing His enthronement as the Son of Man in Daniel. Hence, this life is given in the present, but it has an effect that continues to give life to its recipient, all the way to the point of resurrecting the physical body.

In verse 28, the ones who hear His voice are those in the tombs. They will come forth, contextually, out of the tombs and go into judgment.

There are a few observations to be made here. The "already, not yet" is displayed in what Jesus says each time. In v. 25, He states, *erchetai hōra kai nyn estin hote* "an hour is coming and now is when . . ." But in v. 28, *erchetai hōra en* "an hour is coming when . . ." notice the *kai nyn estin* "and now is" is dropped when referring to the present reality of the future fulfillment. In other words, the resurrection from the tombs is not something occurring when Jesus says this, but the spiritual regeneration of His followers is occurring and will continue to occur in the future. Hence, the "already, not yet" is displayed nicely in the passage, where the spiritual resurrection takes place first and only looks forward to a future physical resurrection which will complete the wholistic creation/restoration of Christ's people.

It is also displayed in the fact that those who hear in v. 25 are given life. There is nothing about a physical resurrection, but in vv. 28–29, the physical resurrection is in view as those who hear His voice are coming out of the tombs.

What is in the *mnēmeiois* "memorials/tombs" (a word John uses fifteen times in his Gospel, always meaning a literal tomb) is not the spirit; it is the body that was buried. This is displayed well in the following eschatological resurrection in Chapter 6:39–54 and the resurrection of Lazarus in Chapter 11 where it is the body of Lazarus, which was buried in the tomb, that is raised as a type of the eschatological resurrection. Like Lazarus' body, the eschatological body is not some other body but the same body with which these who hear His voice come forth from the tomb. The same is true of Jesus' body which is buried in the tomb and in resurrection is raised and comes out from it.

In fact, this is why John uses the resurrection of the body as an analogy to regeneration. Both the spirit and the body are dead and must be given life by God. They cannot be enlivened of their own accord. Hence, God chooses who will be His sheep and thus obey His Son. As the spirit is supernaturally made alive via regeneration, the body is made alive via glorification. This does not refer to the Old Testament saints who, in Matthew 27:52–53, are said to be raised when Christ is crucified as they are also a type of what is to come but cannot be described as made up of the wicked who will also be raised, according to John 5:29, to be judged for their evil deeds. Likewise,

Jesus states here that "all which are in the tombs" will come out, not "some" or a "few." This "all," again, refers to both wicked and righteous alike. But we are told that only some of the OT saints came out of the tombs, and there is no mention of the wicked nor does it seem obvious why the wicked would rise because of Christ's resurrection. Instead, the reference in John 5 is clearly to the general resurrection of all people which was believed by the majority of Jews within Second Temple Judaism to occur at the end of the wicked world. Notice, however, that those who are raised in Matthew are raised bodily out of the tomb and are referred to as *hagiōn* "holy ones/ saints" who had *kekoimēmenōn* "fallen asleep."

> And the tombs were opened; and many bodies of the saints which had fallen asleep (*sōmata tōn kekoimēmenōn hagiōn*) were risen, and came out of the graves after His resurrection and went into the holy city, and appeared to many.

Here, again, we see that falling asleep refers to the physical body that has died, was buried in the tomb, and needs to be raised again to life. The text explicitly says that it is the *sōmata* "bodies" that had fallen asleep, and these are the same bodies that *ēgerthēsan* "were raised" (aorist passive of *egeirō*, the verbal form of the noun *egersis* used to described Jesus' resurrection in the passage). These bodies come out of the *mnēmeia* "tombs." These saints were physically seen by many in the city.

Even though it is clear, then, that Jesus, in John 5:28–29, is not referencing this event mentioned in Matthew, the Matthean text does provide some indication of how the nature of the resurrection was perceived by the New Testament writers. They did not think it was preposterous that the bodies of saints who had been dead for centuries could rise out of their graves alive and well.

This brings me to another point about this Johannine passage. If resurrection is only a spiritual baptism into Christ, as some suggest, what does that have to do with the wicked? We are told here that the wicked also will be raised and go into judgment. The wicked are not united to Christ. They are raised to judgment so that they might answer to the One who destroys both body and soul in *Gehenna*, a reference to the eternal place of damnation (Matt 10:28). Hence, we see that making the "already" aspect of resurrection for the saints all-encompassing and finished so as to exclude the "not yet" aspect of the general, physical resurrection, makes no sense given the fact that the wicked are also raised. It also makes no sense in the light of the rest of the context of the Gospel of John nor of passages like Matt 10:28 where the resurrection refers to the same body that went into the tomb.

Temporal Resurrections in the Old and New Testament

The nature of the resurrection is also displayed in every instance of the dead being brought back to life in the Bible. They are brought back in the same body. We have already noted John's clear reference to Lazarus as well as the Old Testament saints who rose after Christ's resurrection in Matthew, but there are numerous examples in both the Old and New Testaments of other bodily resurrections. Elijah raised the widow of Zarephath's son from the dead, bodily (1 Kings 17:17–24). Elisha raised the son of the Shunamite woman from the dead, bodily (2 Kings 4:20–37). The man who was tossed on Elisha's bones was raised, bodily (2 Kings 13:21). Jairus' daughter was raised from the dead, bodily (Mark 5:35–43). The widow of Nain's son was raised from the dead, bodily (Luke 7:11–15). Peter raised Dorcas from the dead, bodily (Acts 9:36–41). Paul may have been raised from the dead, and of course, it would have been bodily (Acts 14:19). Paul also raised Eutychus from the dead, bodily (Acts 20:7–12). As the author of Hebrews states, "women received back their dead through resurrection" (Hebrews 11:35). This is likely a reference to the Elijah/Elisha narratives where the women were not haunted by a spirit who was raised but were given back their family members in the same bodies in which they died.

This is also displayed in the task of the Messiah spelled out throughout the Book of Isaiah. When John the Baptist doubts in the Synoptics, Jesus tells his messengers:

> "Go back and report to John what you have seen and heard: The blind receive sight, the lame walk, those who have leprosy are cleansed, the deaf hear, the dead are raised, and the good news is proclaimed to the poor." (Luke 7:22 // Matt 11:5)

Notice that the task of the Messiah is to restore the body, the whole person. He heals the body; that is His role. He heals spiritually, but what is spiritual also hails what is ultimately holistic, physical and spiritual together. Hence, He restores the eyes of the blind, He restores the ears of the deaf, He restores the legs of the lame and the skin of the diseased. He restores the whole body, even raising it from death to life. This good news, that life will be restored to their bodies, is proclaimed to the poor who have only the hope of dying in an impoverished condition. But they now have hope of the resurrection through Jesus Christ, the Messiah, who restores the body.

John 5:28–29

This passage seems to be a rather difficult one for Preterists. I say that because the interpretive gymnastics that are performed to make this passage "fit" the preterist concept of resurrection are quite extensive.

As I argued before, this passage clearly teaches the "already, not yet" nature of the resurrection. The Son gives life to the spirit in regeneration, but there is a future aspect to the resurrection that is "not yet." Jesus tells us that this has to do with all bodies, both of the righteous and wicked, coming out of the tombs.

In Birks's analysis, however, the tomb is a metaphor for remembering someone who has died. This is then transformed into a more ethereal concept of death through a linguistically fallacious etymological approach to lexicography. It is confirmed in Birks' mind by a false inference that dead people cannot hear a voice calling them to come forth, so the fact that they hear must refer to the spirit that is not dead (which is probably news to Jesus who calls forth Lazarus bodily from the tomb with His voice). So, Birks changes the verse to read "all who have died" and then forces his foreign definition of "death" into the text. This is all supposedly proven when one "gets into the Greek." Unfortunately, it is rather the case that only when one abuses language, Greek or otherwise, that this argument can possibly be made. (32:58ff.).

As noted, Birks mocks the idea that a dead body can hear and, therefore, obey Jesus' command to come to life and come out of the tomb (missing the theology of John that has God the Father, through the Son, call dead men to life not by their cooperation with God but by His power and authority alone).

> A lifeless body cannot hear. So it's talking about someone who has died. Who hears? Well, it's the person's spirit apart from their body, the person's spirit, which is cognizant, apart from the physical body. So verse 28 of John 5 is not talking about a carbon-based body coming out of the grave, is it? It's not possible." (SCS 9:36:46–37:17)

What seems to escape Birks's notice is that this same language (Jesus shouting in a loud "voice" to a body in a "tomb" that then "comes out" of the tomb later in John) is used in the physical, "carbon-based" resurrection of Lazarus only a few chapters later.

In John 11:38, 43–44, parallel expressions are used to denote that this passage refers back to 5:28–29 as an example of what Jesus is going to do on the last day.

Jesus, quickly walking again, came to the *tomb*. (Now it was a cave, and a stone was placed across it) . . .He shouted in a loud *voice*, "Lazarus, *come out!*" The *one who had died came out*, his feet and hands tied up with strips of cloth, and a cloth wrapped around his face. Jesus said to them, "Unwrap him and let him go." (emphases mine)

In each text, the Son of Man's *phōnē* "voice" is heard by those who "have fallen asleep/are dead" in the *mnēmeion* "tomb." They "come out" of their tombs in resurrection. Both texts are linked in that the resurrection of Lazarus points to the larger resurrection to come. The resurrection of Lazarus, therefore, is meant to communicate that Jesus is not referring to some spiritual idea of resurrection or to some other body that His disciples will receive after they die. Instead, they will receive back the very bodies that went into the tombs as those are what come out of the tombs in the resurrection to which He refers in both passages.

Birks's interpretation, of course, misses the analogy of sleep and waking and misunderstands what actually falls asleep and what actually wakes up. In the "already, not yet" theology of the New Testament, the spirit has already been raised in regeneration so it does not fall asleep. It never dies, as Christ proclaims to Mary and Martha when Lazarus dies bodily. Instead, the body is described as falling asleep because what falls asleep wakes up. This is Jesus' analogy with Lazarus and Paul's analogy within all his writings as well.

What is sown is the seed which goes into the ground. What is raised up is this body which is promised by God, a promise reserved in heaven that God will redeem/restore the whole person, not just part of the person. John, therefore, tells us that Jesus taught a resurrection of the mortal, physical body, the same body that is put in the grave when a person, righteous or wicked, dies.

James Stuart Russell, a full preterist, saw this argument to be obvious and stated that the resurrection to which John is referring is the literal, physical resurrection of everyone in the grave.

> There can be no doubt that the passage just quoted (ver. 28, 29) refers to the literal resurrection of the dead. It may also be admitted that the preceding verses (25, 26) refer to the communication of spiritual life to the spiritually dead. The time for this life-giving process has already commenced –'the hour is coming and *now* is.' . . . The reader will particularly note the indications of time specified by our Lord in these important passages. First, we have 'the hour is coming, and now is:' this intimates that the

action spoken of . . . has already begun to take effect. Next, we have 'the hour is coming,' without the addition of the words 'and now is:' intimating that the event specified, viz. the raising of the dead from their graves, is at a greater distance of time, although still not far off.[36]

Russell concluded, therefore, that the physical resurrection of all the dead and the rapture had taken place in A.D. 70, which is why Christian history is silent on the matter (i.e., all the Christians were raptured in the resurrection, and hence, there was no one left to report it).[37] This was a necessary conclusion for Russell because he did not understand the nature of apocalyptic speech and so believed that the macrocosmic events mentioned in the Olivet Discourse must take place at that time. Again, this sort of *argumentum e silentio* is unnecessary once the distinguishing characteristics of the genre are understood.

In 1 Thessalonians 4:13–17, Paul states:

> But we do not want you to be uninformed, brethren, about those who are asleep, so that you will not grieve as do the rest who have no hope. For if we believe that Jesus died and rose again, even so God will bring with Him those who have fallen asleep in Jesus. For this we say to you by the word of the Lord, that we who are alive and remain until the coming of the Lord, will not precede those who have fallen asleep. For the Lord Himself will descend from heaven with a shout, with the voice of [the] archangel and with the trumpet of God, and the dead in Christ will rise first. Then we who are alive and remain will be caught up together with them in the clouds to meet the Lord in the air, and so we shall always be with the Lord.

We are met here, again, with the imagery of sleep. Notice that Paul has no concept of soul sleep as he longs to be present with the Lord when he departs. Instead, sleep, as he has used it before in 1 Corinthians 15, refers to the dead bodies of believers. Hence, those who are still alive when Christ comes will not precede those who are dead in Christ in terms of being resurrected. They will be resurrected first (v. 16) when Christ descends from heaven, then those who are still alive will join them in the clouds to meet the Lord in the air (v. 17). Those who have fallen asleep, i.e., in their bodies, will

---

36. Russell, *The Parousia*, 123–25.

37. Russell, *The Parousia*, 126. This claim is an odd one as one would suspect a statement from early documents such as the Didache or Shepherd of Hermes or Clement indicating that the event took place before them. Instead, these books indicate that the event is still to come.

be return with Christ at His coming. Paul further explains this by stating the fact that Christ will raise them from the dead, i.e., raise their bodies from the graves, if we keep in line with the sleep metaphor.

The contrast here is between the dead in Christ who are raised first and those who remain alive who are raised second in the resurrection of the righteous. However, as we know from Paul's theology, this second resurrection is an immediate transformation of the body where no death is experienced. The idea here is that those who remain and those who have fallen asleep will receive a glorification/resurrection of the body when Christ returns.

Second Temple Judaism believed that resurrection was of the body. Hence, the Sadducees did not believe in the resurrection because they did not believe that the body would be raised (see their argument concerning which husband a woman who married seven brothers would have if the body were raised and the two would once again become one flesh [Matt 22:23–28 // Mark 12:18–23 // Luke 20:27–33]).

Hence, when these words are used in these contexts, with the same referents contained in other Second Temple contexts, it is a linguistic fallacy to conclude that they might mean something else. The context would have to change contextual referents and mold the words through clearly expressed polemical language. Instead, what we find is that the words are used in accordance with the unmarked meaning that the audience would have assumed. For instance, when Paul addresses the Pharisees, he states that he believes as they do concerning the resurrection: "that there shall certainly be a resurrection of both the righteous and the wicked" (Acts 24:15). There is no indication that he means anything other than they do when they talk about the resurrection.

This is an important point because the concept of the resurrection of the body is expressed throughout popular Jewish literature (e.g., the Enochic traditions that form a basis for Jewish apocalyptic writing found in the Pseudepigrapha and the Dead Sea Scrolls). The New Testament is very much at home when it speaks of the resurrection, and it is not a resurrection of spirits or different bodies but of the very body presently owned by those who are promised resurrection if they follow God and His Messiah. The burden of proof, therefore, is on those who would say that the New Testament does not have a concept that the body of every believer will be raised, using words differently than its religious environment uses them. Certainly, resurrection realities are given new life in the biblical "already, not yet" framework, where future promises have present realities that have been applied already spiritually; but this is an added element brought on by this framework, not a denial of the fundamental meaning of the words that are used in their Second Temple environment nor a rejection of the future, physical aspect of the promises given.

Of course, the most well-known passage is found in the Apocalypse of John. Apocalyptic literature often contains elements of God's Kingdom destroying and replacing other kingdoms, God coming in judgment of the nations, a messianic figure of some sort, and the resurrection of the saints. In this regard, John's work is stock apocalypticism. It also fills out the picture alluded to in the rest of the New Testament.

> Then I saw thrones, and they sat on them, and judgment was given to them. And I [saw] the souls of those who had been beheaded because of their testimony of Jesus and because of the word of God, and those who had not worshiped the beast or his image, and had not received the mark on their forehead and on their hand; and they came to life and reigned with Christ for a thousand years. The rest of the dead did not come to life until the thousand years were completed. This is the first resurrection. Blessed and holy is the one who has a part in the first resurrection; over these the second death has no power, but they will be priests of God and of Christ and will reign with Him for a thousand years. (Rev 20:4–6)

Notice here that there are souls alive and well in heaven with God already. Hence, their *ezēsan* "coming to life" has to do with the resurrection of their bodies. This is, therefore, referred to as *hē anastasis hē prōtē* "the first resurrection," which refers to the belief that there will be two resurrections, one of the righteous and one of the wicked. John splits them here, even though they are joined together elsewhere, perhaps to denote the "already, not yet" nature of the believer's resurrection versus the "not yet" nature of the unbelievers. In any case, resurrection cannot refer to spirit here since John saw the souls previous to the resurrection in heaven with God already. These souls are not in bodies in heaven, and they only come alive when they participate in what is called the first resurrection, i.e., the first raising up. It is important, again, to note here that the imagery of rising is from the imagery of sleeping, which throughout the New Testament has referred to the actual body of the believer who has died.

The second resurrection, even though it is only implied by John's statement of the first, is likewise of the body.

> Then I saw a great white throne and Him who sat upon it, from whose presence earth and heaven fled away, and no place was found for them. And I saw the dead, the great and the small, standing before the throne, and books were opened; and another

> book was opened, which is [the book] of life; and the dead were judged from the things which were written in the books, according to their deeds. And the sea gave up the dead which were in it, and death and the grave gave up the dead which were in them; and they were judged, every one [of them] according to his deeds. (20:11–13)

Here we have what John seems to indicate is the resurrection of the wicked. They are raised, as Jesus said back in John 5, in order to be judged for their deeds. Notice that they are given up from death, the sea, and the grave, a term obscured by our translation of *hadēs* as a place name (although a possible reference to the netherworld, its coupling with the sea and death makes it unlikely to refer to anything but the literal grave).

In order to understand the term "death," we need to look at the concept here that the dead are being given up by the sea and the grave. Are souls in the sea? Do they live there now? The word for seas here is not that for the abyss, which might be synonymous with hell. Instead, it is merely the word that denotes bodies of water. Hence, this refers to those who have been lost at sea. Likewise, therefore, since John is talking about where bodies are buried, *hadēs* simply means "grave." Hence, "death" here refers to the bodies being dead. Death gives up the dead bodies. Neither Second Temple Jews nor the authors of the New Testament believed that the spirits stayed in the grave or that they lived in the water if they died there. They believed that spirits went to the netherworld, either to an unseen realm to be with Jesus or lost in the murkiness of the spirit world. The only thing left in the grave was the body. Hence, the second resurrection, the resurrection of the wicked, is one where their bodies are being raised up from the grave/sea/death itself.

All these passages indicate that the bodies that are buried are the same bodies that are risen. The resurrection, therefore, is of the body. He who is raised is raised a whole person, the whole person he was when he died. To life or to death, to reward or to punishment, the person who goes there goes there as a whole person. Hence, he who gives an account for deeds done in the body will also experience the reward of those deeds in the body.

The Synoptic Testimony

The Synoptic Gospels indicate that the resurrection will be of the actual body one had during his life.

> Do not be afraid of those who kill the body but cannot kill the soul. Instead, fear the one who is able to destroy both soul and body in hell. (Matt 10:28)

If one is inclined to argue that this is a different body than the one an individual had during his life on earth, then why is a body that has not known sin being punished? Other texts make it clear that it is the same body that is resurrected that experiences punishment.

> If your right eye causes you to sin, tear it out and throw it away! It is better to lose one of your members than to have your whole body thrown into hell. If your right hand causes you to sin, cut it off and throw it away! It is better to lose one of your members than to have your whole body go into hell. (Matt 5:29–30)

Notice that it is said it is better to lose one part of your body than to have your whole body thrown into hell. This is not another body or a spirit that is going into hell but "your whole body" from which a part could be taken now in order to avoid the entire body being thrown into the fire. This is also said of the opposite destination.

> If your hand or your foot causes you to sin, cut it off and throw it away. It is better for you to enter life crippled or lame than to have two hands or two feet and be thrown into eternal fire. And if your eye causes you to sin, tear it out and throw it away. It is better for you to enter into life with one eye than to have two eyes and be thrown into fiery hell. (Matt 18:8–9)

Why would one enter crippled or lame if he were getting a different body in the resurrection? The logical inference from the text is that if one were to remove a part of his physical body, he would enter into life with what remains of his physical body. This is said to be better than going into hell with one's body intact. "Life" here is defined as the eternal state of the righteous by Matthew, and this is made clear by Mark's Gospel.

> If your foot causes you to sin, cut it off! It is better to enter life lame than to have two feet and be thrown into hell. If your eye causes you to sin, tear it out! It is better to enter into the kingdom of God with one eye than to have two eyes and be thrown into hell, where their worm never dies and the fire is never quenched. (Mark 9:45–48)

So, the picture that is given to the reader is one where the future resurrected body is the same body that one had during his temporal life which now enters into the eternal state, either to life, i.e., the eternal kingdom of God, or to an eternal wasting away in hell. This inference stands even if one concludes that Christ is using hyperbole concerning the loss of body parts as the physical resurrection to both life and death must be affirmed in order for the hyperbole to make sense.

Likewise, Jesus' encounter with the Sadducees may help one understand what the unmarked meaning of the term "resurrection" was to the Second Temple Jewish audience. The argument given by the Sadducees hinges on the physical resurrection of the same body. The conundrum is that if the same body is resurrected and a woman has been bound in one flesh to more than one husband, then she would end up married to all her husbands in the resurrection since all of their bodies would return and the one flesh union would come back into play. In the scenario given to Jesus, the woman has seven brothers, indicating not only a multiple marriage, which would be seen as sinful enough, but an incestuous one according to the guidelines of Leviticus 18.

Jesus does not answer the question by saying that the resurrection is spiritual or of another body and, therefore, the woman would not be bound by virtue of the body that was made one flesh having been destroyed, which would have put down the objection immediately; but instead, He argues that they are not married or given in marriage in that age and in the resurrection. So, it is a difference of the time period and the understanding that marriage is for *this age*, and not the one to come. The fact that Jesus does not counter their claim by saying that the resurrection is not physical or is that of a different body, i.e., one not bound to previous flesh unions, is a strong indication that He is not disputing the aspect of the resurrection as a raising and transformation of the mortal body which one had during his temporary life in this age.

The Physical Return of Christ

2 John 1:7 states that the one who says that Jesus is not coming back physically is antichrist. This is due to the fact that the present participle, not the perfect as in 1 John 4:2, is used. Don Preston, in a private correspondence with a member of my church, argued that the participle does not have any tense as his way of circumventing the text.

The statement that there is no tense in the participle is overly simplistic in its understanding of tense. I could state that there is no tense in any of the Greek verbs, finite, participle or otherwise, because Greek's verbal system is aspectual, denoting a presentation of an action as wholistic (perfective) or unfolding/processive (imperfective); but this is a generic statement about the verb outside of its uses, not the application of the verbal forms to various syntactical and referential situations within their contexts.

So, for instance, a participle can take upon the "tense" of whatever verb it is attached to in an adverbial syntactical construction when it is a dependent participle rather than asserting an inherent tense of its own. Hence, some have misunderstood this to mean that a participle does not convey tense, but that's simply not true in circumstances where you have the participle function as the only verb in a closed statement, as you have in 2 John 7. In this case, there is no verb from which the participle derives a separate nuance; instead, its tense/aspectual form (in this case, the present form), together with the particular verb *erchomai*, denotes either a present or future referring action. What this means is that either John is saying that antichrist is denying the proposition that Jesus *is coming* in the flesh right now or gnomically (i.e., from time to time), or that Jesus Christ *is coming* in flesh in the future. To take it as present-referring makes no sense here. Hence, you have a present participle that is future referring as is a typical use with the verb *erchomai*.

Hence, the grammars note this fact. Perschbacher states that an "independent or absolute participle is used as a finite verb when no other finite verb is present."[38] Although Wallace miscategorizes this particular use in 2 John 7, he does classify the type of participle I would argue this is as "independent verbal participles." He states that what is "included in this category are those participles that function as though they were finite verbs and are not dependent on any verb in the context for their mood . . . The participle can stand alone in a declarative sense as the only verb in a clause or sentence. In such instances, the participle may be treated as an indicative verb . . . This usage is apparently due to Semitic influence, for such occurs in Hebrew and Aramaic."[39]

Wallace alludes to this possibly being linked to Semitic influence as the present participle in the Hebrew of the time period is very commonly used as the verbal idea in a clause.

All grammars note that the idea that the participle does not convey time is a generic statement about the construction apart from any context, and that this is not true in application when the participle, in fact, conveys antecedent, contemporaneous, or subsequent time to the main verb or speech. Furthermore, the instances where it stands alone, it functions as a finite verb. This is when there is no other verb or deictic indicators, from which it gains its tense, presented along with it. This is the case both in 1 John 4:2 and in 2 John 7. In fact, even in the substantival forms that are more adjectival, a tense is seen when it is not adopting the tense of a

---

38. Perschbacher, *New Testament Greek Syntax*, 411.
39. Wallace, *Greek Grammar Beyond the Basics*, 650–53.

dominant verb. The "one who has come" refers to the one who has come already, and the "coming one" refers to one who is coming, i.e., in the future.

For instance, take the use in John's Apocalypse (1:4, 8; and 4:8) where Jesus is described with participles of different tenses, as *ho ōn kai ho ēn kai ho erchomenos* "the one who is, the one who was, and the one who is coming" (again, present participle, future-referring). Is Preston suggesting that these are not meant to convey tense so that they should just be translated, 'the one who exists, the one who exists, and the one who exists"? What does this concept do to the numerous other passages in the NT that convey the Son of Man's future comings and the coming of the future age that are referred to with the present participle which everyone agrees is future referring in those contexts? For instance, Matthew 16:18 (present participle of *erchomai*, future-referring); 24:30 (present participle of *erchomai*, future-referring); 26:64 (present participle of *erchomai*, future-referring); Mark 10:30 (present participle of *erchomai*, future-referring); 13:26 (present participle of *erchomai*, future-referring); 14:62 (present participle of *erchomai*, future-referring); Luke 18:30 (present participle of *erchomai*, future-referring); Luke 21:27 (present participle of *erchomai*, future-referring); Hebrews 10:37 (present participle of *erchomai*, future-referring).

Hence, the participle here conveys the same idea. It functions alone as the verbal idea of the clause. Furthermore, John purposely uses the present participle, as opposed to the perfect participle in 1 John 4:2, to show the scope of their denial (i.e., that Jesus is coming physically). 1 John 4:2 conveys the past incarnation/coming. 2 John 7 conveys the future coming. The docetic Gnostics denied both the physical first coming and the physical second coming.

Furthermore, the participles typically correspond to these past, present, and future connotations in their aspects (i.e., aorists and imperfects are typically applied to past events, or that which is antecedent to the main verb when there is one, presents are typically applied to contemporaneous actions or what is contemporary to the main verb when there is one, and so on for the future). In cases where you have certain verbs, like *erchomai*, the present can refer both to present and subsequent actions to the time the author is speaking or to the main verb (as is true in English as well). In short, Preston has an oversimplified view of the Greek participle that does not take the evidence into account nor does he seem to understand the Greek tenses with their specific uses with certain verbs, like *erchomai*, which never uses a future tense, given his statement that there is no future tense here.

So, neither one of his statements (the participle does not convey temporality in general and that there is no future tense here) refutes the argument that 2 John 7 is conveying a physical future coming of Christ.

He seems to have no problem being completely dogmatic that the perfect participle in 1 John 4:2 absolutely conveys Christ's first coming/incarnation. Yet, we only get this from the tense of the participle. He, therefore, has to affirm of 1 John 4:2 what he denies in 2 John 7 in order to explain away the passage. There is no reason to play these games. If the participle does not convey a time reference, then he cannot refer to the perfect participle in 1 John 4:2 to argue that the instance in 2 John 7, in comparison to 4:2, is past referring either.

Hence, the evidence shows that the participle is, in fact, applied to events according to its tense, especially so when used as a singular verbal idea as we have in these two passages. That the present use with *erchomai* is often used either as present, present-referring or present, future-referring is clear; and when speaking of the coming of Christ, apart from its historical use in narrative description, it is often, if not always, used as present, future-referring.

There is simply no substantial objection to the fact that this must be taken as a future reference to Christ's second coming, not the first. The only reason one might try to come up with reasons against this is that it does not support a preconceived idea that one wishes to maintain, namely that of a traditional mistranslation or full preterism. We can see that there is no hesitation in taking the perfect participle in 1 John 4:2 as conveying tense when it supports one's position. This is simply because this is the natural reading of the tenses unless some other contextual circumstance exists. There is no such circumstance in 2 John 7, and the natural reading of this text is to read it as a future event.

Therefore, John purposely goes from saying that these heretics deny Jesus *has come* physically to saying that they deny that Jesus *is coming* physically. He *is coming* in the same way that the Son of Man throughout the Gospels and in Revelation is said to be coming, i.e., in the future to the author's speaking.

Now, of course, the idea that a future tense is needed to convey a future idea is easily dismissed. Present participles that speak of His second comings are numerous, and there are numerous present tense forms of *erchomai*, as noted before, that are future-referring when referencing His comings. This is true of other referents as well. For instance, notice the switch in tense from present, future-referring to aorist, past-referring in Matt 17:11–12. These participles clearly refer to a future event in the context. Yet, modern grammars would say the same thing about the verb; it does not convey tense, but aspect. That does not mean that it is not applied temporally to a passage. A distinction must be made between the unmarked grammatical semantics of a verbal form with the contextualized verbal form which often conveys tense.[40]

This is not to mention the numerous future events, such as the Spirit's coming, that are described with the present participle and are future-referring. The grammars are clear that the participle is applied to various situations and is used by the author to convey tense. Participles are subordinate to other verbs and deictic indicators in the context when they exist, but, as said before, none exist here so the participle functions as the verbal idea of the sentence (as the present participle often does in late Biblical Hebrew), and the tense indicates a future reference, as it does in numerous other places.

All this to say, Preston's points are all incorrect and evidence a superficial understanding of the language. The participle here conveys a future idea, the present is future-referring in the context, and there is absolutely no justification for ignoring it and plugging in the verbal idea of the perfect participle from 1 John 4:2 instead.

As Lieu states:

> Particularly striking here, however, is that the present participle "coming" (*erchomenon*) replaces the perfect participle of 1 John 4:2, "having come," while the prepositional "in flesh" instead of preceding the participle follows it, although it is a moot point whether this gives it less significance. A number of translations ignore this present tense and treat it as if it were past, "has come," merely repeating 1 John 4:2 (NRSV); this, however, is not what the participle means, and to translate so fails to explain why the author, if dependent on the passage in 1 John, has made the change—even if he had an aversion to the perfect he could have used an aorist tense. Similarly, attempts to suggest that the present tense expresses a timeless truth or continuous reality clash both with the inherent idea of the verb and with the precision implied by "in flesh."
>
> It is, however, the nature of the verb that the present participle can have a future reference: "Jesus Christ (as) the one to come in flesh." The earliest known writer to cite 2 John, Irenaeus, used a chain of Johannine passages—2 John 7; 1 John 4:1–3; John 1:14; 1 John 5:1—to make this precise point: "knowing the same Jesus Christ, to whom were opened the gates of heaven because of his enfleshed assumption, who also in the same flesh in which he suffered, will come [future] revealing the glory of the Father (*Against Heresies* 3.16.8). The future fleshly coming

---

40. Cf., for instance, the uses of the word *eimi* in places like Revelation 1:8 or 17:8–11.

was a common concern of the period, more frequently made by an appeal to Acts 1:11 ("in the same manner"). Although rarely taken up by translations and less favored among modern commentators, a continuing line of interpretation has seen in 2 John 7 a defense of the expectation of a fleshly parousia. Such a reference cannot be excluded, and might cohere with the warning against eschatological loss of a reward in the following verse.[41]

Lieu here alludes to modern commentators, largely of the more liberal variety, who do not care to take this statement as referring to the future advent of Christ. One might assume that this is for the obvious reasons that many liberal commentators share the same assumptions about the Second Coming that the Docetic Gnostics held, i.e., that the Second Coming is a spiritual event, not a physical one where Christ literally returns in the same body with which He rose from the grave. The large number of conservative commentaries who assume the parallel, however, may evidence that it is simply a tradition that many find hard to give up, even though it is without contextual, grammatical, and syntactical warrant.

For instance, Dodd goes so far as to say that the text's plain reading to anyone who knows Greek would obviously convey the idea that the author was referring to Christ's Second Coming. He then, however, proceeds to denigrate the author of the Second Epistle by saying that he must not be versed in the subtleties of the Greek language: "We shall perhaps do best to assume that our writer is not skilled in the niceties of Greek idiom, and to understand the present passage in light of the First Epistle."[42]

Apart from appealing to an idea that denies the meaning of the text as it is written, Dodd is correct to admit that the Greek is clear enough to convey the idea that the present participle references the future coming of Christ, not His incarnation. This is because the Docetic Gnostics not only denied that Jesus had come in the flesh but, because of their denial of His physical entrance into the world, they also denied that he would return in the flesh. If Christ had not come in the flesh in the first place, it was hardly true that He would return in a physical body that He never took on in the world. One, perhaps, sees this same denial in Paul's reference to the heresy of Hymanaeus and Philetus in 2 Timothy 2:17–18. The heresy with which Paul is addressing throughout the work is a form of Gnosticism. Hence, the two men are likely spreading Gnostic ideas about the resurrection, which enabled them to assert that it had already taken place since Christ was not returning physically and the resurrection was not a physical event.

---

41. Lieu, *I, II, & III John: A Commentary*, 253–54.
42. Dodd, *The Johannine Epistles*, 149.

John is likewise addressing Gnosticism and is refuting the same types of claims. Hence, John intentionally changes the tense of the participle from perfect, which is past-referring in the context of 1 John 4:2, to the present, which is future-referring in the context, in order to combat the same heresy that denied the physical appearance of Christ, both in His incarnation, as John addresses in 1 John, and in His return, as John now addresses in his second epistle.

Hence, the text should read as follows:

> Because many deceivers went out [aorist: past-referring] into the world, those who do not confess [present substantival participle: present-referring] Jesus Christ is coming [present: future-referring] in flesh. This is [present: present-referring] the deceiver and the antichrist."

The statement evidences that this refers to the second coming of Christ. Along with a rudimentary understanding of Greek grammar, Preston offers nothing but the same old argument that it must somehow mean the same thing as 1 John 4:2, even though John plainly changes the tense from perfect to present.

Acts 1:9–11

> After he had said this, while they were watching, he was lifted up and a cloud carried him from their sight. As they were still staring into the sky while he was going, suddenly two men in white clothing stood near them and said, "Men of Galilee, why do you stand here looking up into the sky? This same Jesus who has been taken up from you into heaven will come back in the same way you saw him go into heaven." (Acts 1:9–11)

One of the issues involved in interpreting what most people throughout history thought to be a pretty straightforward statement about Christ's return is correctly identifying the genre in which a text appears. Obviously, this text, when read literally, would negate much of preterist thinking since it indicates that Christ will return visibly.

In an effort to refute a literal reading of the text, Preterists argue for a more symbolic and/or limited interpretation that is congenial to a preterist eschatological paradigm. For instance, in his foreword to a reprint of J. Russell's *The Parousia*, Ed Stevens argues the following.

> The Acts 1:11 reference to the return of Christ is easy to apply to AD 70 when we realize it is speaking of the reverse of the visible *ascent* of Christ in Theophany form. His *descent* would follow the same Theophany pattern as His *ascent*, meaning it would be visible like His departure. He ascended visibly with clouds and angels in the presence of a few disciples, and the two angels (Acts 1:10-11) promised that He would descend visibly "in like manner" in that same Theophany pattern to only those disciples whom He wished to see it. Both the going away and the return were "cloud comings" (Theophanies) accompanied by angels. He left the same way He would return (in clouds with angels) to appear to His anxiously awaiting disciples . . . They expected His return before all of that generation died. Some of them were promised to remain alive until His return, and that they would literally "see" it before they all died (Matt. 16:27-28 and John 21:22f).[43]

With many preterist interpretations, there is a tendency to allegorize the text, which expands the possibilities of its interpretation. This is done, precisely, because the text, if taken literally, would indicate a visible return of Christ in the flesh. Hence, the clouds are seen as imagery that represents God's presence in terms of God displaying His glory and judgment. In *that sense*, Christ returns physically in terms of a physical judgment upon Jerusalem and display of His presence and glory. The language is interpreted, therefore, to simply refer to the symbolism of theophany and not a literal, visible, and physical return of the man, Jesus Christ, to the earth. Stevens, however, seems to see the literalness of the text; but with his view that Christ returned in A.D. 70, he must make the argument that Christ literally appeared in the clouds and returned to earth, limiting His appearance to only the eyes of the apostles. How this might square with other texts, like Revelation 1:7, that indicate that even Christ's enemies will see Him is unclear. One can only imagine that the two hermeneutics would be combined so that the preterist can have his cake and eat it too by saying that Christ's enemies saw the storm cloud theophany, but His disciples saw Him (even though the text says that all will see *Him*).

Other Preterists, however, see the text as only symbolic, theophanic language, which merely presents Christ as returning in judgment, so that what is seen is the judgment of Christ, not Christ Himself in any literal sense.

The exegetical problem with this allegorical interpretation is that it ignores the genre and context which provide the necessary indicators that something is to be understood as symbolic. Luke's writing is not simply

---

43. Stevens, "Foreword," x.

narrative, but it is a historical narrative that is written to a Gentile in an effort to give an account for the rise and hope of Christianity, which is the restoration of the kingdom of God that will be restored to the world and ruled by the Davidic King, Jesus Christ. One would find it difficult to find much symbolism in the book that is not also meant to convey what literally takes place. Acts is not a prophetic, poetic, or apocalyptic book that would assign its imagery merely to the symbolic. This means that direct speech within the book seldom, if ever, takes the form of allegory but instead describes something literal to its readers. The exception to this might be when the author depicts what is said in a vision.

Second to this, there are no referents in the text that indicate that this statement refers to the destruction of Jerusalem in A.D. 70. This is precisely why Stevens brings in other contexts that he believes provide the necessary referents that this text is missing. This is, however, a subtle admission that nothing in this text indicates that the return of Christ to which the angel refers is identical to the event of A.D. 70, and therefore, it is a standalone passage that describes the nature of the macrocosmic event itself, i.e., the literal manner in which Jesus will return in the macrocosmic event, not how He will return in A.D. 70.

Finally, much is made of the fact that "in like manner" can be used in analogies of things that are not literal. This is obvious, but it misses the fact that the genre and context indicate that there is no figurative analogy here. The analogy is between Christ physically ascending into heaven and Christ physically returning from heaven. This is also made clear by the use of the collocation *houtos trepon* "in this exact way," where *houtos* "this" refers to the physical ascension into the clouds. It is in *this* way that Christ will descend. Hence, the only difference is in the direction, not the nature of the movement.

Likewise, Revelation 1:7 states,

> Look! He is returning with the clouds, and every eye will see him, even those who pierced him, and all the tribes of the earth will mourn because of him. This will certainly come to pass! Amen.

The question becomes, "Who pierced Jesus in Johannine thought?" The Jews? The Jews certainly participated in His death by betraying Him, but it was the Romans who actually pierced Him according to John.

> Then, because it was the day of preparation, so that the bodies should not stay on the crosses on the Sabbath (for that Sabbath was an especially important one), the Jewish leaders asked Pilate

to have the victims' legs broken and the bodies taken down. So the soldiers came and broke the legs of the two men who had been crucified with Jesus, first the one and then the other. But when they came to Jesus and saw that he was already dead, they did not break his legs. But one of the soldiers pierced his side with a spear, and blood and water flowed out immediately. And the person who saw it has testified (and his testimony is true, and he knows that he is telling the truth), so that you also may believe. For these things happened so that the scripture would be fulfilled, "Not a bone of his will be broken." And again another scripture says, "They will look on the one whom they have pierced." (John 19:31–37)

In Revelation, John quotes his translation of Zechariah 12:10 that he gave in John 19:37 rather than the LXX translation of the prophecy which may be an indication that he is referencing the Roman soldier, as a representative of Rome, who pierced Jesus. According to John, therefore, the passage that is applied to Christ, i.e., Zechariah 12:10, is ultimately fulfilled not by the Jews, as it may or may not be in Zechariah's context (the text is rather ambiguous), but by the Romans in its ultimate fulfillment at the cross. In fact, even the passage in Zechariah indicates that the Jews are looking *to* YHWH for salvation as God pours out His Spirit of favor and supplication upon them so that they repent of their sins and are cleansed of sin. They are not killing Him. This is not the context of Revelation, which is one of final judgment of the enemies of Christ and His people.

This would mean that the enemies who see Jesus with their very eyes are the Romans, representing the entire wicked world at the time of John, which is also the group opposed to Christ throughout the Book of Revelation. What originally is said in Zechariah 12 about the tribes of Israel being restored to YHWH in repentance now becomes about the tribes of the entire earth who are judged for persecuting Judah. Hence, *tēs gēs* here should be expanded to the idea of the earth, and not just the land, as it is consistently applied throughout the Apocalypse as that which clearly displays that the entire earth is in view (see 3:10, where *gē* parallels *oikoumenē* and 14:6, where the *gē* is parallel to "every nation, tribe, language, and people"; see also 1:5; 5:13; 6:13; 7:1; 10:6; 12:4, 9, 12; 13:3, 8, 14; 14:7; 17:2, 8, 18; 18:3, 23; 19:19; 20:8–9; 21:1, 24).

The enemies of Christ and His people are the Roman Empire with its Roman Emperor who is even depicted as entering into a war against Christ (19:11–21). The Jews may or may not be understood as playing a part (if the word "Jew" is to be taken literally and not a figure for true and false Christians in 2:9 and 3:9), but the main enemy, either way, remains the pagan

Roman Empire throughout the book. It is the entity ruled by the beast, killing Christians who do not worship the beast and his image and pressuring Christians to compromise rather than to remain faithful.

What this means is that the typical preterist interpretation of this passage that claims the Jews merely saw Christ in terms of the physical manifestation of judgment upon Jerusalem makes little sense. First, the text states that every eye will see Him, not just those who pierced Him. Second, it says that they will see Him, not just His glory or judgment or something that surrounds Him. Third, the Johannine context implies that the Romans, who represent the wicked world, will see Him. There is no indication that any of this occurred in the first century. Because of this, these texts have yet to be fulfilled.

Chapter 5

Preterist Prooftexts concerning Time References

I have argued that misunderstanding the macrocosmic/microcosmic nature of apocalyptic speech allows the preterist to take any time references found within texts of an apocalyptic nature as referring to the Olivet Discourse, or to any other microcosmic situation occurring around the time. The genuine understanding of the nature of apocalyptic speech (the joining of micro and macro events together as a singular event in order to describe the micro in terms of the macro) negates this idea. Hence, even if all these time reference texts referred to A.D. 70, then, due to the nature of apocalyptic speech, they still would not support the false inferences made by full preterism that claim that all eschatological prophecy has been fulfilled but only the claim of partial preterism that the microcosmic events have been fulfilled but the macrocosmic events these smaller events only picture are still future.

The exegetical freedom to discover to what event each text in its own right refers, through a proper understanding of the genre, allows the interpreter to see that many of the words and phrases understood by preterists to be referring to the Olivet Discourse have been misapplied to that event and, in fact, do not convey the ideas that preterists think they do when proper exegesis is employed.

The following chapter will discuss what are normally considered to be the "time references" that supposedly make the argument that preterism is true. Again, as stated before, even if these passages were taken as preterists often take them, then it still does not prove preterism as true. This is why the nature passages are more important than the time passages, simply because they can prove or disprove whether preterism is the correct interpretation of biblical eschatology.

Does the Greek Word Mellō Mean "About to"?

The argument made is that the word *mellō* means "about to" in the sense that whatever is being said is something that is soon, or "about to," to occur. There are Preterists who argue that the word, in general, refers to something about to come, and there are Preterists who argue that the word when used in a particular grammatical construction means "about to." I'll discuss the former first and then the latter.

Verses that use *mellō* need to convey the idea of imminence through context. The word does not inherently mean "about to come." If this were true, then even in verses, like Romans 5:14 where Adam is a figure of Christ who was *tou mellontos* "the one to come," would have to be translated as "the one about to come." Was Christ the one who was about to come after Adam? The time between Christ and Adam, even in a strictly literalistic timeline, is around 4,000 years or so. If 4,000 years later constitutes what is "about to come," then the expression really does not indicate imminence.

Again, in Matt 11:14, Jesus speaks of John as the predicted Elijah who was *ho mellō erchesthai* "the one who was to come." The word here simply means "destined" or "going to." He was Elijah who was destined or going to come. Now, if the word meant "about to come," it would make little sense here since not only has John already come, but there are hundreds of years between John's coming and the prediction made in Malachi. Matthew 17:12 evidences the same idea.

In Acts 13:34, Jesus is said to be raised from the dead, "no longer *mellonta* ["destined/going to"] decay." Now, if the word that I have translated as "destined" or "going to" means "about to," then is Jesus only saved from a near death rather than death *en toto*? Is Jesus only no longer about to decay, or is he no longer going to decay, period, regardless of whether it is a little time from when this is spoken or thousands of years from the time this is spoken? The translation of "about to" makes no sense here because it is not the meaning of the word.

The translation "about to" is a contextually referential translation that usually is taken from narrative contexts where everything that is said and done can be seen as taking place immediately or imminently in the context. Hence, things are "about to come" because in the narrative context that's contextually understood. It has nothing to do with the word *mellō*, which simply means "going to," "destined to" happen. Anything beyond this needs the context to supply the rest, whether it be the event that is going to happen or the time concerning when that event will occur. To assign a time-indicating reference in one context to another that does not supply the time frame is to commit the illegitimate referential transference that is common among those interpreters who employ exegetical fallacies.

Therefore, the word really just means something that is "going/destined to happen," or "going/destined to come." The context nuances the word in terms of when it comes. Hence, the word is not a deictic marker. In other words, it doesn't convey how long away something is from the time it is spoken. The context does that. Hence, the word can refer to something that is distant or something that is imminent, depending on the context.

What most Preterists confuse is the difference between *meaning* and contextual *referent*. This is the linguistic fallacy called *illegitimate referential transference*. What often happens is that the word's "meaning" is taken from contextual "referents" found elsewhere. Most of these are narrative contexts where events are all "about to happen" because narrative tends to speak of the immediate future of X occurring soon in the narrative. Narrative very seldom drifts out of the immediate. An exception might be to talk about something in the distant future, such as the destruction of Jerusalem which will not occur for another forty-five years or so after the Olivet Discourse takes place; but this is the nature of context, such as in narrative, not the meaning of *mellō*. The context can refer to an X that is "about to come," "coming in the more remote future," or "going to happen in the very distant future." Genuine deictic markers are needed to secure such nuances. The word cannot do that itself as it is not a word that conveys time.

Hebrews 10:1, for example, says that the Law was a shadow of things to come, referring to those things that would come about in the New Testament age. The Law was given around 1,500 years before that age. Does 1,500 years constitute what is "about to come"? Again, the word simply does not inherently refer to something that is "about to come." Context must bear that out.

Then there is the more specific argument that perhaps *mellō*, when used with an infinitive, conveys the idea of imminence. Supposedly, the lexicons state this idea. Now, part of the problem here is that this is an improper way of reading a lexicon. A lexicon is not arguing that a particular construction always means such and such. What a lexicon does is simply state that grammatical construction X is used with word Y with a meaning of Z in a specific text. But most lexicons will also go on to indicate that grammatical construction X is used with word Y with a meaning of M in other contexts.

That is because the lexicon is not arguing that the grammatical construction means Z or M but is simply noting that the grammar is used *in particular contexts* to convey this or that meaning. It is not often saying that the grammatical construction itself conveys that meaning. In the case of *mellō*, it does not. In fact, the infinitive is said to accompany the word with multiple contextual nuances.

For instance, Thayer, a common lexicon used by Preterists, states that the infinitive can be used in contexts that refer to something that is "on the point of doing or suffering something." But then it notes that the infinitive is used in contexts where the word just refers to an intention that someone has, irrespective of conveying anything about the time the intention would be fulfilled. Likewise, the infinitive is used with the word in contexts that indicate things that "will come to pass . . . by fixed necessity or divine appointment." Again, the infinitive is used of things that "we infer from certain preceding events will of necessity follow," again, without indication of time reference. Finally, Thayer states that the word with the infinitive is used "in general, of what is sure to happen," again, without any time reference indicated. This is true of all the aspects/tenses in which the infinitive with *mellō* may appear.

Likewise, BDAG, the most preeminent of the modern New Testament Greek lexicons, tells us that the infinitive with the word can mean to "be on point of, about to" but then goes on to explain that the infinitive is used in contexts that indicate other meanings as well, like "certainty that an event will take place in the future," and that this construction with *mellō* is used to express something that will occur in the future. It also just denotes an intended action, as Thayer noted. Additionally, this construction appears in contexts that reference what is simply "destined, inevitable," something that will "certainly" happen. It is used in contexts of something that happened in the past, and something that was destined to come from a past perspective, in contexts that talk about promises made long ago and were destined to be fulfilled. How could something that already happened be spoken of as something that is "about to happen" in the immediate future? In short, the lexicons are not arguing that *mellō* always means "about to" with this particular construction. They are simply noting the grammatical constructions that exist in the various contexts with various contextual meanings.

In fact, I would argue that *mellō* does not have the connotation of "about to" at all but that this translation of the word is a referential one. In other words, the idea that *mellō* is a time indicator that indicates something that will occur soon is actually being drawn from the context and not from the word at all. In fact, one can put that phrase into any temporal context as a viable translation because the *context*, not the *word*, indicates these events are about to take place. Furthermore, one does not even need the word *mellō* to exist in the text at all. For instance, imagine if one were to take the following biblical narrative that does not contain the word at all and do just that.

> But now I am *about to* go to the one who sent me, and not one of you is *about to* ask me, 'Where are you *about to* go?' Instead your hearts are filled with sadness because I have said these things to you. But I tell you the truth, it is to your advantage that I am *about to* go away. For if I do not *soon* go away, the Advocate will not *soon* come to you, but if I am *about to* go, I will *soon* send him to you. And when he *soon* comes, he will *soon* prove the world wrong concerning sin and righteousness and judgment—concerning sin, because they do not believe in me; concerning righteousness, because I am *about to* go to the Father and you will *soon* see me no longer; (John 16:5-10)

In Romans 15:25-26, we could just as easily put the phrase "about to" in our translation: "But now I am *about to* go to Jerusalem to minister to the saints. For Macedonia and Achaia are pleased to make some contribution for the poor among the saints in Jerusalem." One can do this in a narrative or any context that indicates that something is about to happen. The word *mellō* is not even needed. The word itself clearly does not convey that concept as there are many instances where imminence is not indicated contextually and even would contradict such a meaning. It is, therefore, not the word that is supplying this meaning but the individual contexts in which the word may sometimes appear. This makes sense in terms of things that are going to happen, especially in narrative where they are going to happen soon in the context. But since the word does not carry this meaning over with it to other contexts, it cannot supply the meaning in contexts where imminence is not indicated by some other time indicator.

Hence, all the verses that supposedly indicate the imminence of the Second Advent that have only *mellō* as a supporting argument are actually begging the question[1] and, therefore, do not support the idea that these things are "about to happen."

The "Last Days"

Many preterists, as well as many others in other camps, think that the phrase "last days" means "the final days of the age." Gary North argues that the last

---

1. Texts often used include Matt 3:7; 12:32; 16:27; Luke 3:7; 24:21; John 14:22; Acts 17:31; 24:15, 25; Rom 4:23-24; 8:13; Eph 1:21; Col 2:16-17; 1 Tim 4:8; 6:19; 2 Tim 4:1; Heb 1:14; 2:5; 6:5; 9:11; 10:1, 27; 13:14; James 2:12; 1 Pet 1:6; 5:1; Rev 3:10; 12:5.

days were the time of the New Testament before and during A.D. 70 and so limits them to "the early days of the church of Jesus Christ."

> The last days spoken of in the New Testament were eschatological last days for national Israel, not for the New Covenant Church. The "last days" were in fact the early days of the church of Jesus Christ. How do we know this? How do we know that we are not now living in the last days and never will be? How do we know that the New Testament was written in the last days, which came to a close over 1,900 years ago? Because the New Testament clearly says so. The author of the Epistle to the Hebrews specifically identified his own era as the "last days." He wrote that God "Hath in these last days spoken unto us by his Son, whom he hath appointed heir of all things, by whom also he made the worlds" (Heb. 1:2). He was quite clear he and his contemporaries were living in the last days. (North, Preface, xiv).

Keith Mathison, when commenting on 2 Timothy 3:1, also argues that the phrase often refers to the "last days of the Jewish age" and "not a prophecy of conditions at the end of the world."[2] David Chilton argued that "the Biblical expression *Last Days* properly refers to the period from the Advent of Christ until the destruction of Jerusalem in A.D. 70, the 'last days' of Israel during the transition from the Old Covenant to the New Covenant."[3] Michael Sullivan argues that the New Testament phrase is linked to its use in Isaiah 2:2–4; he claims that since both refer to the destruction of Jerusalem, the phrase signifies that particular judgment in A.D. 70.[4]

Contrary to the claim of these authors, the preconceived notion that the phrase, appearing only five times in the New Testament,[5] refers to the

---

2 Mathison, *Postmillennialism: An Eschatology of Hope*, 215.

3. Chilton, *The Days of Vengeance*, 16 fn 35, 51.

4. Sullivan, "The Eschatological Madness of Mathison," 80. The claim that Isaiah 2:2–4 is linked to the event in A.D. 70 is a rather difficult stretch to make. Beside the problem of needing to play with the text in order to get global peace established forever in the first century, this is yet another case of illegitimate referential transference. The reference of one text cannot be assumed in another, even if that text is quoted (and it is not in any of these passages).

5. The use of *ep' eschatou tōn chronōn* in 1 Peter 1:20 may be an additional variation of the plural phrase. See also *ep' eschatou chronou* in Jude 1:18 which parallels 2 Peter's *ep' eschatōn tōn hēmerōn* (3:3). If *eschatos* is understood as equivalent to ʾaḥēr in these passages, then the referential idea is that of the future which may be an ongoing time period rather than the terminal point of a time period. Hence, the passages are merely arguing that "in the future, there will be mockers..." 1 Peter 1:20 contrasts Christ who, although He was foreknown before the foundation of the world, has been manifest "upon the last times," i.e., the present and future time period in contrast to the ancient time before the world. Notice that the period of the "last times" here is that in which

final days of something is simply due to a misunderstanding of the terminology that is itself due to the common English translation of the phrase as "last." The New Testament phrase *en eschatais hēmerais*, in 1 Timothy 3:1 for instance, is taken from the Hebrew *bᵉ 'aḥᵃrît hayyōmîm* "in/upon the last/latter days" and is the common Hebrew expression that means "in the future."[6] Although a future time can refer to such a thing as the "end days," the context would have to dictate this and not the terminology as the phrase often contrasts "former" or "beginning days," i.e., the past. It does not, therefore, necessarily or even usually refer either to the final days of the world, an age that ends, or anything else.

For instance, in Hosea 3:5, God promises blessings in the "last days" to Israel if it returns to Him after it is punished in the exile. This clearly indicates what God will do in future days ahead as opposed to the judgment they have received for their past and present sins.

> For the sons of Israel will remain for many days without king or prince, without sacrifice or *sacred* pillar and without ephod or household idols. Afterward the sons of Israel will return and they will look for the Lord their God and David their king; and they will come trembling to the Lord and to His goodness in the future.

Again, in Genesis 49:1, Jacob assembles his sons to tell them what will befall them in the "last days." These warnings include Simeon and Levi being dispersed in Israel rather than inheriting land like the other tribes (something that happens in Joshua's day), Zebulun's tribe being situated at the seashore (also in Joshua's day), Issachar becoming a slave to other peoples (days of the judges), Dan becoming the judge of the other tribes (days

---

God has made Christ known to people and is something that references his earthly ministry, not solely His second coming in A.D. 70 or beyond.

6. For thorough discussions on the Hebrew word-group (*'aḥar, 'aḥᵃrê, 'aḥᵃrît*) used in the biblical and Qumranic literature, see Shemaryahu Talmon, *Literary Motifs and Patterns in the Hebrew Bible: Collected Essays* (Winona Lake, IN: Eisenbrauns, 2013), 137–56, *Dictionary of Classical Hebrew,* 193–201, *Theological Dictionary of the Old Testament,* 204–212, *Hebrew and Aramaic Lexicon of the Old Testament,* 35–37, *Theological Dictionary of the New Testament,* 152–59, *Brown-Driver-Biggs,* 31. I would also contend that the Greek term, for the most part, has not altered the meaning of the Hebrew in any way for the Jewish author and, instead, must be assumed in the Greek New Testament to have the same connotations unless context dictates otherwise. For the LXX's use of the term *eschatos,* see Takamitsu Muraoka, *A Greek-English Lexicon of the Septuagint* (Louvain: Peeters, 2009), 294. Unfortunately, many scholars in the past, e.g., Kittel (*TDNT* 2:697–98), merely assumed the meaning not only of the Greek term but even of the Hebrew phrase and simply ignored the temporal referents made clear by the contexts in which the words appear.

of Joshua and Judges), and tribal trouble between Gad and other groups (again, Judges). In other words, they all have to do with blessings and judgments which will happen to the tribes within their biblical futures. They concern how prosperous or lacking in prosperity (in terms of war, food, riches, wisdom) each tribe will be. This is not concerning the end of the world or the end of national Israel, but instead, the phrase, "the last days" merely means "future days" or "in the future."

Again, in Numbers 24:14, the phrase is used to refer to "future days" when Israel's king will rise up and crush the Moabites, Amalekites, Kenites (Saul and David accomplish this), not "final days" when all nations will be destroyed and replaced with God's kingdom. Even though one might certainly read this as a microcosmic foreshadowing of that larger event, it is clear that this specifically speaks to David's cleansing of the land from the oppression of foreign peoples (2 Sam 8). Hence, the term is talking about "future days," future from Balaam's perspective, not "final days."

An angel comes to Daniel in 10:14 and tells him that he has come to give Daniel understanding of what will happen to his people b^e 'ah^arît hayyomîm (LXX: ep' eschaton tōn hēmerōn). What he reveals to Daniel is found in Chapter 11, which moves from the Persian to Seleucid Empire and ends with the death of Antiochus IV in 164 B.C. In other words, the phrase does not refer to the end of an age or the world but to what will happen to Daniel's people "in the future."

In Deuteronomy 4:30, the phrase refers to the post-exilic period when Israel will return from the exile and worship YHWH after being punished. In 8:16, it refers to God's intent to discipline Israel in the wilderness in order to do good to them in their future lives in the land of Canaan.

In LXX Proverbs 31:25 (English v. 26), the noble woman has prepared her household so well that when she enters the hēmerais eschatais "last days," i.e., "future," she laughs at it instead of being in distress from lack of preparation. The text refers not to the final time of something but, instead, merely to the future for which she has prepared.

Ecclesiastes 1:11 contrasts those who lived in the past with those who will live "in the last," referring merely to people who live in the future. In fact, the term "last" in biblical literature by itself is often misunderstood as meaning "final" in older scholarly literature. Instead, it is clear that the term has a wider range of meaning and can be related more to the idea of the "latter" or what comes "after," referencing a point in time as a departure for what is to follow. For instance, Moses speaks of Israel's continued rebellion against God upon "the last of my death" (Deut 31:27) and "the last of my end" (v. 29), which means "after my death" and "after my end." In LXX Job

8:7, *prōta* and *eschata* are contrasted as the first part of Job's life (i.e., before he got sick) with Job's future (i.e., after he will be made well).

In fact, it is important to note that the LXX translates the Hebrew *'aḥar/ 'aḥᵃrê/ 'aḥᵃrît* "after" as *eschatos* "last" and the Hebrew phrase *'aḥᵃrît yommîm* "after days" as *eschaton hēmeron* "the latter days." Hence, one encounters passages like Haggai 2:9, where the splendor of Solomon's temple in the past is contrasted with the second temple's splendor in the future, as well as Isaiah 41:22 which contrasts the former things with latter things (i.e., past things versus future things).

Whereas *'aḥar/ 'aḥᵃrê/ 'aḥᵃrît* and *eschatos* can refer to the uttermost limit of something (e.g., a body of water or the earth, numbers or a list of something, and even of days when speaking temporally with a plurality of days), it is most often referring to the future from the person's perspective, not some period of time at the end of the world or the end of an age.

This is more likely what Paul and Peter mean by statements that indicate mockers will come in "the last days." The phrase likely means "future" not "final days" as popular opinion often interprets it. Hence, "in these latter times/present and future days in contrast to the former days, mockers will come with their mocking." Jesus' prediction that He will return becomes, in the apostle's day and beyond, a source of mockery for the people of God. This was not an issue in the past before Christ came and made this prediction.

As such, other than contrasting what occurred in the past with what is now and/or will occur in the times to come, the passages in which this phrase occurs cannot be considered time-reference passages, marking an imminent end. They merely refer to the time to come versus the past. In fact, what both Paul and Peter describe in each of their passages are things that both occurred in their days and continually occur throughout their future. Mockers still come with their mocking concerning the coming of Christ. People still seek out teachings that tickle their ears and are corrupt. These are not things of the end that only occurred in the days of the apostles before A.D. 70 but things that occur in latter days, after days, future days as opposed to the days in the past which begin in the days of the apostles and continue on into the indefinite future.

Marvin Pate explains this commonly held view among scholars of different eschatological paradigms.

> The "already-not yet" understanding of New Testament eschatology, the latter days/future eschaton has been inaugurated and continues on to its consummation; but from the time of Christ to the time of His second advent, one is living in the future time predicted by the prophets in the past. It is this latter period, as

opposed to the former Old Testament period, that is called the latter/future days.

The New Testament clearly states that the age to come or the last days dawned with the first coming of Christ (Acts 2:16–21; 1 Tim. 4:1; Heb. 1:2; 1 John 2:18). A generation ago, C. H. Dodd expanded on this truth by pointing out that the early church (especially as it is depicted in the book of Acts) attributed eschatological significance to the life, death, and resurrection of Jesus Christ in a number of ways: (1) In Jesus the messianic age dawned (Acts 2:16; 3:18, 24) through his ministry, death, and resurrection (2:23–33). (ii) By his resurrection, Jesus has been exalted to the right hand of God as messianic head of the new people of God (2:33–36; 3:13). (iii) The Holy Spirit is the sign of the presence of the eschaton (the final age) as well as the proof that Jesus currently reigns in heaven in power and glory (2:23). (iv) The messianic age will shortly reach its consummation in the return of Christ (3:21). (v) An invitation is always extended for people to receive Christ and the life of the age to come (2:38–39).[7]

Hence, the author of Hebrews argues that the "last days," i.e., the present and future, as opposed to days of the past, will be characterized as the new age where God has communicated to His people through the Son.

> After God spoke *in the past* in various portions and in various ways to our fathers through the prophets, *in these latter days* he has spoken to us in a Son, whom he appointed heir of all things, and through whom He created the world. (Heb 1:1–2; emphasis added)

Not only do we see the contrast between the *palai* "old *times*" and the *ep' eschatou tōn hēmerōn toutōn* "upon the latter of these days" or "upon these latter/future days," but the verse also contrasts the mode of communication that characterizes these future days of the Son with the one that characterized the previous days of God speaking in various, diverse manners. The old days saw God speak to His people through the prophets via various means (e.g., visions, angels, signs, dreams, etc.), but in the future era, God has spoken through His Son. Each of these modes of divine speaking characterize the entire era. To this very day, God has spoken through His Son. We are not in a different era than that of the auctor. We are in the same time period where God has spoken through His Son. This means that

---

7. Pate, *Four Views on the Book of Revelation*, 92.

the church, to this very day, is in the latter days the auctor describes as they would stretch from the time of the Son into the unforeseeable future.

Gary DeMar acknowledges this and argues for it by asserting that "the Hebrew word often translated 'last days' means nothing more than 'in future days.'"[8] DeMar, however, asserts that "the last days are not way off in the distant future. The end came to an obsolete covenant in the first century. In AD 70, the 'last days' ended with the dissolution of the temple and the sacrificial system."[9]

In other words, even though DeMar understands that the phrase refers to future days as opposed to past days, he still seems to think that it means "end of days" and argues that this phrase in the New Testament refers to the end of the days of the old covenant. As I have argued, it does not refer to the end of anything. They are not literally last days of anything, as though they refer to the final days of something. DeMar appeals to 1 Corinthians 10:11, but this verse says that the *telos* of the ages (plural) has come upon Paul and the Corinthians.[10] In other words, all of the ages, either from eternity's "past," or all of the past ages of the earth's existence, have existed with the goal of God bringing salvation and holiness to the church. That is why Demar states this in the context of arguing that what happened to Israel in the past happened to it as an example to correct and guide the church. The statement in 1 Corinthians has nothing to do with the end of the Old Covenant in context.

In the New Testament, the latter days, as opposed to the former, are characterized by the kingdom of God that was promised by the Prophets. The kingdom is the gathering of God's people that is made up of the remnant of Israel and the other nations. This gathering of the kingdom begins with the earthly ministry of Christ and His apostles, and it has not ended since. In fact, this kingdom will never end, and hence, the "future days" have no terminus. Hence, contrary to DeMar and others, they did not end in A.D. 70, and there is no Scripture that ties the phrase to that event. It must be read into the text via eisegesis.

Again, Preterists have misunderstood the terminology that has been used by the biblical authors due to their biased understanding of the English word "last"; but the Greek word does not exclusively mean "last" but rather *eschatos* can mean "latter, future, time after former times, or final in a list." When used of a plurality of days in the Bible, especially in contrast,

---

8. DeMar, *Why the End of the World Is Not in Your Future*, 90.

9. DeMar, *Last Days Madness*, 38. See also his conclusion in *Why the End of the World*, 92: "The 'last days' were operating in the first century and referred to the close of the Old Covenant era (see 1 Cor. 10:11)."

10. DeMar, *Last Days Madness*, 39.

either explicitly or implicitly, to other days in the past, it refers to present and future days in contrast to those former days. It is the stock way the LXX translates the Hebrew idiom "after days" with *eschaton hēmeron* referring to future days in contrast to past days, and the New Testament adopts this usage.[11] Hence, the argument that sees some sort of time indicator of the "final days of Israel," or any other final days, in the various phrases that incorporate the "last days" often may be a case of a mistranslation that expounds upon the limitations of the English word not the semantic range of the Hebrew, Aramaic, and Greek words or their contextual referents used in biblical literature.

The Time Is Almost Here or the Time Is Now Here?: The Misunderstanding of the Word "Near"

We are met with a series of verses that use the word *engus*, which most people think conveys the idea that the time of Christ's coming or the end is "near." They interpret the English word "near" as something that is almost here, but still yet to come.

What a thorough study of the word bears out is that it actually conveys the idea that something is currently accessible, within one's reach, because it has come into the sphere or proximity of one's presence. By "near," the English reader thinks of the idea as something that is almost here. It is something that is on its way but not quite here yet. This is a great example of why English glosses are not sufficient to convey the concepts of words from a foreign language. The receptor language may carry nuances in it which are not carried by the original language that the translator is attempting to bring over into his target language. In other words, when an English person thinks of the word "near," he thinks of the two nuances the English word has and then assigns them to the Greek word *engus*; but the Greek word has the idea that something is within the proximity of one's grasp. It is accessible.

Hence, the word near in English can convey something that is in one's presence, in a spatial sense, or something that is close to arriving but not

---

11. This is the "latter" in relation to a former thing as Lexicographers have noted (see under the meaning 2a in BDAG). Certainly, confusion is brought in by the use of the Greek word itself since it often refers to the final element in a list, but this is an issue of illegitimate referential transference when common use in secular Greek literature is understood as the reference over common use of the term in the LXX and New Testament passages cited. As noted before, these texts do not evidence the use of the phrase as meaning "final days" in the Greek New Testament. Instead, the New Testament authors were heavily influenced in their translation of Hebrew and Aramaic terms by the LXX and followed it on numerous occasions.

currently in one's presence. The same can be said of the temporal idea of "near." In other words, if something is "near," it is either in your present time frame or it is about to be in your present time frame but is not currently in your present time frame. This thinking, however, is completely fallacious. The word *engus* doesn't have a nuance that indicates something is "almost but not currently in one's presence." It is something accessible, within arm's length, something that one can reach out and take hold of. Hence, an old translation of the term was "at hand."

Instead, the word simply conveys the opposite of something remote or something not currently in one's presence or present. Likewise, its verbal form *engizo*, specifically in its perfect form, refers to something that has already come and is in one's presence.[12]

For instance, James states, "You also be patient and strengthen your hearts, for the Lord's *parousia* is near" (5:8). James encourages them to wait on the judgment of the *parousia*. This is interpreted to mean that James believes a *parousia* is close to happening. As stated before, that is a possible interpretation of the text since the apostles believe that a/the coming of Christ is imminent. However, the word *engus* likely refers to one of the many judgments that Christ will place upon His church as He purges and, therefore, receives the rule over His kingdom. What James would be saying to his audience, instead, is that they should be patient and encouraged that the judgment of Christ is currently being made, and therefore, has already become accessible to them. They are not without recourse when others oppress them since Christ is present among them and they have access to His royal judgments. This interpretation is strengthened by the fact that 5:9 proclaims to them, "Behold, the Judge is standing before the gates!" He is not on His way. He is not planning to come from His current dwelling. He has arrived. He is already here and ready to judge. Hence, *engus* does not mean "almost here" but instead conveys the idea that something is within arm's length, within one's proximity, and can be accessed at any time. The Judge is standing at the gates so Christians can come and make their pleas before Him when oppressed. The better translation of *engus* in many cases, therefore, might be "here" instead of "near," which can convey the idea in English that something is close to entering one's presence but has not yet come into that presence. This would mean that what is "near" is not yet accessible but is close to becoming accessible, which is the opposite of what the word actually means.

---

12. The verbal form *engizō* can be a bit more fluid since some of its verbal forms can convey the movement of something that is coming into the presence of something else, i.e., "will draw near," "is drawing near," etc.

Another example often cited is 1 Peter 4:7, which states, "the end of all things is *near*." There are, of course, numerous issues concerning not only what the word *engus* means but what nuance of the word *telos* ("termination," "maturation," "goal," "outcome," etc.) is being conveyed. It is context that must explain the referent of the word, so it's crucial becomes necessary to understand the message of 1 Peter. The context says nothing of the Old Covenant coming to an end or anything about Old Covenant Israel, as many Preterists would argue.[13]

Hence, Peter is not talking about the end of "all things" concerning the Old Covenant only. Instead, the book encourages Christians to enter into maturity through suffering under unjust authorities which it lists as unjust leaders within the Roman government, disobedient husbands, and harsh masters. These are the scattered Christians throughout Asia Minor, so their unjust authorities are not Jews in Jerusalem. Hence, it would do little good to bring any sort of relief to them by telling them that all things within old covenant Israel were at an end. That does little to comfort someone being oppressed by Nero or other Roman authorities. It does little to comfort the wife of an unjust husband or the slave of a wicked master. Therefore, the interpretation of the "all things" as referring to the old covenant is a case of the context replacement fallacy.

It is possible, however, that Peter is telling his audience that all these authorities are coming to an end, and therefore, they will no longer be oppressed by them in light of their destruction. This would be another indication of Peter's belief concerning the imminence of the eschaton. He may be very well using the final return of Christ, as it is used throughout the New Testament, as a major motivation for sanctification in a world passing away, which is the thrust of the book. The believed imminence of Christ's return, since it is not known when He will return, functions as a motivation for believers to focus their lives on what may at any time turn from the fallen world to the redeemed one. Since believers claim to be a part of that redeemed world, they ought to live accordingly.

Even within this view, with his use of *engus* expressing something currently accessible, Peter would be not focusing on an end that is "about to come but not yet here" but rather an end that has already come. In other words, this would be an indication of the "already-not yet" concept in the New Testament where he is encouraging his audience to look at the fact that what Christ has done has spelled the end for all unjust authorities and, therefore, the end of all of these things has truly come. Like an antibiotic

---

13. DeMar, *Last Days Madness*, 37.

administered to an infection, it is simply a matter of its slow death, but its end has, indeed, already taken place.

However, it is also possible, given the context, that the word refers to the maturation of the believer as the outcome of his perseverance through adversity. The word *telos* often refers to result or outcome as the "end/goal" of a process or activity.[14] In fact, the term is used four times in 1 Peter and every other time it refers to the result or outcome of a person's behavior. It twice refers to the outcome of a believer's faith and faithfulness (1:9; 3:8[15]) and once to the result of the behavior of the wicked world which does not follow Christ (4:17). Peter's point in the context would be that Christians should no longer live in the same manner that the pagans live their lives. They should take upon suffering from unbelieving authorities as Christ suffered and push on toward Christian maturity because it is, in fact, accessible to them now. In fact, the "all things" would likely refer to their suffering as the means to their maturity. It is like saying, "The end is in sight," referring to the Christian persevering to become like Christ in maturity. The *telos* "mature outcome" of all of those things is accessible, at arm's length. Hence, they should persevere since their suffering is producing the maturity of Christ in them. The goal is attainable.

Therefore, since Christ suffered in his body, arm yourselves also with the same attitude because *whoever suffers in the body is done with sin.* As a result, they do not live the rest of their earthly lives for evil human desires but rather for the will of God. For you have spent enough time in the past doing what pagans choose to do—living in debauchery, lust, drunkenness, orgies, carousing and detestable idolatry. They are surprised that you do not join them in their reckless, wild living, and they heap abuse on you. But they will have to give account to Him who is ready to judge the living and the dead. For this is the reason the gospel was preached even to those who are now dead so that they might be judged according to their earthly lives in

---

14. LSJ 1772–74. This use is related to the idea that *telos* refers to the end goal of a process (BDAG 887–88). Its cognates bear this meaning out. The verb *teleioō*, the adjective *teleios*, and the adverb *teleiōs*, and the synonyms *teleiotēs* and *teleiōsis* all are used often to refer to the maturation of a person or process. Hence, Peter argues, "Like obedient children, do not comply with the evil urges you used to follow in your ignorance, 1:15 but, like the Holy One who called you, become holy yourselves in all of your conduct.

15. The Greek states, "But the *telos* is for all to be harmonious, compassionate, brotherly in one's love, kindhearted, humble in spirit, not returning evil for evil," etc. This clearly refers to the goal in Christian maturity and not an end of all these things. In fact, it might be translated, "The goal is everything harmonious, compassionate, brotherly in love," etc. In other words, either way, the *telos* itself that is accessible in 4:7 is actually a state of Christian maturity.

regard to the body but live according to God in regard to the spirit. The *telos* of all things is *engus*. Therefore, be alert and of sober mind so that you may pray. Above all, love each other deeply because love covers over a multitude of sins. Offer hospitality to one another without grumbling. Each of you should use whatever gift you have received to serve others as faithful stewards of God's grace in its various forms. If anyone speaks, they should do so as one who speaks the very words of God. If anyone serves, they should do so with the strength God provides so that in all things God may be praised through Jesus Christ. To him be the glory and the power for ever and ever. Amen. (4:1–11)

Words for "maturity" or someone who is "grown up" are cognates of the word *telos* because the word can refer to an end state of something as a result and not merely the annihilation of a thing. Since maturity is accessible through all their trials, Christians are to persevere through them, knowing they are producing the mature character of Christ in them.

The full passage above, as well as the letter as a whole, indicates that the issue is one of perseverance for the purpose of becoming like Christ in Christian maturity. The context can be understood as eschatological, but it is more than likely just ethical in nature.

Either option is viable. The option that is not viable is a preterist understanding as the context indicates either that this has nothing to do with the second coming but is instead about persevering in Christian maturity or, if it is about the second coming, that the second coming will put an end to *all* unjust and oppressive authorities (at least to the ones to which Peter is referring in context—i.e., the unjust Roman government, disobedient husbands, and harsh masters), which did not happen in A.D. 70. Hence, what is accessible is either the maturation of a Christian who is becoming like Christ in His character, as the context seems to indicate, or that Peter believes that the very end of all things, especially all abusive authority, is already here and so Christians should live accordingly.

This understanding of *engus* helps the reader further understand the texts that state, "the kingdom of God is near" or the "time is near." These are often understood by Preterists to mean that the kingdom of God, the time, the end, the Lord's judgment of His *parousia*, etc., is soon approaching but has not yet arrived at the time these things were written down by the apostles.

In fact, both James and 1 Peter, cited above, are in the perfect aspect form which conveys the stative idea that the Lord's presence and the *telos* "maturity/end goal/completion" of the ages has come already and exists at the time of the author's writing.

The specific *parousia* "presence" of the Lord in James refers to the eschatological judgment of Christ (i.e., the macrocosmic event) that is present in a small part now (the microcosmic situation) and is ready to render judgment. In fact, we are told that the judge is not on his way, but instead the judge stands (perfect aspect) at the gates. The gates were the place of judgment which means that the Lord is already in the place of judgment and the verdict of his eschatological *parousia* is something that Christians will experience in their lives and something to which they will have access not just in a distant future but now since it has already arrived.

Likewise, in 1 Peter 4:7, the statement that "the end/culmination of all things is *near*" is not a statement that the culmination/maturation/end goal is about to come but that it has come already. Peter presents the "end" as the current state of all things as he is writing, not as something that is on its way but has not yet occurred. Since a maturation of all things is accessible, Christians are to take hold of this new state of all things and abandon their former lives of immaturity and futility as though they were still living in an age when the maturation of all things in Christ was not yet attainable.

Luke 21:31 is an interesting verse as it indicates that the meaning is not "almost here." "When you see all these things happen, know that the kingdom of God is *engus*." Now, if the word means "almost here," rather than "here," then that creates quite a problem since the phrase, "all these things" includes the Son of Man arriving in the clouds of heaven which would mean that redemption is not almost here, but it has, in fact, arrived. Likewise, in v. 20, the surrounded Jerusalem indicates that the city's abandonment by God has come (again, perfect aspect) rather than conveying something that is coming but has not yet arrived.

The verbal idea, however, is more fluid in that one could take it to mean that something is in the process of drawing near, mainly when appearing in the present aspect, but it would be unlikely that the perfect form would be the best choice to convey this idea.

The noun *engus* is much more concrete. It conveys something that is in one's presence, spatially or temporally. It conveys the idea that something is here more than it conveys the English concept of something that is near but not here. Hence, a better translation might be "here," "accessible," "within one's reach," etc. The common translation "at hand" would have sufficed if it did not now take upon itself different connotations within certain circles that interpret the phrase "at hand" to refer to something that is almost here rather than something that is here. The misinterpretation of the word *engus* has led to the misunderstanding of a series of verses. For instance, Matthew 24:32 states:

"Now learn a parable of the fig tree; When its branch is yet tender, and it puts forth leaves, you know that summer is near."

One would think this verse confirmed the idea that summer is almost here but not quite due to the fig tree blossoming in spring. However, what it fails to note is that there is no spring in ancient Israel. Ancient Israel only had two seasons: winter and summer. There were many festivals, harvests, rains, etc., that also tracked time but only two actual seasons. Hence, the fig tree does not blossom in winter but in summer. When you see it blossom, it tells you that summer is here. It has arrived already. It is not on its way but has come.

The point of the analogy conveys the same idea, "So also you, when you see all these things, know that he is near, right at the door" (Matt 24:33). He is not in His place. He is not on the road on the way to the house; He has arrived. He is at the door. He is here.

Hence, when Paul says, "the word is near you" (Rom 10:8), he means that it is there in their presence at that time and, therefore, accessible now, not something that is on its way, but not yet in their presence. It is not at a distance anymore. It has arrived in their proximity. They can access it right then and there. Hence, he follows up by clarifying where this word that is "near" is actually located, i.e., "it is in your mouth and in your mind."

Philippians 4:5 encourages Christians to be gentle as they are mindful of the presence of the Lord since "the Lord is near." He is encouraging them, not that the Lord is on His way, but that He is in their presence.

Ephesians 2:13 says, "But now in Christ Jesus you who used to be far away have been brought near by the blood of Christ."

All the benefits of the kingdom have been made accessible to the believer through the blood of Christ. They are his to access "now."

In Matthew (e.g., 3:2; 4:17; 10:7), the preaching of the gospel is framed in the message, "Repent, for the kingdom of Heaven is engus." It is clear that the kingdom of Heaven has been made accessible to them right then and there through the very preaching of the gospel. It is in their presence and accessible to them.

The grammar of engus in Luke 10:9 indicates that the message of the gospel was that "the kingdom of God has come upon you" (BDAG 270 s.v. ἐ᾽γγίζω 2; W. R. Hutton, "The Kingdom of God Has Come," ExpTim 64 [Dec 1952]: 89–91; and D. L. Bock, Luke [BECNT], 2:1000). The idea it expresses in these contexts is that the kingdom has been made accessible to them.

In fact, Luke 17:20–37 states that "the kingdom of God is in your midst." It was present with them then and there.

Christ also indicates that the disciples will long to see the day of His coming (i.e., the macrocosmic event) and will not see it. So, if the kingdom of God is something that is still to come from the standpoint of the apostles who are proclaiming that it is near, then this poses quite the conundrum since it is said to be in their midst and yet it is something that is not yet in their midst. This problem is removed when we understand the word properly. Instead, the kingdom of God has come already. It is there, in their midst. Everything else stated is an indication that it is here and has already come (Matt 12:28; Luke 21:31).

Mark makes this more explicit by stating the proclamation as "the time has been fulfilled and the kingdom of God is here (*engus*). Repent and believe" (1:15). The time is not about to be fulfilled but "has been fulfilled" already. The kingdom of God, therefore, is now accessible. One can reach out and take hold of it, and the way to take hold of this kingdom that has now come is to repent and believe.

In Matthew 12:28, Jesus argues that "if I cast out demons by the Spirit of God, then the kingdom of God has already come upon you."

Hence, as Paul indicates to the Corinthians, the end of the ages "has come" (perfect aspect, 1 Cor 10:11). It is not on its way in twenty some odd years. It has already come by the time Paul writes to the Corinthians as he presents it as the state in which they live. The kingdom of God is here, "in your midst." The end/the maturity of the age to come/the goal of the ages is among us, here, at hand, where one can reach out and grab it because it is not "on its way shortly" but rather has arrived and is standing in one's presence. The time is here. The judge is in the gates ready to render a verdict. He walks among the lampstands, His churches. He is at the door. He is here. That is what *engus*, and in most cases *engizo*, actually means. *Engus*, in the New Testament, does not typically, if at all, carry the English nuance "almost but not yet in one's presence." Yet, it is that English nuance upon which the preterist supports his belief. In reality, if one were to believe that *engus* means "approaching," it would still not support the preterist argument as this could very well refer to the judgment in A.D. 70 without referring to the final judgment of the macrocosmic event.

In truth, none of these verses supports the idea that the end, the kingdom of God, the *parousia* of Jesus, etc., "is nearing, but not yet arrived" but rather that the end, the eschatological presence of the Lord, the kingdom of God, etc., is *here*. It has come. It is standing in the midst of them right then and there in the late twenties A.D. It has arrived and is present with the apostles *long before* A.D. 70. This is a strong argument for the already-not yet teaching of the New Testament where the end is broken up between the spiritual fulfillment of the end, taking place from the first coming of Christ, to the physical fulfillment, taking place at the second coming. It is accessible now so that Christians (before and after A.D. 70) do not need to wait until the end of this world to receive its power, blessings, and judgments. Hence, there is a sense in which the coming kingdom is already here, and words like *engus* describe that present reality, even in the pre-A.D. 70 period.

Now, if one wishes to argue a preterist version of the "already, not yet," where these verses merely convey the "already" nature of the kingdom, then he cannot also claim that these verses convey the "not yet" aspect of what happens in A.D. 70 since the word "near" is not talking about something that is shortly approaching but about something that has already come. In other words, everyone who has a concept of the "already-not yet" can accept these verses into his system as they do not convey the imminence of the "not yet," as they are so often said to do so by Preterists. Instead, they convey the imminence of the "already" aspect of the kingdom, maturation of all things, Christ's kingly presence as judge, etc., long before the events of A.D. 70 ever occur.

What Must Soon Take Place?

The word *tachu* is relevant as a time reference only in the Book of Revelation. It is repeated at the beginning and the end of the book (2:16; 3:11; 22:7, 12, 20), forming an *inclusio* that creates a general feel for the whole book, indicating that Christ's coming/judgment of the matters discussed therein will fall *tachu*.

Preterists often argue that, since the word means "soon," the events in Revelation must be taking place in the first century, in John's day. I, of course, agree that the events are taking place in the first century and in John's day but do not agree that the word must be understood as "soon" in order to get this idea nor do I agree with the non sequitur that this somehow means that the event described therein is the destruction of Jerusalem in A.D. 70. That idea just does not pan out when one reads the book carefully, as I will show later.

The microcosmic/macrocosmic interpretation of Revelation allows one to look at the contextual evidence for either of the two most prominent meanings put forth by scholars, "soon" or "suddenly," without a dog in the race since either translation fits into that interpretative paradigm. Since I believe the events taking place in the background of the book refer to the persecution of Christians during the reign of Domitian toward the end of the first century A.D., understanding the term to mean either "soon" or "suddenly" makes sense within this context either way.

BDAG relates that *tachu* can refer to a brief period of time with an emphasis on the speed of an activity, or it can just refer to something that is done "without delay," "quickly," "at a rapid rate" (993). In other words, one meaning may be that it describes the *time* frame in which the action is performed (i.e., "soon"), and the other meaning, and what I think is more likely the case in the context of Revelation, describes the *manner* in which the action is done ("quickly," "suddenly").

In fact, the word *tachu* itself seems to be used mainly in the New Testament to describe things that are done quickly in terms of manner (Matt 5:25; 28:7; 28:8; Luke 15:22; John 11:29), although one occurrence in Mark 9:39 is ambiguous and could be interpreted either way. The translation "soon" seems to be a more suitable meaning of its cognate *tacheos*, which does not appear in the Apocalypse. However, its other cognate, *tachos*, which does appear in Revelation twice (1:1; 22:6), is more ambiguous, sometimes evidencing a meaning of manner, i.e., "quickly" (Luke 18:8; Acts 12:7; 22:18) and sometimes so ambiguous as to possibly have either meaning (Acts 25:4; Rom 16:20; 1 Tim 3:14). Although, even here, BDAG states that the word can refer to a period of time that focuses on the "speed of an activity or event" (992). It may be that both words are used to convey both the brief time and sudden manner in which Christ's judgment will befall the church so the distinction may be arbitrary in the end.

Revelation is made difficult not so much by the argument of the book itself but because our presuppositions of what the book is about often do not accord with what the book says, and hence, it becomes incomprehensible. Its interpretation either must be constructed from an obscured symbolism due to these end-time events taking place in the distant future, or they solely make up a symbolic description of some past event where everything was brought to an end. One is either reading the Bible with a modern newspaper in his hand or he is reading it with an ancient newspaper in his hand, attempting to mark when the end has or will occur. Both of these positions tend to think that the Apocalypse is about detailing the "end" (whether the end of a covenant age or the end of the world), whether in literal or symbolic form. Both positions, however, could not be more wrong.

The Apocalypse is not about the end of anything. It simply references the end (what I refer to as the macrocosmic event) and puts it together with an immediate judgment that Christ is making upon the churches, arguing that if Christians align themselves with the world via a compromised form of idolatry or worldly living (i.e., worshiping the beast), they will meet the same fate as the world, typified in the Roman Empire. This judgment consists of a microcosmic event in terms of the fact that it is not a universal or cosmic event but rather a localized event that foreshadows the larger one, and the smaller judgment should be seen in light of the larger event. What this means is that the book is not attempting to describe the macrocosmic event but merely is attempting to place the microcosmic event in the context of the macrocosmic event, whatever it may look like, in order to communicate a message to the first century church concerning Christ's coming to *it* in judgment (e.g., "I am coming to *you*" 2:5, 16; 3:3). In fact, the Book of Revelation is made up of a series of apocalyptic scenes that do not always match up with one another because it is not John's purpose to describe the details and chronology of the end but instead to argue to Christians that who they choose to follow today is a choice for what eternal destination they will enter as each person will share in the inheritance of their federal head (whether that be Christ or the beast).

Hence, even though the words *tachu* and *tachos* convey more of an idea that pertains to something takes place suddenly, or someone doing something quickly/hastily, rather than conveying the time frame it is an irrelevant distinction since Christ is saying to the churches that He is coming quickly to render judgment upon them (which is why the rest of the book should be read in light of the ecclesiastical letters in the beginning of the book, which function as the book's key). He is already at the door, judgment is about to take place for these churches, and He will come suddenly like lightning and like a thief in the night to render His verdict. Hence, the churches that have disobedient members are told to repent of their living like the world and those who are living faithfully need to stand firm in light of their future reward. The book further argues that those who live in a Christless antinomianism really belong to the world and will receive its judgment. The Apocalypse, therefore, is not concerned with describing end time events but rather merely references various commonly held, apocalyptic themes of the end times in order to convey the concepts of the visible and invisible church and how their daily choices display where their respective allegiances truly lie.

The book has absolutely nothing directly to do with the fall of Jerusalem, which must be inserted into a text that does not reference the event. (Notice that the church in Jerusalem is not even one of the churches addressed.) Christ's "coming" in the context is His coming to judge these churches (and by extension the church as a whole), and this microcosmic event is merely linked to His future macrocosmic, eschatological coming in the flesh where every eye will see Him, including the Romans who pierced Him. This joining of the microcosmic and macrocosmic events together as a single event is a common literary feature in apocalyptic literature. It does not intend to convey the idea that the micro-event and the macro-event actually occur at the same time or that the microcosmic event *is* the macrocosmic event. To read it as such is to misunderstand the ancient worldview at work in these apocalyptic texts.

The book itself is set in the backdrop of Domitian's persecution as the book is primarily concerned with condemning Christians who compromise and "eat food sacrificed to idols" (2:14, 20) in order to participate in the larger culture. This has its specific reference in John's work to those who participate in idolatry and the imperial cult (e.g., worshiping the beast and his image is condemned numerous times throughout the book, Rev 11:7; 13:4, 12–14; 14:9, 11; 15:2; 16:2; 17:3–7; 19:19; 20:4). As the beast is the Satanically-empowered enemy of Christ and His people, worshiping the beast is antithetical to worshiping God through Jesus Christ. Jesus Christ, in Revelation, therefore, comes to judge His Church concerning the matter.

When Christ tells the church that He is coming *tachu*, He is not saying that He is coming *soon* since He is actually already there among them (2:1). What He is saying is that when judgment falls, it is going to fall suddenly and without warning. In fact, the rebuke He gives is already part of that judgment. It has already begun, and unless they repent, they will be removed from the eternal reward that only belongs to His people (2:5).

This sudden judgment is captured in the image of a thief who comes quickly in the night (3:3). It is sudden and before one knows it. In fact, the "thief in the night" imagery is supplemented with other images throughout Scripture that describe judgment as a sudden event for which people living in unrepentant sin are not prepared. It is described as birth pangs coming upon a pregnant woman (1 Thes 5:3) and a trap that suddenly springs on the one it traps (Luke 21:34). The word in Luke is *aiphnidios* "suddenly." The only way to avoid a surprise judgment that suddenly falls is to repent and be ready by living in faith, love, and hope (1 Thes 5:8). The final imagery is lightning flashing from one side of the sky to the other (Matt 24:27; Luke 17:24). Lightning is not flashing "soon" but suddenly and without warning.

This is what *tachu* most likely conveys in these texts. It is not that the trap shuts "soon" or that birth pangs come upon a woman "soon" or that the thief comes "soon" or that lightning flashes "soon." It is that the trap shuts suddenly, abruptly, without warning. Birth pangs come upon a pregnant woman seemingly out of nowhere. They fall upon her suddenly and without warning. The thief does not come soon in the night but rather quickly. He comes without warning and with great haste so that he can quickly leave with one's goods. The lightning flashes quickly across the sky. It is sudden and without warning.

This suddenness is the type of judgment conveyed throughout the book. All the plagues fall upon Babylon the Great in one day (18:8) and with a sudden violent force (v. 21). In another description the city, the mountains, and all the islands of the world fall with a sudden, violent earthquake (6:14–17; 16:20).

The Lord conveys with the word *tachu*, then, that those who do not repent will also be overtaken suddenly along with the world (2:16; 3:3). Since they wish to partake of the benefits of attending the festivals that honor the gods and the emperor, they can also partake of its sudden judgment and destructive end that leads to the lake of fire and brimstone.

Hence, the message of the book is a message of repentance and encouragement so that the faithless are restored to right worship and those who have overcome the beast by not loving their lives even to death are encouraged. The suddenness of Christ's judgment strikes fear in the hearts of the unfaithful with the goal of their repenting of their sin, and it gives hope to the faithful so that they might persevere to the end.

Did Jesus Say John Would Live until He Returned?

Some of these perceived time statements are actually just loose readings of texts that are taken out of context. One example of this is found in the Gospel of John. In John 21:18–23, we have the following scene described.

> "I tell you the solemn truth, when you were young, you tied your clothes around you and went wherever you wanted, but when you are old, you will stretch out your hands, and others will tie you up and bring you where you do not want to go." (Now Jesus said this to indicate clearly by what kind of death Peter was going to glorify God.) After he said this, Jesus told Peter, "Follow me." Peter turned around and saw the disciple whom Jesus loved following them. (This was the disciple who had leaned back against Jesus' chest at the meal and asked, "Lord, who is the one who is going to betray you?") So, when Peter saw him, he asked Jesus, "Lord, what about him?" Jesus replied, "If I want him to remain until I come back, what concern is that of yours? You follow me!" So, the saying circulated among the brothers that this disciple was not going to die. But Jesus did not say to him that he was not going to die, but rather, "If I want him to remain until I come back, what concern is that of yours?"

Preterists often take this passage as a statement by Jesus that John would remain until Christ comes. What is odd about this interpretation is that it is the same mistake made by "the brethren" whom John is trying to correct. A rumor goes out among them that John is not going to die, but John must correct them by saying that Jesus did not say that he was not going to die but only said "*if* I want him to live until I come . . ." The hypothetical is meant to convey to Peter that it is none of his business what Jesus does with another disciple.

The fact that some preterists ignore the hypothetical "if" is simply an oddity that can only be explained by a willingness to find proof texts in any place one can.

But what is even more fascinating about this verse is that, once placed back into its context, it ends up being a text that would reject the preterist understanding of Christ's second coming as it ties the idea that once Christ comes back physical death will be abolished.

Notice that the context here is that Jesus has just told Peter how he is going to physically die. Peter then asks Jesus how John is going to physically die. Jesus responds by saying, "If I want him to remain until I come, what is that to you?" This is an important statement in that it basically has Jesus stating that if John were to remain until He comes, he would never physically die.

In fact, this is clearly the implication as the brethren miss the hypothetical, as do modern preterists and, therefore, conclude that John is not going to physically die. John merely corrects them by pointing out that it was a hypothetical statement and that those who think he will not die because Christ is coming back in his lifetime have simply missed the "if" in the statement.

If the second coming of Christ is about the destruction of Jerusalem and the establishment of the new covenant over the old, as preterists suggest, however, what exactly does this have to do with whether John will physically die or not? If Jesus, John, and the early Christians taught by them understood the second coming to refer to the destruction of the old covenant and the city, what would John remaining until Christ returned have anything to do with whether he would physically die? Christians physically died before A.D. 70, and they physically died afterward. The only implication of this is that they all viewed the second coming of Christ as an event that would end physical death, and therefore, whoever was still alive at His coming would never die.

There are strange ways that some try to get around this. For instance, the idea that Lazarus is the disciple whom Jesus loved here and that the brethren think he won't die because he was raised by Christ is not only nowhere in the text but it ignores what is in the text, which is that the statement is directly linked to Peter's question about the beloved disciple dying and the implication of Jesus' response, i.e., that if he remains until Jesus comes he will not die. This is not even to mention that the disciple whom Jesus loved is clearly one of the eleven as the upper room is made up of

Jesus and the twelve (Matt 26:20; Mark 14:17; Luke 22:14), and the disciple whom Jesus loved is one of the twelve (the one who leaned upon him at the supper and asked who would betray him—v. 20). These types of explanations are another instance of the context replacement fallacy. Either way, this interpretation has no merit as it ignores the context of the statement in an attempt to create an alternative context which can then be used to reinterpret the scene.

However, the implication of Jesus in the context is clear. If John were to have remained until His coming, he would not have physically died. This means that Jesus believed His own coming would mark the end of physical death itself. This also means that the early Christians understood the statement this way because they believed that the coming of Christ would mark the end of physical death. Rather than a proof text for preterism, this passage actually contradicts it.

The Synoptic Gospels and the Destruction of Jerusalem

The strongest argument made by preterism concerns the time statements surrounding the destruction of Jerusalem in the Synoptics. The Olivet Discourse is often a fall back passage when one is getting hammered with another passage that indicates that resurrection is of this physical body or Christ's return is physical, etc. However, as apocalyptic discourse, these passages cannot be read as though they are some literal layouts of the coming of Christ.

The following six statements made in the Synoptic Gospels make up the sum total of what I would consider time statement evidence that the Synoptics are talking about the fall of Jerusalem in A.D. 70 (I think a couple other verses often cited are actually referring to something else). Notice, then, the scarcity of verses that actually address the fall of Jerusalem in the New Testament. It is comprised of only six statements.

1. "The axe is already laid at the root of the trees." (Matt. 3:10; Luke 3:9).

2. "His winnowing fork is in His hand." (Matt. 3:12; Luke 3:17).

3. "'When the owner of the vineyard comes, what will he do to those vine-growers?' '. . . He will bring those wretches to a wretched end, and will rent out the vineyard to other vine-growers, who will pay him the proceeds at the proper seasons' . . .'Therefore I say to you, the kingdom of God will be taken away from you, and be given to a nation producing the fruit of it'. . . When the chief priests and the

Pharisees heard His parables, they understood that He was speaking about them." (Matt. 21:40–41, 43, 45; Luke 20:15–16, 19).

4. "This generation will not pass away until all these things take place." (Mark 13:30; Matt. 24:34; with some variation in Luke 21:32).

5. "These are days of vengeance, in order that all things which are written may be fulfilled." (Lk. 21:22).

6. "Daughters of Jerusalem, stop weeping for Me, but weep for yourselves and for your children. For behold, the days are coming when they will say, 'Blessed are the barren, and the wombs that never bore, and the breasts that never nursed.' Then they will begin to say to the mountains, 'Fall on us,' and to the hills, 'Cover us.'" (Lk. 23:28–30).[/NL 1–6]

Of course, there is complete agreement that these texts refer to the destruction of Jerusalem in A.D. 70. Since one can take them as such without holding to full preterism, these are not verses that prove preterism. Many partial preterists, and even those outside preterism, would agree that these are talking about the destruction of Jerusalem.

The problem, however, is that preterists tend to draw false inferences from these verses, making certain unwarranted conclusions which stem from a lack of familiarity with apocalyptic literature and speech. These conclusions, or non sequiturs, can be summed up in the following two premises that preterists use to interpret not only the Olivet Discourse but other passages as well.

1. That any macrocosmic language used to describe a microcosmic event means that the microcosmic event is the macrocosmic event, and hence, the macrocosmic language is either to be taken at face value and dated as occurring at the time of the microcosmic event or it is merely hyperbole.

2. That there is only one "coming" and *parousia* of Christ rather than multiple comings and instances of Christ's future *parousia* breaking into the here and now.

These two assumptions can be seen in the argument of James Russell, as well as countless Preterists who follow the same line of reasoning.

> How plainly does St. Luke, in his record of the prophecy on the Mount of Olives, represent the great catastrophe as falling within the lifetime of the disciples: 'And when these things begin to come to pass, then look up, and lift up your heads; for your redemption draweth nigh' (Luke xxi.28). Were not these words

spoken to the disciples who listened to the discourse? Did they not apply to them? Is there anywhere even a suspicion that they were meant for another audience, thousands of years distant, and not for the eager group who drank in the words of Jesus? Surely such a hypothesis carries its own refutation in its very front.[16]

Russell goes on to argue that if this argument does not suffice, Jesus makes it plain by telling the disciples that their generation will not pass away until the *parousia* takes place. The reason why Russell makes this argument is because he only sees a single event being described in the discourse: "Words have no meaning if this language, uttered on so solemn an occasion, and so precise and express in its import, does not affirm the near approach of *the great event* which occupies *the whole discourse* of our Lord."[17]

In other words, the fact that Jesus tells his disciples that their generation will not pass away until all these things take place, coupled with the understanding that there is only one event being referenced and that event is the singular *parousia* with none other to follow, causes Russell, and Preterists like him, to conclude that the *parousia* occurred in A.D. 70.

The problem with this, of course, is that it assumes what it concludes. Of course, if one assumes that there is only one manifestation of the *parousia*, then there would not be another after it; but this assumption must be proven by looking at other apocalyptic texts, asking whether they speak of two events, noting the contextual referents of all apocalyptic texts in the Bible to see if they only speak of one event, and then looking at the nature passages to see if the nature of the event describes that of A.D. 70 or can only be interpreted as a time yet to come.

To start, let us examine the first assumption, i.e., the idea that if cosmic language is applied to a local event, the cosmic event is either occurring at the same time or it is merely a hyperbolic way of describing the microcosmic event.

Part of the thrust of many apocalyptic texts is to take an event that is occurring in the author's day and place it within the context of the future restoration of God's people and judgment of the world. This is done for a variety of reasons, but the main one seems to be that it provides perspective to those who are witnessing the microcosmic event in their own lifetime.

For instance, in Daniel, under the persecution of Antiochus IV, the people of God were hopelessly being oppressed and killed for worshiping YHWH. What Daniel did was to take that persecution and place it in the

---

16. Russell, *The Parousia*, 83.
17. Russell, *The Parousia*, 83.

context of the ultimate end, the macrocosmic event in an effort to give the faithful perspective. They may die for their faith, but there will be a resurrection of the dead. They may lose their possessions and property now, but they will take possession of the whole world in the future. Hence, Daniel took the two events and mixed them together as one, precisely to argue that the microcosmic event is really a spark of a larger fire to come; the persecution of God's people will end in victory.

In Daniel, then, the kingdoms are all wiped away. As the Aramaic states, "In the days of those kings [i.e., the Seleucid kings in the second century B.C.] the God of heaven will raise up an everlasting kingdom that will not be destroyed, and there will be no kingdom that is left for another people. It will break in pieces and bring about the demise of all these kingdoms. But it will stand forever."

Here we see that all the kingdoms of the earth will be utterly destroyed, and there will be no other kingdom left for another people. Only the people of God will rule in the kingdom of God. Yet, we know that this did not happen in the second century B.C. In fact, it has not happened yet at all. One might argue that the kingdom of God is spiritual and exists in the world today, but that is not what this passage teaches. It does not say that the kingdom of God will exist side by side with kingdoms of other people. According to this, there are no other kingdoms left. Instead, what the author of Daniel has done is to combine the event of Antiochus' persecution, which becomes clearer as the reader progresses through the work, with the macrocosmic event in the end.

Again, in Chapter 12, we are told of the great victory and resurrection of the saints.

> "Now *at that time* Michael, the great prince who stands *guard* over the sons of your people, will arise. And there will be a time of distress such as never occurred since there was a nation until that time; and at that time your people, everyone who is found written in the book, will be rescued. "And many of those who sleep in the dust of the ground will awake, these to everlasting life, but the others to disgrace *and* everlasting contempt. "And those who have insight will shine brightly like the brightness of the expanse of heaven, and those who lead the many to righteousness, like the stars forever and ever. (Dan. 12:1–3 NAS, emphasis mine)

This text clearly has macrocosmic language all over it. We are told that all these things happen "at that time." This, of course, raises the question: "At what time?" The answer is found in the preceding chapter which indicates the time that this all occurs is the time of Antiochus IV and his demise. Ulrich argues for this very idea.

> Mattathias and his sons (the Maccabees) took a stand that eventually led to the defeat of Antiochus IV (1Macc 2:42–48) and the restoration of proper worship (1Macc 4:36–58). The writer of 1Maccabees saw the hand of God at work in these events (1Macc 3:19, 4:55) and compared them with the Exodus from Egypt (1Macc 4:8–9), the victories of David (1Macc 4:30), and the deliverance of Hezekiah (1Macc 7:41). The Maccabean victory may not have been the final defeat of evil, but it was one of Goldingay's partial realizations in the long sweep of redemptive history."[18]

It is important to note that *ûbāʿ ēt hahî'* "now, at that time" refers to the time that is described in the paragraphs before, i.e., the time of Antiochus IV's death. The resurrection and eternal victory of the saints is said to happen at the time of the localized victory over Antiochus IV and his persecution of the Jews. Obviously, the resurrection does not literally occur at this time, and the Jews (and people of God in general) will go on to suffer under other oppressors; but the localized victory and demise of a major oppressor of God's people is joined as a singular event with the final victory over death and oppression which will take place in the resurrection of the dead and final judgment. This local victory is a picture, a type, and even a part of the final one.

Therefore, despite the forced idea that Chapter 11 somehow splits at the end and refers to Rome, the entire book, chapter, and flow of narrative indicate that there is no change in person or time. Daniel has joined the microcosmic and macrocosmic events together in order to argue that, despite the severity of oppressive powers and even death among God's people, if they trust in God, they will have the final victory in the end.

Likewise, 1 Enoch, one of the most important books in Second Temple Judaism, is an apocalyptic book that takes the event of the flood and combines it with macrocosmic language to convey that the flood was a foreshadowing of a larger event to come at the end of the fallen world. In the context of the flood, Enoch tells his readers that the flood will bring about a total destruction of the wicked, something it also does in the biblical narrative, but this destruction soon takes on another event all together in that the wicked are removed from the earth forever. They will never again set foot on it. The righteous will live upon it forever instead, and it will never again be corrupted by the wicked. This clearly does not happen in the flood,

---

18. Ulrich, *The Antiochene Crisis and Jubilee Theology*, 48.

and the author of Enoch knows this. So why does he present the flood as a futuristic judgment of the world in which the wicked are wiped away in fire (fire itself seems odd for a cosmic deluge)? Because he is combining the flood event with what he sees as the future judgment of the world. They are two events spoken of together as though they are a singular event because, in the author's mind, they are.

In the apocalyptic mind, all microcosmic events are like streams of water that flow from the larger ocean of creation. On one side of creation, the inauguration of creation at the beginning, there is an ocean from which creational language is drawn, and on the other side of creation, there is destruction and re-creation that ends in the consummation of creation, the finishing of everything God has made and the filling up of His earth full of His covenant people, which was His original purpose in creation. Hence, everything is creation. Every event is a part of that larger event. All is one in that regard. All removal of chaotic agents and ordering of chaos into its telos is a creation event. Hence, events like the exodus have creation language attached to them not as an act of hyperbole but to display the unification of the two events as one. The exodus is a creation event. Likewise, an event like the destruction of Babylon contains destruction and re-creation language since such events are also one with the future renewal of the cosmos.

This is the multifaceted view of apocalyptic speech. It combines events together in an effort to view the microcosmic, localized event within the framework of the larger cosmic one to come. As such, the prophets can place the destruction of cities in the context of that larger cosmic event, and Second Temple/New Testament authors, especially within an apocalyptic context which is characteristic of this practice, can do the same with events such as the persecution under Antiochus IV, the flood event, Christ's coming to His churches in judgment in Revelation, the Mount of Transfiguration, Christ coming to render a verdict for the oppressed workers in James, and Christ coming as a judgment upon the city of Jerusalem and its leaders. All of these things can be described in terms of the macrocosmic events of Christ's final return and consummation of His kingdom because they are all a part of that final consummation in one way or another. They are microcosmic events occurring in time that are branches from a larger tree which exists in both the past and the future. They are the kingdom to come, the final creation completed, reaching back into our age.

Now, that all negates the preterist idea that if macrocosmic language is intermingled with the description and reference to a microcosmic event, then this somehow means that there either is no macrocosmic event or that the microcosmic event is the macrocosmic event. A proper understanding of apocalyptic speech helps us identify the falsity of the claim that the presence of macrocosmic language must imply that the final macrocosmic event is occurring at the time and place of the microcosmic event (whether literally or figuratively)). Within these Synoptic passages, like the Olivet Discourse, there are two combined events, not one.

However, it is important to note the finer distinction that there are not two events *addressed* here. There is only one event that is being addressed, i.e., the destruction of Jerusalem and its temple. The macrocosmic event is not being addressed. It is, instead, presented along with the microcosmic event as a way of placing the microcosmic event within the context of the macrocosmic event. As such, there is one event being addressed, not two. One event is merely meant to be read in the light of the other, but the other is not currently being addressed by the author. To give an example of this, it would be like saying that your husband is your Superman. He flies you away to exotic places, protects you from arch enemies when he helps you overcome your Lex Luthors in life, and his kryptonite is ice cream. One could say there are two references here: one to a woman's actual husband and one to a comic book superhero; but although there are two references, only her husband is the subject being addressed. She is not providing commentary about Superman directly, even though some information about Superman can be gleaned from what is said. Likewise, in a passage where the localized event is at issue, the reference to the macrocosmic event in the future functions only to place the one in the light of the other. Therefore, when Jesus says, "This generation will not pass away until *all these things* take place," "all these things" is not talking about the macrocosmic event, which is merely providing the eschatological context to the event and is not literally being addressed, but rather the microcosmic event which is. The same can be said of most apocalyptic texts where a microcosmic event is in view (e.g., those in Daniel, Revelation, Enoch, etc.).

So, what about the other claim? What about the idea that there is only one coming, only one *parousia*? In some way, I have already given an answer above. If smaller events in time are all a part of the larger event in the future and can be spoken of as one singular event, then there can be many smaller events that are in some way connected to the larger one.

But if this is true, one might ask whether there are some statements made in the New Testament that confirm this idea. Indeed, there are texts that confirm this idea of multiple "comings"/"parousias."

For instance, in Luke 17:22, Christ states to the disciples that "the days are coming when you will desire to see *one of the days* of the Son of Man and you will not see it." Not only does this seem to indicate that there is more than one day/time that belongs to Christ's coming but that the main day that they long to see will not be seen by them within their lifetimes.

Again, in a verse cited by many Preterists, but not read closely, Christ reveals to the priestly court that *"from now on,* you will see the Son of Man sitting at the right hand of the Power and coming on the clouds of heaven" (Matt 26:64).

Using the same macrocosmic language from Daniel, Christ argues that this will be a continuous thing that occurs, not forty years from His court hearing but "from now on." This is because the language of Daniel, where the Son of Man "comes" has to do with His coming up to the Father to receive His kingdom. This is why his reception of the Father's blessings on the Mount of Transfiguration is considered a "coming" and a "parousia" by the Synoptic Gospels which place the prediction of His coming in parallel to His ascending to the Father on the mountain. It is also why Peter joins them together in his epistle (2 Pet 1:16–18). This is not because this event fulfills all that the Bible predicts about the *parousia* but because it is a small part of the larger event to come.

It is also why Christ's judgment over His Church, as its King, can be referred to as His coming (Rev 2–3) and why James can refer to His coming to render a fair verdict to His oppressed people as His *parousia* (4:7). As Luke indicated, there are many days of the Son of Man, not just the final one. There are many receptions of His kingdom, many times He will come in the clouds of heaven from the time He speaks to the priests to His final return. Indeed, he sits at the right hand of God the Father in His ascension to the Ancient of Days precisely to put all of His enemies underneath His feet as he collects His people from all the nations. The *parousia*, in that sense, is continually occurring until the day He hands the heavenly throne over to the Father (1 Cor 15:24–28) in order to rule under Him as the Davidic King upon the earth, thus uniting all heaven and earth and dispelling all chaos (i.e., demonic powers and kingdoms, death) from both.

Therefore, the preterist's assumptions are false inferences on both accounts. To say that macrocosmic language means that the macrocosmic event is occurring, and therefore, if it does not happen literally, it all needs to be reinterpreted into something spiritual is a non sequitur. To say that this must be true because there is only one coming and manifestation of the *parousia* is also false.

Without these two assumptions, there is simply no reason to read the Olivet Discourse, one of many instances of Christ's coming and *parousia,* as the final one. In fact, in light of the nature passages, it becomes obvious that the preterist reading is not the correct reading of the text.

Hence, Preterists are right that all six of these statements in the Synoptic Gospels refer to the microcosmic event of the destruction of Jerusalem. Their assumptions about how to read apocalyptic/prophetic speech, however, have led them to misunderstand the nature of the larger event to which some of its language gives witness.

The Last Hour

Along the lines of misunderstanding terms, there are a few phrases that are misunderstood such as John's statement concerning "the last hour" (1 John 2:18) or Paul's statement that "the night is almost gone" (Rom 13:12). These statements are interpreted by Preterists to refer to the small remaining time that exists until the end of the age in A.D. 70. However, there is no indication of a time frame at all in these phrases. Preterist interpreters have simply misunderstood the metaphor that is being used.

For instance, in 1 John, we are told what John is talking about just a few verses before. He makes the statement, "On the other hand, I am writing a new commandment to you which is true in him and in you, because the darkness is passing away and the true light is already shining" (2:8).

John is not describing the last hour of an age but giving us the imagery that the apostles often give to the "already-not yet" time period in which believers find themselves, which is described as the last hour *of night*. He is referring to the time of night when it is still dark, but light from the sun has shone in it, mixed with it, so that both light and darkness exist *at the same time.*

He says this because the type of proto-Gnostics he is addressing in the epistle seem to have an over-realized eschatological idea that the new age has already come. Their view of resurrection and Christ's spiritual return would foster this idea. Hence, many think the dark age is gone and they themselves have been spiritually resurrected to new life where they are free from moral constraints and are without any guilt of sin (1:5–10).

John counters this by arguing that Christians still sin and are in need of confession and the advocacy of the Righteous One, Jesus Christ, to forgive them, as well as having a need to walk according to His commandments (2:1–6). The new age of amoralism, where one need not be concerned about his or her sin anymore, has, therefore, not come. Christians are still bound to the commandments of Christ, specifically those concerning loving fellow Christians by providing for their needs in a world where they lack them.

Likewise, John's entire point is to argue that the proof that Christians are still in a time of darkness is that there still exist false prophets in the world, which is the spirit of antichrist (2:18). If false prophets exist, then the time of darkness is not fully gone. Instead, the light has broken in as it does in the last hour of night when darkness and light exist together at the same time.

John, therefore, does confirm that the light has come, and the darkness is passing away, but the two exist now together until the darkness is completely gone (i.e., when sin and false prophets are no more). It is this coexistence of the two that he calls "the last hour," referring to the last hour *of night*. John proves that darkness still exists with the light, that it is still the last hour of night and not the full day by citing the fact that there are many antichrists who have appeared in the world. Hence, the kingdom of the devil is not gone but merely going as the world/darkness is passing and the light is growing in the last hour of night.

Paul makes this imagery clearer in Romans 13:12 where he uses terminology that talks about the far advancement of night (*hē nux proekopsen*) in the hour that the day has come ("is here" "in one's presence," *engizo* in the perfect aspect). The time of night described is the time that John also talks about in his epistle. It is the time when night is coming to an end and the light is beginning to come out, even though it is still the time before the dawn. Paul states that this is "already the hour for you to awaken from sleep," which is a reference to the early morning hour when one often wakes up. His exhortation is to the Roman Christians to see that light has broken into the world and they should, therefore, live accordingly. They ought to live not according to the pattern of the world that is passing away, described by night and darkness, but according to the light which has shined in the darkness, described by the day. 2 Peter 1:19 uses a similar concept, evidencing that this is a common metaphor in the early church to describe the existence of two kingdoms and two ages existing simultaneously together, one where Christ is honored and followed in righteousness and one where the world still follows the devil and his pattern of rebellion and sin.

"Moreover, we possess the prophetic word as an altogether reliable thing. You do well if you pay attention to this as you would to a light shining in a murky place, until the day dawns and the morning star rises in your hearts."

Peter expresses the need here for the church to give their ear to the testimony of the apostles to withstand the onslaught of heretics in the church as a "light shining in a dark place." This is needed until the day dawns and the morning comes in terms of spiritual maturity/glorification.

The author of Hebrews has this same concept in mind when he states that Christians need to remain faithful "as they see the day drawing near [*engizo* "further into their presence" in the present aspect, 10:25]."

None of these expressions conveys when the sun will fully rise and the night will be completely over. They all convey the idea that, while there are false prophets, sin, antichrists, heretics, and heresy (i.e., the things of the night) in the world, the night is still here. The assurance that the apostles give to Christians is that the darkness is on its way out not on its way in. The light, however, is on its way in, and the first light of day, even though still dark outside, has come.

The Passing Away of the Mosaic Law?

One of the time indicator arguments that Preterists like to use concerns the Mosaic Law. Jesus said in Matthew that "until heaven and earth pass away not one *yōd* or *tittle* would pass away from the law until all is accomplished" (5:18).

One of the arguments that is extrapolated from this is that if heaven and earth have not yet passed away, then Christians are still under the law. Hence, since Christians are under grace and not the law, heaven and earth must have passed away. Since the literal cosmos has not passed away, Preterists must be right about their allegorical interpretation of the phrase, "heaven and earth," which actually refers to the old covenant in this context.

Another argument is that the law would still be in effect for Jews outside of Christ, and this means that Jews would be able to achieve salvation by following the Mosaic Law outside of Christ.

Let us first examine the claim that Christians would be under the law if the Mosaic Law had not passed away. The biggest objection is that it clearly is not true when we look at the pre-A.D. 70 claims of the New Testament, specifically concerning what Paul claimed. Paul argues that the only reason he may still practice the ritual law is to gain an opportunity with those whom he wishes to evangelize; but he clearly states that all things are lawful for him (1 Cor 6:12) and that he is not under the law any longer.

In 1 Corinthians 9:19–21, Paul states: "For since I am free from all I can make myself a slave to all, in order to gain even more people. To the Jews I became like a Jew to gain the Jews. To those under the law I became like one under the law (though I myself am not under the law) to gain those under the law. To those free from the law I became like one free from the law (though I am not free from God's law but under the law of Christ) to gain those free from the law."

Again, in Romans 6:14–15, he states of the Roman believers: "For sin will have no mastery over you, because you are not under law but under grace. What then? Shall we sin because we are not under law but under grace? Absolutely not!"

He argues further,

> So, my brothers and sisters, you also died to the law through the body of Christ, so that you could be joined to another, to the one who was raised from the dead, to bear fruit to God. For when we were in the flesh, the sinful desires, aroused by the law, were active in the members of our body to bear fruit for death. But now we have been released from the law, because we have died to what controlled us, so that we may serve in the new life of the Spirit and not under the old written code. (7:4–6)

It is clear that the Apostles, as Jews, were not under the law. Yet, Preterists must argue that the law is still in effect until the temple/old covenant passes way in A.D. 70. If it is not true that the New Testament Jews are under the law before A.D. 70, it is certainly not true that they would have to be so after A.D. 70, whether the law remains or not.

Furthermore, the Judaizers in Galatia would have been in the right for insisting that the Gentiles be circumcised and follow the ritual law since everyone would have been supposedly still under it. Paul would be in the wrong because he would have been stating that the Galatians were free from the law while they were still under it. Of course, some Preterists argue that only the Jews would have been subject to the law if it were still in effect but, of course, as discussed above, Paul is a Jew.

Peter, also a Jew, is said to be one who does not follow the law either. Paul says to him in Galatians, "If you, although you are a Jew, live like a Gentile and not like a Jew, how can you try to force the Gentiles to live like Jews?" (Gal 2:14; see also v. 12). Paul's statement to Peter indicates that Peter was not following the rituals of the old covenant law but instead was living like a Gentile in terms of these rituals (not in terms of the moral law which is affirmed throughout the New Testament as evidence of redemption). The Jewish ritual law has been fulfilled in Christ, and it is no longer a boundary marker for those who belong to YHWH. Instead, since all the ritual law has been fulfilled in Christ, to be Jewish is to belong to the Jewish Messiah via faith in Him.

Therefore, when Paul contrasts himself with the Judaizers, he describes them as those who have slipped in to spy on Paul and other believers' freedom.

> Now this matter arose because of the false brothers with false pretenses who slipped in unnoticed to spy on *our* freedom that *we* have in Christ Jesus, to make *us* slaves. But *we* did not surrender to them even for a moment, in order that the truth of the gospel would remain with you." (Gal 2:4–5; emphasis added)

Instead, Paul argues that neither he nor the Galatian believers are under the law but rather free from it, and this he said long before A.D. 70.

> Now before faith came we were held in custody under the law, being kept as prisoners until the coming faith would be revealed. Thus the law had become our guardian until Christ, so that we could be declared righteous by faith. But now that faith has come, we are no longer under a guardian. For in Christ Jesus you are all sons of God through faith. For all of you who were baptized into Christ have clothed yourselves with Christ. (3:23–27)

> For through the law I died to the law so that I may live to God. I have been crucified with Christ, and it is no longer I who live, but Christ lives in me. So the life I now live in the body, I live because of the faithfulness of the Son of God, who loved me and gave himself for me. I do not set aside God's grace, because if righteousness could come through the law, then Christ died for nothing! (2:19–21)

If heaven and earth, i.e., the old covenant, need to pass away before one can be free from being *under the law*, then how did Paul and early believers become free before A.D. 70? Obviously, "heaven and earth" passing away was not needed. Let us now address the idea that the Jews can still be saved through the law if it is still in effect, thus arguing that there are two ways of salvation.

There seems to be a presupposition in this argument that the law is a vehicle of salvation in the Old Testament and, therefore, would remain one until the old covenant is done away with in A.D. 70. This, however, is a dispensational idea that the Bible does not support. The law is only the vehicle of salvation for one person, Jesus Christ. Through His federal headship, all are saved when they are united to Him by faith. The vehicle of salvation for everyone else is unification with Christ via faith. Apart from faith, everyone, being under the law, must obtain his own salvation and this is why everyone outside of Christ will be damned. Hence, once faith comes no one is condemned by the law, having already paid the penalty of the law for their sins and obtained the salvation from perfect obedience to God through the Person and work of Christ in His life and death and resurrection. There is no need for Christ to return to free us from the condemnation and justificatory obligations of the law. In New Testament theology, Christ returns to bring salvation in terms of the body and makes salvation complete via glorification, not justification which is obtained by faith whether one lived during the Old or New Testament era. It is clear from the New Testament, therefore, that there is no transitional period in the way that Preterists imagine. What was left of the external religion of the old covenant ended at the cross of Christ (1 Peter 2:24). However, it was never a vehicle of salvation for anyone but Christ alone. The one who would see life from the law was to obey all of it. Only Christ has ever done this. Therefore, as Paul argues, the law, as a vehicle of salvation via perfection, is an instrument of death to everyone else. Hence, it has been, is now, and always will be that the vehicle of salvation is being united to Christ by faith, whether for old covenant believers or new. Old covenant believers were united to Christ via faith in YHWH and looked toward the cross with sacrifices and ritual law. New covenant believers have received Christ not in the shadows of rituals that looked forward to Christ but as the substance of Him who has now been revealed. The suggestion that the law itself would pass away while men are still outside of Christ and continue to sin is an odd one. With what standard will men be judged now? Every passage that speaks of judgment speaks of a judgment according to one's works. Paul himself states that the law exists to hold all men accountable to God.

> Now we know that whatever the law says, it says to those who are under the law, so that every mouth may be silenced and the whole world may be held accountable to God. For no one is declared righteous before him by the works of the law, for through the law comes the knowledge of sin. But now apart from the law the righteousness of God (which is attested by the law and the prophets) has been disclosed—namely, the righteousness of God through the faithfulness of Jesus Christ for all who believe. (Rom 3:19–22)

The distinction between those under the law and those saved by grace via faith in Christ is not "old covenant versus new covenant" but rather damned versus redeemed. In other words, God is not going to do away with the law until all men have been judged for their sins. Notice that the law is not merely for Israel as Paul means to argue that the law exists both in special revelation via Moses and in natural revelation via creation and conscience. The law does not pass away before it holds all men accountable and brings them into judgment. Neither Jew nor Gentile is free from the judgment of the law before or after A.D. 70 if, in fact, they are not united to Jesus Christ through faith.

"But we know that the law is good if someone uses it legitimately, realizing that law is not intended for a righteous person, but for lawless and rebellious people, for the ungodly and sinners, for the unholy and profane, for those who kill their fathers or mothers, for murderers, sexually immoral people, practicing homosexuals, kidnappers, liars, perjurers—in fact, for any who live contrary to sound teaching." (1 Tim 1:8–10)

In this regard, the law cannot pass away until all men are judged, and that occurs when the old heaven and earth pass away in preparation for their renewal into an eternal state. Hence, the idea that there are two covenants in effect during A.D. 30–70 simply misses the point the New Testament is making. The old, external covenant was never a means to salvation for anyone but Christ. It was, is now, and will continue to be a vehicle of condemnation for those outside of Christ.

However, the law also has another function for those who are already justified by Christ. For those who have turned from self-love to Christ-love, the moral law is instruction/guidance/direction of what love looks like. In fact, the preface of the law in Deuteronomy presents the law as an expression of loving God with one's whole being. Indeed, Paul continually argues that the law is fulfilled in loving one's fellow covenant members who represent God/Christ. Law is condemnation for those sinners attempting to use it as a vehicle to be justified before God, but it is a teacher of what love of God and fellow believers looks like in various situations.

It is this aspect of law that Jesus is talking about in Matthew as Matthew presents Jesus as arguing that one must, as a kingdom member, observe the law in terms of using it as a way to love God and the least of these brothers of Christ.

In fact, preterists tend to only quote part of the verse, but the entire verse makes it clear that the law to which Jesus is referring is the "law OR the prophets," i.e., the Scripture. Specifically, He is referring to moral commands found in the law which are for kingdom members, those in the new covenant, since they are commands to love God or other believers in a particular way that new covenant members are to put into practice. The text reads:

> Do not think that I have come to abolish the law or the prophets. I have not come to abolish these things but to fill them up. I tell you the truth, until heaven and earth pass away not the smallest letter or stroke of a letter will pass from the law until everything takes place. So anyone who breaks one of the least of these commands and teaches others to do so will be called least in the kingdom of heaven, but whoever obeys them and teaches others to do so will be called great in the kingdom of heaven. For I tell you, unless your righteousness goes beyond that of the experts in the law and the Pharisees, you will never enter the kingdom of heaven. (Matt 5:17–20)

Notice that there is nothing here about being "under the law" until heaven and earth pass away. To say that a text that tells us that the law will not pass away until all is accomplished means everyone is under the law until it passes away is a non sequitur. It says it will not pass away until everything is accomplished not that it will pass away once everyone is no longer under it. In other words, the terminology is not that of using it as a vehicle of justification but one of verification that one is loving God and one's fellow believer as well as the evidence brought forward in one's judgment to verify the claim that he knows Christ and has loved Him through the least of these who represent Him.

Jesus then continues to argue that following the law evidences one's allegiance to Christ as Lord, and those who do not follow it are called "lawless" and told that Christ never knew them. This is because Matthew will present the greatest of commandments, as do the other Gospels, as loving God with one's whole being and loving one's fellow covenant community members who represent God. The moral law expresses love toward one's fellow Jewish believer, wife, and even fellow Gentile believer (which is what Matthew is primarily about). But what is even more telling than this is that Christ explicitly states that anyone who breaks even the least of these commands and teaches others to do the same will be called least *in the kingdom of heaven*. The one who keeps them will be called greatest *in the kingdom of heaven*. In other words, these commandments, in terms of the way that Jesus is using them here in Matthew, are for those in the kingdom, not just for those outside of it. This is the entire point of the Sermon on the Mount and the Gospel of Matthew in general. If one is truly a disciple of Christ, he will do the good of the law. If one is not truly in Him, he will practice lawlessness. It is the fruit from a good tree. In fact, the reason why the Jewish leaders are condemned is because they do not bear the fruit of the kingdom (Matt 3:7–10), and hence, the kingdom is taken away from them and given to a nation who will bear the fruit of it (Matt 21:43).

Yet, if the law passes away for those in the kingdom, why is Jesus telling those in the kingdom that they are to observe and teach others to observe even the least of the commandments of that law? The kingdom *is* the new covenant community, the eternal kingdom that exists on this side of eternity. While living here, kingdom members must observe what the Scripture (for Matthew that is the Old Testament) has commanded because it has commanded them to do those things that are expressions of true love for God and one another.

Now, let us put it all together. If the law here exists for believers in the kingdom to use as a guide to love one another until all is accomplished, then they will be judged as to whether they loved Christ and one another by it, and yet, they are free from seeking justification before God through it, as Paul argues, because it is only a vehicle of condemnation for every sinner. Believers, before and after A.D. 70, are no longer "under the law," but the law still exists for them to direct their love toward God and one another. In one regard (according to the Pauline sense), the external law has passed away as a vehicle of condemnation for those in Christ Jesus, but it still remains to judge all outside of Christ and to give direction to believers who want to know what love looks like.

So, love is demonstrated through taking principles of the law, like not murdering, and applying them in ways that don't degrade the humanity of one's brother because the law was meant to give examples of what love looks like rather than existing as an exhaustive list of morality. Love looks like taking the principle of the law against adultery and applying it to directing one's desires toward one's spouse rather than a stranger, and it looks like reconciliation rather than divorce. Love and reconciliation to God and fellow believers is the core context of the law in Matthew. All who claim to love God and nullify the Scripture in these areas are pretenders, or as more commonly translated, "hypocrites."

This is the same as the original law which directed Israelites to love God through their fellow covenant members by not stealing their goods, locking up their dangerous animals, making right any debt owed through wrongdoing, etc.

The simple point is that the law never passes away on this side of creation. It exists to shut all men up before God and hold them accountable; it was a tutor which taught us we needed a sacrifice and a Savior. It exists to judge all men outside of Christ. As a guide, it even exists to judge whether we truly love one another and shows us where to direct our professed love. This distinction is seen in Luke 16:16–17:

> The law and the prophets were in force until John; since then, the good news of the kingdom of God has been proclaimed, and everyone is urged to enter it. But it is easier for heaven and earth to pass away than for one tiny stroke of a letter in the law to become void.

Here we see the concept that the law and prophets, i.e., the Scripture, are in force until John. Christ's advent ends this. Yet, in the same breath, Jesus tells them that it is easier for heaven and earth to pass away than for one tittle of the law to become void. So, we have both the idea that, for those in the kingdom, the law is not in effect over them in terms of judgment and that the law is still in effect in other ways until the very ending of heaven and earth. Also notice that "heaven and earth" cannot mean the old covenant/law represented by the temple if it is easier for it to pass away than the tiniest letter of the law to become void. If they are the same thing (i.e., law = old covenant = heaven and earth = temple), then it would be just as easy to pass away. In fact, it would be nonsensical for Jesus to argue that it is easier for the law to pass away than for even a tittle of the law to pass away. In fact, Luke's parallel to Matthew's statement here makes it clear that the intention is not to say that the law must completely pass away in order for grace to come but that the law continues to be in effect even once the kingdom has come. It is merely important for one to realize how it is to be viewed. This is likely why Matthew adds the statement by Jesus that He did not, in fact, come to do away with the law but instead to fill it up, establish it further, bring out its fullest intention and expression among the covenant community, and indeed, within the world as a whole until all things are accomplished.

This is why historically reformed theologians have made the case that there are three uses of the moral law: (1) As a civil fear for all people, (2) As a tutor that brings one to Christ, and (3) As a guide that confirms what love looks like and directs it to its fullest expression.

The distinction made by the New Testament authors between the moral and ritual law is also important because it separates the law as law and gospel. The ritual law is gospel, and it is fulfilled by Christ alone. The moral law is fulfilled by Christ in terms of justification (thus, the second use of the law), but the third use remains for those who are in Christ as a confirmation that one is loving God and fellow believers in the way that he or she should. This is Matthew's point. Those who abolish even the least of the moral laws and teach others to do the same are teaching contrary to loving God and fellow Christians and, therefore, will be considered least/of no position in the kingdom of heaven (5:19–20), i.e., they are false believers who practice lawlessness (7:21–23; 13:41).

This brings us to an important discussion. preterists tend to confuse the old covenant with the moral principles of the law. The old covenant is actually the external packaging of the moral law/justice as it existed in external images, which display a picture of holiness and salvation written on tablets of stone, as opposed to the new covenant which is that same moral law written upon the minds, i.e., onto the actual being of the individual believer. The new covenant is not a different morality but a different law/covenant in terms of the means of its communication to the new covenant community. In other words, it is about where the law is written, i.e., how it is communicated, but it is the same law. I will address this further in the discussion concerning Auctor's quote of Jeremiah 31:31–34 in Hebrews 8:6–9:1.

For now, it suffices to say that the claim that heaven and earth must have passed away or else the Jews, or even the Gentiles, would still be under the law, or the claim that the Jews could still be saved under the old covenant if the law is in effect, is a false inference that stems from misunderstanding both the need of the law until the end and the context of Matthew which argues for a continued use of the law for believers.

This explains why Paul can say he is not under the law and, yet, that he delights in the law of God in his inner being (Rom 7:22). He also notes that believers are called to fulfill the moral law as evidence of a Spirit-filled life.

> For you were called to freedom, brothers and sisters; only do not use your freedom as an opportunity to indulge your flesh, but through love serve one another. For the whole law can be summed up in a single commandment, namely, "You must love your neighbor as yourself." However, if you continually bite and devour one another, beware that you are not consumed by one another. But I say, live by the Spirit and you will not carry out the desires of the flesh. For the flesh has desires that are opposed to the Spirit, and the Spirit has desires that are opposed to the flesh, for these are in opposition to each other, so that you cannot do what you want. But if you are led by the Spirit, you are not under the law. Now the works of the flesh are obvious: sexual immorality, impurity, depravity, idolatry, sorcery, hostilities, strife, jealousy, outbursts of anger, selfishrivalries, dissensions, factions, envying, murder, drunkenness, carousing, and similar things. I am warning you, as I had warned you before: Those who practice such things will not inherit the kingdom of God! (Gal 5:13–21)

When Does the Old Covenant Pass Away?

I mentioned in the previous post that there seems to be some confusion on the nature of the new covenant in Jeremiah. This confusion is compounded by a statement, often misread, in the Book of Hebrews. In Hebrews, the auctor makes the following observation after his quotation of Jeremiah 31 concerning the new covenant.

> When he speaks of a new covenant, he has made old the first. Now what is growing old and wearing out is already fading away. (Heb 8:13)

What Preterists often think this means is that the author of Hebrews is arguing that Jeremiah predicted a future time (i.e., in the first century A.D.) when the new covenant was going to come, and the old covenant would grow old and soon pass away. The common interpretation of the passage is to understand it as the author arguing that the old covenant is currently in the process of passing away in his own day but that it has not quite occurred yet. Hence, Preterists see this as a reference to the coming of Christ in A.D. 70 since that is the big event about to happen and when the old covenant, in the preterist paradigm, is said to have passed away completely.

First, one ought to point out again that in Jeremiah 31, the difference between the old and new covenants is where they are written and how they are communicated (i.e., externally and internally versus only internally without the external). Jeremiah is addressing the Jewish community that is in exile and is going to be without a temple, sacrifices, and any of the external means through which God had communicated the law to them.

The text is arguing that God will write His law upon their minds and hearts so that they will be directly taught of God rather than having a need for physical demonstrations and illustrations of holiness through ritual or an external law written on tablets of stone. In other words, Jeremiah is arguing that much of the ritual law is only a form of communication of the moral law and that one does not need temples, sacrifices, etc., in order to obey it. Hence, once they are brought back from exile, if they do not have a temple where they can sacrifice or other ritual means to observe some of the ritual law, the essence of the law, which is moral in nature, can still be observed in the new covenant which YHWH makes with them since it does not require the externalities to exist in order for internal obedience to the law of YHWH to exist.

Instead, the new covenant will see the law written upon the very beings of the exiles themselves. "But I will make a new covenant with the whole nation of Israel after I plant them back in the land" (Jer 31:33). In fact, the whole context relates God's restoration of Israel from the exile, the rebuilding of the temple, and the re-establishment of the Levitical priesthood. But the renewed covenant is needed, one that differs from the first in terms of where it is displayed, because none of the external pictures exist after they are wiped out by the Babylonians.

Fast-forward to the auctor's time. He is drawing from this idea in order to make the argument that the Old Testament teaches the necessity of Christ. Christ, after all, is the capstone of the new covenant and, indeed, even its foundation. He argues that the reason why Christ's blood of the new covenant is necessary is because the old covenant is no longer in effect. It has already passed away. The external religion, which existed in rituals and sacrifices, was a shadow of the covenant to come in Christ. Hence, once Christ came, the shadows became ineffectual and unnecessary. This is what the author of Hebrews picks up on in Jeremiah. The shadows in rituals were already passing away when God wiped them out through the Babylonians. The author argues that this is because He was establishing a new covenant to come. The lack of necessity for Jews to practice the external rituals and the making of the new covenant with the Jewish exiles displays the fulfillment of the ritual code in One to come. Hence, they began to pass way and grow old at the time of Jeremiah. Once Christ came, they passed away completely.

His argument is that because Jeremiah used the word "new," Jeremiah was implying that the external covenant written on tablets and existing in rituals was "old." The author then points out that what is old is worn and is already passing away.

Where many people have misunderstood what is being said, it seems rather clear that the author of Hebrews is saying this *of Jeremiah's day, not his own*. In other words, Jeremiah, not the author, used the word "new." Jeremiah, not the author, implied by his use of the word "new" that the external covenant was old. Jeremiah, not the author, was implying that what is old is worn out and already fading away. In Jeremiah's day, the Old Covenant is fading away because God is promising to bring about the new covenant when He brings Israel back from the exile in the fifth century B.C., which means that the old covenant was old and worn out in the sixth century B.C. In fact, that is the context of the Book of Jeremiah. The old is already passing away and the new is already coming so that the exiles can worship God even without the external religion of a temple, which has been destroyed, and rituals, which cannot therefore be performed, because the law will be written, not on external tablets that they can see, but only on their minds and hearts from that point on.

So, Auctor is not arguing that the old covenant is currently passing away in his own day, as though it did not take its last breath at the coming of Christ and His finishing work on the cross, but rather that if it was already fading away in Jeremiah's day, then it was certainly finished off by Christ in His death, resurrection, and especially ascension.

Hence, his entire argument in Hebrews is that Christ has already fulfilled the sacrificial laws, He is already fulfilling the priesthood by being at the right hand of God the Father, He has a better tabernacle in the presence of God the Father to do His priestly work, etc. There is simply no need for the old external covenant when one has the new better one now. This is his argument to Jews leaving Christianity. It is not that they will have something better in terms of the covenant in the future but that they currently (before

A.D. 70) already have it through Christ's fulfilling the rituals seen in the external covenant law via His death, ascension, priesthood, tabernacle, etc.

The text of Hebrews 8:13 is simply being misread.

Imagine if I said that Napoleon once said that he had a new sword, and by "new" he implies his other sword was old, and what is old is wearing out and already fading away. It is well understood that I am not saying that the sword is becoming worn out and is already fading away in my own day, but in his.

Or to put it in logical terms: Author X, who lives in Time M, used the word Y in Time M. The word Y implies Z in Time M. What is Z implies B and C. If Author X implies that word Y is occurring in Time M, then Z is occurring in Time M. If Z is occurring in Time M, and it implies B and C, then B and C are occurring in Time M.

One can argue that this statement made by Jeremiah is only a prophecy of the future and not meant for the returning exiles, and perhaps even exiles, but this would simply ignore the context of Jeremiah and that of Hebrews as well.

The idea that a "new" covenant implies that the other one is now old and fading away at the time the word "new" is voiced is the logical implication of what is said since it is Jeremiah, in the sixth century B.C. who says/implies it, and not Auctor in the first century A.D. This also takes seriously the context of Jeremiah which presents the new covenant in the context of God restoring the exiles to their land and restoring their living and worship there. And it is also the context of Hebrews where Auctor argues that there is currently no need for any externally communicated old covenant since the new covenant has already come and Christ has, and is, currently fulfilling the role of the old covenant ritual law in a far superior way than the shadow did in its own day since He is the substance of what was to come.

What is old in Jeremiah's day is worn out in Jeremiah's day and is already fading away in Jeremiah's day. When Christ comes, He removes any further need of its remaining elements and takes over the roles those external elements played in the worship of God.

Hence, this is not a time reference that indicates any sort of transition period. As argued before, there is no transition period. The new covenant is celebrated as having already come when Jesus hands the disciples the wine, which symbolizes the new covenant in His blood. This same new covenant is celebrated by the early church in communion, as evidenced in 1 Corinthians 11:25–26. The new has come. The old has faded away as a necessary means to worship God. This is Auctor's point. The superior has come, so the inferior has already passed away. The renewed and superior is necessary. The old and inferior is superfluous. Trading in the former for the latter, therefore, is foolish. Jewish Christians should not turn back to an old covenant religion that is now obsolete.

The Antinomians under the Judgment of Christ's Final Victory

Jude 1:4, 14–15 states: "For certain persons have crept in unnoticed, those who were long beforehand marked out for this condemnation. . . .About these also Enoch. . .prophesied, saying, 'Behold, the Lord came with many thousands of His holy ones, to execute judgment upon all, and to convict all the ungodly. . .'"

Preterists often dissect this verse by making it sound as though the final judgment Enoch speaks of is specifically talking about these actual false teachers in Jude's day. The question is whether this passage is talking about these specific men only or these types of men, the group that makes up false believers, of which these first century men are a part. The context makes it clear that this is a type of men that make up the group considered to be false believers. That is why the references are to Old Testament false believers. These men are a part of that group. But none of that is quoted in order to make it seem like this verse is only talking about these men and not the larger group of which they are a part.

It is the same thing here as we have in many places in the Bible and elsewhere, where the contemporary wicked will be placed in the larger context of those who have been predetermined for destruction.

Jesus does the same thing with the Pharisees. "Rightly did Isaiah prophecy of you . . ." But it is clear that the prophecy in Isaiah is of disobedient and unbelieving Israelites in his own day. How can Jesus say that it is about the Pharisees? Because they are a part of the larger group that is being condemned. It is simply absurd to suggest that Jude is talking only about these specific false believers and no other false believers in other churches, throughout time, etc. The partial quotation that leaves out that fact seems to indicate that the preterist who quotes the passage this way knows it must be edited to give credence to his interpretation. The same can be said for 2 Peter 2:3 and any time a general judgment is associated with a people, whether for damnation or salvation. The New Testament speaks to the part as partaking in the judgment of the whole. That is simply a common way of speaking for all languages throughout time.

The Way into the Holy Place

In Hebrews 9:8–10, Preterists argue that the temple still stands as a symbol that the old covenant remains. Hence, the old covenant is still in effect until it is destroyed in A.D. 70. This confusion may stem from the way the text is often translated in various Bible translations. The text is often translated similarly to the following:

"The Holy Spirit is signifying this, that the way of the [heavenly] Holy Places has not yet been revealed, while the outer tabernacle is still standing, which is a symbol for the present time. Accordingly, both gifts and sacrifices are offered which cannot make the worshiper perfect in conscience, since they relate only to food and drink and various washings, regulations for the body imposed until a time of reformation."

It is suggested by some preterists that the Holy Place referenced here is the temple and it currently stands in Auctor's day as a symbol that will be taken out of the way when the new covenant age is brought to fruition in A.D. 70. The problem is that Auctor nowhere talks about the temple. He does not use the word even once. He makes no reference to it at all. What Auctor is talking about is what the tabernacle *in the Pentateuch* symbolizes to the Israelites in the Pentateuch. He is arguing that the tent of meeting is a symbol for the old covenant because he wants to show the temporal nature of that covenant as it was communicated through rituals, which then also were meant to be temporary.

We know this because not only does he not refer to the temple (and the temple is never referred to in Hebrews as the tabernacle—they are two different structures) but also because he describes the tabernacle he is talking about, and it is not the second temple that is standing in the first century. That tabernacle has the ark of the covenant in it (v. 4). That is a dead giveaway that he is talking about the tabernacle in the Pentateuch as the ark is lost after the exile, and the second temple does not contain it. If someone wants to take issue with that and argue that they have a replica inside, he mentions that the ark has Aaron's miraculously budding rod and the two tablets of stone carved out by Moses in it. He is simply not talking about the second temple. These passages are completely taken out of context.

Neither does the use of the present tense indicate that he is talking about a present situation. Often when the New Testament authors relate a larger narrative, they use the present tense to describe the narrative in a more vivid fashion ("it has [present aspect] the golden pot and Aaron's budded rod" v. 4) in order to place the audience back into the context of the story. Storytellers today do the same thing. This may be deceiving to the English reader when one does not realize the practice of storytelling is being utilized. It should be noted that many New Testament authors would often shift from perfective narrative tenses to imperfective aspects (like the present tense) for the purpose of storytelling. In 9:1, Auctor does just that. Notice that he speaks of this as something in the past.

"The first covenant *had* (imperfect) regulations . . ."

"There had been (aorist passive) a tabernacle . . ."

The point is simply that Auctor is arguing the old covenant has already passed away at the cross. It is no longer valid in God's eyes in his own day. Everything pertaining to the tabernacle has passed away, and thus, all that it symbolizes (i.e., the ritual expression of teaching the law) is displayed as having existed as a temporary placeholder until the time of Christ and the church that it represented would appear. The passage is simply being ripped out of context by preterists to make it refer to the second temple; and the book of Hebrews is thus horribly misunderstood as somehow supporting the idea that the author is talking about his own time as the time of the old covenant.

The translation that states it is a symbol for the present time is misunderstood as well. Auctor is actually saying that it is a symbol for them, the ancient Israelites. Hence, a better translation would be to understand that "the present time" refers to "that present time" referenced throughout the context.

> This was a symbol for the time then present, when gifts and sacrifices were offered that could not perfect the conscience of the worshiper. They served only for matters of food and drink and various washings; they are external regulations imposed until the new order came. (9:9–10)

There are two ways one can understand the verse. It can be translated as "this had been a parable for the contemporary time period," i.e., time period and people in Moses' day about which Auctor is speaking; or it can be understood as referring to the tabernacle in the Pentateuch serving as a parable of the old covenant up to Auctor's own day. Either way, since this is about the tabernacle, it must refer to a time when the tabernacle existed, which means that it must refer to Moses' day and not Auctor's since the tabernacle does not exist beyond the time of Solomon's temple. The temporary nature of the tabernacle symbolizes the temporary nature of the ritual communication of the holiness of the law, i.e., the old covenant as the manner by which the moral law was communicated and its external versus internal nature. In contrast, the moral law is now written on the hearts/minds of God's people. The tabernacle signifies this in the Pentateuch to the people, and it can continue to symbolize the temporal nature of the first covenant to the Auctor, his audience, and to us a couple thousand years later. That is because the tabernacle exists both for Auctor and us in the text of the Torah, not as a temple literally standing in Jerusalem. He is not talking about the temple but the tabernacle, which signifies that he is talking about a symbol found in the Pentateuch that describes the tabernacle at Sinai. There is no tabernacle standing in Auctor's day.

So, what this passage does not mean is that the tabernacle is still standing in the form of the temple in Auctor's day. That is not what Auctor is referring to. He is immersed in the Pentateuch and attempting to take his audience there. This passage, then, also is taken out of context, and in order to get a temple out of a tabernacle one simply has to change the context and ignore what Auctor is actually saying.

The Antichrist Is Already in the World

John indicates that the antichrist is already in the world. It is suggested that the antichrist marks the time of the end. This may or may not be true, but we will grant for argument's sake that this is what John is saying.

Preterists will often quote this passage: "This is that of the antichrist, of which you have heard is coming, and now is already in the world" (1 John 4:3).

In context, John, in his typical already-not yet fashion, sees the antichrist as already present through the spirits of false prophets who have gone out into the world. Specifically, he is speaking of the alternate christs offered up by the proto-gnostics. So, through these people, who have the same spirit as antichrist, the antichrist has already come—not because he is already here but because those who typify him are.

John states: "Who is the liar but the person who denies that Jesus is the Christ? This one is the antichrist: the person who denies the Father and the Son" (2:22).

Notice, the person who denies that Jesus is the Christ (something proto-gnostics were doing by divorcing the divine Christ from the human Jesus) is the antichrist.

However, in 4:1–3, John makes it clear that he is talking about the *spirit* of antichrist (*to tou antichristou*, where the neuter article has *pneuma* as its antecedent) that has gone out to many false prophets in the world. In fact, in 2:18, John flat out says that he is talking about these many antichrists (plural) that have already gone out (same terminology used of the spirit of antichrist displayed in the false prophets) into the world. It is the spirit of the antichrist (4:3) in these false prophets that displays the presence of the antichrist. This is a part of John's continual use of the "already, not yet" in his theology. Again, this is just another text taken out of context by preterists.

Putting the Prophets to Death

Another passage taken out of context is Revelation 18:24: "And in her [the Great City Babylon] was found the blood of prophets and of saints and of all who have been slain on the earth."

This is then compared to texts like Matthew 23:35–36 // Luke 11:50–51 where the Lord sent them messengers and prophets who they persecuted and killed.

> Woe to you! You build the tombs of the prophets whom your ancestors killed. So you testify that you approve of the deeds of your ancestors, because they killed the prophets and you build their tombs! For this reason also the wisdom of God said, 'I will send them prophets and apostles, some of whom they will kill and persecute,' so that this generation may be held accountable for the blood of all the prophets that has been shed since the beginning of the world, from the blood of Abel to the blood of Zechariah, who was killed between the altar and the sanctuary. Yes, I tell you, it will be charged against this generation. (Luke 11:47–51)

Notice first that the text says that God will send them prophets and messengers as a prediction made in the past. The generation to which Christ is referring is only being charged for the bloodshed from Abel to Zechariah, not for the deaths of the New Testament apostles and prophets, so "apostles and prophets" here do not refer to New Testament apostles and prophets. They instead refer to the *apostoloi*/*mal'ākîm* "messengers" and prophets sent to Israel in the Old Testament.

Revelation, however, is not referring to messengers and prophets of the Old Testament as is made clear by the context of the book. Instead, these are the prophets, apostles, and saints of the New Testament who overcome the beast, i.e., Domitian, by the blood of the lamb and the word of their testimony (6:9–11; 7:14; 12:11; 18:20).

In 20:4, we see that these people are New Testament believers, not anyone who was executed between the times of Abel and Zechariah.

> Then I saw thrones and seated on them were those who had been given authority to judge. I also saw the souls of those who had been beheaded because of the testimony about Jesus and

because of the word of God. These had not worshiped the beast or his image and had refused to receive his mark on their forehead or hand. They came to life and reigned with Christ for a thousand years."

Notice that these people are beheaded because they would not worship the beast and his image, i.e., Domitian, and because of their testimony about Jesus and the gospel. Notice also that the nation killing them is Rome. The Roman Emperor Domitian executed people for treason. To refuse to worship him or his image was treason against Rome and the gods. Consider then the manner of execution. It is not stoning or most of the ways the prophets are said to have died (e.g., sawed in half, thrown off cliffs, stoned to death, stabbed, etc.). Instead, they are beheaded, which is the most common manner of execution for Roman citizens. The Roman government would likely crucify Jews, and Jews would stone others to death, even though they are not officially allowed to execute anyone at the time, but this death in Revelation is by beheading by the entity which Paul describes in Romans as not "having the sword for nothing." The sword is a synecdoche for the death it causes via beheading.

So, this is not Israel killing Old Testament prophets and messengers. It is Rome executing New Testament Christians, who live long after Zechariah, for the treason against gods and men that results from refusing to worship its emperor, Domitian. The cross references, therefore, are deceptive in that two different contexts with different characters involved are at play. The preterist who uses this passage as a proof text has simply failed to note this and is, therefore, committing both an illegitimate referential transference and the fallacy of context replacement.

The Coming of Christ in the Apocalypse of John

Revelation 2:25 is quoted as a reference to Christ's return in A.D. 70. "Nevertheless what you have, hold fast until I come."

The problem with this interpretation is that Christ's coming in context is not about the destruction of Jerusalem in A.D. 70 but encouraging believers to remain faithful under the pressure of the beast to worship him and his image. If they are faithful, they will receive the reward of confirmation that they are Christ's true people. If they are not, they will have their lampstands removed from His presence. As Christ warns them, "Therefore, remember from what high state you have fallen and repent! Do the deeds you did at the first; if not, I will come to you and remove your lampstand from its place—that is, if you do not repent" (2:5).

This text, and the book itself, is all about encouraging Christians to remain faithful. Christ's judgment of the world and the false church is seen as something that breaks into history before the time of final judgment. Christ's coming in Revelation 2 is an ongoing process whereby He judges His church to keep it pure. Hence, this continual, but not final, coming that is referred to in Revelation 2–3 is merely one of Christ's methods of receiving His purified kingdom/bride. It is not the macro coming, which is future, but a micro coming, which is present with the believers in the first century. Hence, He is coming to *them* (2:5, 16, 21–23; 3:3, 19–20).

So, this is Christ coming to His churches and disciplining them. He is viewed as both coming and having already come and judged some churches/people; but this is not talking about the final judgment and coming of Christ, which the book depicts as something still to come after His people have overcome the world by His blood and their testimony, when the total destruction of the world's kingdoms takes place.

Crushing Satan Underfoot

There are a few verses left that are largely taken out of context. For instance, Romans 16:20 says, "the God of peace will soon crush Satan under your feet." The context is not the eschaton but overcoming false teachers at Rome. The heretics are referred to as their source, i.e., Satan, and the God who brings shalom to His community will soon give victory to the faithful over these heretics. There is no mention of the end times. That is simply being assumed because of the use of Genesis 3:15, as though it were Christ crushing the serpent. Paul is clearly using this as his framework, but he applies it in way of application to this smaller victory of the saints over Satan's minions. It is simply eisegetical to insert some sort of time reference about the end of the age here. As Morris concludes, "Nothing in the context indicates that Paul is looking to the parousia, and it is better to see the promise of a victory over Satan in the here and now."[19]

Remaining Parousia Passages in the Synoptics

As I have argued, the non-preterist interpreter has no need to interpret these passages used by Preterists as referring to either the destruction of Jerusalem in A.D. 70 or other events in the first century or beyond. The understanding of apocalyptic speech I have given in this book frees the interpreter

---

19. Morris, *Romans*, 517 who also cites Wilckens, Fitzmeyer, and Calvin as in agreement.

to allow the context to guide his interpretation. Having said that, however, it seems clear that the last remaining *parousia* passages in the Synoptics, which are often interpreted to support preterism, are actually not referring to the destruction of the temple in A.D. 70 at all. These are Matthew 10:23 and Matthew 16:28//Mark 9:1//Luke 9:27.

Not Finished Going through the Cities of Israel until the Son of Man Comes

In Matthew 10:23, Christ tells the disciples that they will not finish going through the cities of Israel until the Son of Man comes. It is these last few words, "the Son of Man comes" that I think leads the preterist to assume that Jesus is talking about the second coming. Hence, it is argued that the gospel is preached to the entire world, according to the New Testament, before A.D. 70, the end is to come after it is preached to the whole world, and certainly the cities of Israel are included in that. Hence, since the disciples themselves are the ones doing the preaching, and they preach the gospel to the whole world (again, including Israel) before A.D. 70, this must mean that the disciples will be alive when Christ returns.

There are a couple of issues with this interpretation, however. In the context, Christ is sending the disciples out to the cities of Israel *during His earthly ministry*. Verses 10:5–10 make this clear.

> Jesus sent out these twelve, instructing them as follows: "Do not go to Gentile regions and do not enter any Samaritan town. Go instead to the lost sheep of the house of Israel. As you go, preach this message: 'The kingdom of heaven is near!' Heal the sick, raise the dead, cleanse lepers, cast out demons. Freely you received, freely give. Do not take gold, silver, or copper in your belts, no bag for the journey, or an extra tunic, or sandals or staff, for the worker deserves his provisions.

Notice that the disciples are told not to go to the Gentiles, which is the opposite of what Christ will command them to do at the end of the book in the Great Commission (Matt 28:16–20). This tells us that this mission is a more localized one and one that comes before the other in Christ's earthly ministry.

Christ also tells them not to bring provisions with them. This is also the opposite of what He will command them later when they go out to the nations after He leaves them (Luke 22:35–38). Again, this indicates that the mission in Matthew 10 is not the same one as the Great Commission later.

There is also a problem in harmonizing what is said here with the idea that this refers to the global mission that ends with Christ's return. Jesus states that the disciples will not finish going through the cities of Israel until the Son of Man comes. He does not say that they will finish before He comes. He states that it is not until the moment He comes that they will finish. His coming marks their completion of the mission and that they have gone through all the cities. It is the point of their finishing.

The worldwide mission is said to be completed long before Christ comes. Preterists are fond of quoting Paul who states that the gospel has been proclaimed in all creation under heaven (Col 1:23), that the voice of those who preach the gospel has gone out to the ends of the world (Rom 10:18 quoting Psalm 19:4), that it is bearing fruit and growing in all the world (Col 1:6).

But Christ says that they will not finish going through the cities of Israel *until* He comes. What this indicates is that the Son of Man coming is throwing off the preterist interpretation. They are reading an eschatological coming into the text when Christ is simply referring to Himself as the Son of Man who will come to them at the point when their temporary mission during His ministry is completed. And, indeed, the preaching itinerary of both Christ and the disciples indicates that they would have covered all of Israel within His earthly ministry.

One might argue that the lost tribes of Israel were scattered among the nations, and hence, Christ is referring to the whole world, but the problem with this is that the text clearly states that Christ tells them NOT to go into any of the cities of the nations/Gentiles. They are not even to go into the towns of the Samaritans. So, it is clear that this is referring to the northern towns of Israel, where the northern tribes were once located and still had members of those tribes in them. Again, the disciples would have completed this task within a short time frame. Northern Israel is not that big. So, His coming has to do with His coming to them at the completion of their mission, not some eschatological coming in A.D. 70 or otherwise.

Now, what of the argument concerning the end taking place once the gospel is preached to the whole world as in Matthew 24:14? I think there is a twofold fulfillment of this in terms of the micro-macro argument. The end for Israel in the destruction of the temple in A.D. 70 occurs after the gospel has been proclaimed to the whole Roman world. Matthew 24 is about the destruction of Jerusalem in A.D. 70 so this would make sense. So, in a microcosmic manner, it is fulfilled in the same way that the destruction of Jerusalem is a microcosm of the larger destruction of the world to come.

However, it should be noted that it is not clear whether Christ is referring to the world in the same way that Paul is. Christ uses the word *oikomene* which refers to the literal creation of the world, the entirety of the created order, the whole inhabited earth. Paul merely uses *kosmos* or *ktisis* in his hyperbole but does not seem to be quoting Christ or alluding to the prediction in Matthew 24.

I would also argue that Paul is speaking in hyperbole, not literally. In fact, all must conclude this as the gospel had not, in fact, been proclaimed to all the world as a literal fulfillment. It had in terms of a representative fulfillment, a micro fulfillment of what would come. The idea that Paul did not know of the world outside of Rome, of course, is complete nonsense. Everyone was well aware that a larger world existed outside of the Roman Empire. So, Paul's declarations here are meant to be hyperbolic, but Christ's prediction seems to be literal. Furthermore, Paul conveys the idea that this message being heard by all the nations is from his own personal proclamation, as though he is the one personally to have told the entire world the gospel, which is another indicator that he is using hyperbole here and is not literally saying that every nation has heard the gospel from his own lips. The idea instead is that the gospel has gone out not only to Israel but to the entire world, all of creation in a sense, and has spread beyond the borders of Israel to the farthest boundaries of the Western Empire and to much of the East, covering the expanse of the entire Roman world (cf. 1 Clement 5:5–6). Hence, one could argue that the entire world had the gospel preached to it in a hyperbolic manner since Rome was not the entire world but made up the entire Empire that ruled Paul's world. The gospel had not yet gone to China or to the tribes in the African bush or to the Barbarian tribes outside of Rome, etc., all of which Paul would have known to exist. But he uses hyperbole to show just how extensive the preaching of the gospel, i.e., his own work, truly was.

He likely states this as a counter to the claims of Judaizers that the gospel is for those who become Jewish. In any case, his claim uses hyperbole to counter the idea that it is for the Jew and not also for the Gentile. Hence, the two books in which he makes these statements are Romans and Colossians, two books dealing with heretical Jewish teaching. But it is also clear that the gospel was meant to go out to the entire world, all of creation, not only in the hyperbolic sense in which Paul is using it but literally. This is only being fulfilled recently in our own time.

Since Christ's prediction is literal and Paul's claim is hyperbolic, and because there are clear microcosmic and macrocosmic fulfillments of this prediction (no one would argue that the gospel is actually proclaimed to the entire known world of the first century audience), one can say that this both had a fulfillment in the first century but also needed to be fulfilled in the future if it was to be fulfilled literally.

In conclusion, Matthew 23:10 is not talking about some eschatological fulfillment but merely stating that the disciples will not finish their work of going through the northern towns of Israel before Christ comes to them to end that temporal ministry.

The Mount of Transfiguration

In Matthew 16:28, Christ indicates that some of the disciples will see Him coming in His kingdom. This is taken by Preterists as an indication that Christ will return in their lifetimes. However, it seems clear instead that this is a reference to the Mount of Transfiguration scene to follow. There are numerous reasons for understanding it this way.

1. The parallels indicate that this is a reference to God beginning to give the kingdom over to Christ.

   > And he said to them, "I tell you the truth, there are some standing here who will not experience death before they see the kingdom of God come with power." (Mark 9:1)
   > But I tell you most certainly, there are some standing here who will not experience death before they see the kingdom of God." (Luke 9:27)
   > I tell you the truth, there are some standing here who will not experience death before they see the Son of Man coming in his kingdom." (Matt 16:28)

   The Son of Man coming in His kingdom is a parallel idea to the kingdom of God coming with power and the kingdom of God itself. We are told that the kingdom of God has already come. We are also told that the kingdom of God comes with power in Jesus' ministry. It also comes with power in the ministry of the apostles and the church in the coming of the Holy Spirit. But the point I would make here is that I think that Preterists miss the complexity of this verse by assuming that there is only one coming of Christ, only one reception of His kingdom, rather than many as the New Testament indicates. They do not understand the micro-macro nature of apocalyptic speech, the already-not yet nature of a future fulfillment also being fulfilled in smaller ways before the time, and hence, they conclude by the language preceding Christ's statement in the Synoptics that this must refer only to the Second Advent and not anything that might come before and would be spoken of as one with it even though separated by time.

2. The placement of the narrative.

There is more to indicate that the fulfillment, at least the initial fulfillment of Christ's coming/reception of His kingdom is on the Mount of Transfiguration.

First, it is important to note that every single Synoptic places the Mount of Transfiguration scene immediately after Christ's statement concerning the kingdom of God. This is significant since the Gospel authors seem to have no problem moving things around to present the sayings of Jesus and the events of His life in an order that suits their theological themes. Yet, even with differing themes and the recasting of many events, this one is placed immediately after what Christ says here in every one of the Synoptic Gospels.

Narrative makes its arguments this way. When an author places things together in a narrative, he is often meaning to communicate that the one goes with the other. The surrounding text gives context to what comes before or after.

3. The mimicking of language from the Daniel 7 "Son of Man coming in the Clouds" narrative in the Mount of Transfiguration Scene.

The language of coming, as we have seen in the other Gospel presentations of what Christ said, is actually the language of the Son receiving the kingdom. It is a royal conferment, the transference of sovereignty from the Father to the Son. This idea is taken from Daniel 7. In Daniel 7, the Son of Man comes on the clouds of heaven and ascends to the Ancient of Days, i.e., the Father, and receives the kingdom from Him. God is described as white as snow, like wool, and glowing like fire.

In the Mount of Transfiguration scene, Jesus is the one glowing, a display of His deity, but he ascends to the Father on the mountain, they are enveloped in a cloud, and the Father confirms the authority/power the Son has and that all should now listen to Him. Even the declaration by the Father, i.e., the Ancient of Days, that Jesus is His one beloved Son is terminology of kingship as the anointed king was considered God's son.

The coming language of Matthew 16:28 is, therefore, explained as reception of the kingdom/conferment of the kingdom by the Father to the Son. It is a fulfillment of Daniel 7 (not *the* fulfillment but *a* fulfillment), where God gives His majesty to the Son in the clouds of the sky here upon the mountaintop.

So, the Mount of Transfiguration is a beginning fulfillment that is witnessed by a few of the disciples a few days after Christ proclaims that some will not taste death until they have seen the kingdom of

God (Luke 9:27)//the kingdom come with power (Mark 9:1)//the Son coming in/into His kingdom (Matt 16:28), i.e., the Son starting to be given the kingdom by the Father.

4. Peter links them together.

But there is even more than this that indicates that the Mount of Transfiguration fulfills this prediction, at least in part. Peter links the two ideas together himself. In 2 Peter 1:16–18, Peter states the following:

> For we did not follow cleverly concocted fables when we made known to you the power and *parousia* "coming" of our Lord Jesus Christ; no, we were eyewitnesses of His majesty (i.e., royal conferment). For He received honor and glory from God the Father, when that voice was conferred to Him by the Majestic Glory: "This is my dear Son, in whom I am delighted." When this voice was conveyed from heaven, we ourselves heard it, for we were with him on the holy mountain.

Notice, the idea that power and royalty were given to Christ on the Mount of Transfiguration, and this is referred to as Christ's *parousia* "coming." Peter argues that this is what was proclaimed to Peter's audience, and that it was not a story made up by the apostles but rather what they themselves saw on the mountain.

The disciples will also witness Christ's reception in His resurrection, His ascension, the coming of the Holy Spirit at Pentecost, etc. Some will see it in His destruction of the temple in A.D. 70 as well. There are many "receptions/comings" of His kingdom that will lead up to the final and ultimate coming and reception of His total kingdom in the end. Indeed, as we have noted, He states to the priests before His death that "from now on, you will see the Son of Man sitting at the right hand of Power and coming in the clouds of heaven" (Matt 26:64), which indicates an ongoing reception of the kingdom. (Note the contradiction between sitting at God's right hand and coming in the clouds that arises if taken literally, yet both convey the reception of power in the Bible.)

Luke even records that the ultimate day, the final coming, will not be seen by the disciples even though they will see other days, other comings, which precede it. In Luke 17:21, Christ argues that the disciples already have seen the coming of the kingdom but, in v. 22, that they have not yet, nor will they, see the final coming of Christ in their lifetimes.

Hence, the most natural understanding of Christ's words is to see them in light of the Mount of Transfiguration first. If there are other fulfillments the disciples will see, and there are, then they are secondary to the fact that Christ's prediction is already fulfilled with some of the apostles a few days later.

Belief in the Imminence of Christ's Return

One of the arguments that Preterists often give is that the apostles seem to believe that Christ was returning in their lifetime.

Paul states that the "time is short" and that the "form of this world is passing away" (1 Cor 7:29, 31)[20] and that Christ will give "us" rest when He returns with His holy angels and burns up his adversaries.

> For it is right for God to repay with affliction those who afflict you, and to you who are being afflicted to give rest together with us when the Lord Jesus is revealed from heaven with his mighty angels. *With flaming fire he will mete out punishment on those who do not know God* and do not obey the gospel of our Lord Jesus. They will undergo the penalty of eternal destruction, *away from the presence of the Lord and from the glory of his strength*, when he comes to be glorified among his saints and admired on that day among all who have believed—and you did in fact believe our testimony. (2 Thes 1:6–10; emphasis added)

> And I say this, brothers and sisters: The time is short. So then those who have wives should be as those who have none, those with tears like those not weeping, those who rejoice like those not rejoicing, those who buy like those without possessions, those who use the world as though they were not using it to the full. For the present shape of this world is passing away. (1 Cor 7:29–31)

The apostles simply speak to believers in a way that these events (i.e., Christ's return, resurrection from the dead, transformation of their bodies, destruction of the wicked, etc.) will happen to them. Peter does the same as

---

20. It is very possible that Paul is talking about death rather than the second coming here. As he emphasizes the person as the one who will be as one who did not weep, who did not possess, who is not married, etc. In this way, it may be that the form of this world is passing away in terms of the believer's death, and the "time" that he refers to is one's lifetime. However, if referring to the second coming, this text contradicts preterism as sorrow, marriage, and commerce for the Corinthians does not pass away in A.D. 70.

he speaks of sharing in this glory that is to be revealed when Christ returns and rewards the believers to whom he is speaking (1 Pet 5:1–4).

Now, what preterists will say is that Paul includes himself in this rescuing and, therefore, believed that the Lord would come back in his lifetime. Yet, Paul was martyred by Nero before the Lord is said to return in A.D. 70. Peter was specifically declared by Jesus as one who will not see Christ's second coming as he will die instead (John 21:18–23). The problem, of course, immediately emerges that if Peter and Paul are dead, then they are not going to be around for Christ's return, nor be relieved and given rest from the enemies through the event since they are not a part of the event in A.D. 70 when Christ supposedly does this.

If it is true that these apostles believed that the Lord would come back within their lifetimes, then everyone, including preterists, must conclude that they were wrong. Paul was wrong. Christ did not return to deal out fire on his enemies and give to him relief from persecution. Peter was wrong since Christ did not return in his lifetime. Both Peter and Paul died before the destruction of Jerusalem in A.D. 70. They were reported to have died under the persecution of Nero in the mid-60s as James Crossley sums up, "the evidence of Peter and Paul dying in Rome being fairly secure (cf. e.g., 1 Clem. 5.1–7; 6.1; Ign., Rom. 4.2–3; Iren., *Adv. haer.* 3.3.2; Eus. *HE* 2.25; 3.1.32)."[21]

But there is more than this to consider and that is the nature of what the apostles believed was going to happen. In 1 Corinthians 7:29–31, notice what Paul says of this age to come. He is arguing to the Corinthians that they might want to think twice about getting married since the time is short and those who are married will soon be as those who are not. The present pattern of the world that is passing away includes the marriage institution. It also includes buying things, weeping, and rejoicing about the things of the present world. Did all that end in A.D. 70? Did commerce end in A.D. 70? Did having joy and sorrow about situations that arise in the world end in A.D. 70? Did the form of this world pass away in A.D. 70 because God knocked down a city in the Middle East? Paul's entire point concerns marriage among the Corinthians to whom he is speaking. He is arguing that one needs to consider the brevity of time until those who are married will no longer be married. As Christ argued as well, the age to come is one in which resurrected saints do not marry (Luke 20:35), something that would cause a problem if marriage was restored once a person's body was restored and the one flesh union made in that body was reestablished, as the Sadducees point out.

---

21. Crossley, *The Date of Mark's Gospel*, 7.

One might argue that marriage and buying ended in Jerusalem at that time, but then why is Paul arguing that the Corinthians in Corinth might not want to get married because the time is short and marriage is going to come to an end? Paul's argument would make no sense. If marriage ended in Jerusalem, it certainly did not end in Corinth or any other city to which believers could move if they wanted to get married.

Furthermore, the enemies upon which Christ deals out a fiery destruction are in Thessalonica, not Jerusalem. And, as discussed before, Paul historically is relieved from their persecution by his death, not Christ's return.

This is not even to mention the fact that the apostles believed the coming of Christ will do away with death, sin, sorrow, the wicked and their kingdoms and bring about a resurrection of the dead for both the righteous and the wicked. None of this happened in A.D. 70.

So, were the apostles wrong? This is a possibility since we believe that the Scripture is inspired to instruct Christians not in timelines but in theology and ethics. Their sacred writings are inspired and inerrant not they themselves, lest we argue that the apostles were made little omniscient gods to fulfill their ministry; and the purpose of those sacred writings is not to present all knowledge to the Christian but a comprehensive Christian worldview constructed by the divine theology and ethics that are expressed through the apostles' language and cultural ideas that themselves only function as vehicles of that presentation.

In fact, we know that the apostles do not know when Christ is returning because Christ Himself repeats to them twice that no one knows when He is returning in terms of the macro event, nor does it belong to them to know.

In Acts 1:6–7, the apostles ask when He will restore the kingdom to Israel. He replies that such knowledge does not belong to them but is solely the Father's prerogative to know such things. This is reminiscent of His response to the apostles' question in the Olivet Discourse concerning the macro event. He relates to them the micro event and says that it will happen within some of their lifetimes, but the timing of the macro event is said to only be known by the Father. Not even the Son knows it so, obviously, Jesus could not be revealing when it was occurring. Hence, the timing of Christ's return is not something God ever revealed to the disciples.

But there is another interesting possibility and that is that what is given to men, even commanded of them, is to look forward to Christ's return. In other words, the expectation of Christ's return is something the New Testament considers important. It's so important that it provides the basis for our sanctification. In fact, it seems that the New Testament authors believe it to be a necessary element in motivating believers to purify themselves.

Jesus places it as the basis for treating one's fellow Christians well in Matthew (24:42–51). In Mark's version, one reads the common theme of using the imminent return as a reminder of Christ's coming judgment found in all the Synoptics.

> "But as for that day or hour no one knows it—neither the angels in heaven, nor the Son– except the Father. Watch out! Stay alert! For you do not know when the time will come. It is like a man going on a journey. He left his house and put his slaves in charge, assigning to each his work, and commanded the doorkeeper to stay alert. Stay alert, then, because you do not know when the owner of the house will return—whether during evening, at midnight, when the rooster crows, or at dawn—or else he might find you asleep when he returns suddenly. What I say to you I say to everyone: Stay alert!" (Mark 13:32–37)

The ignorance of His disciples as to when He will return plays into the command to stay alert. If one knew the timing of the event, one would merely be tempted to doze off until that time. So, looking forward to His coming and not knowing when He will come plays a vital role in staying alert, something God considered necessary for Christians to have in terms of motivating them toward sanctification.

Likewise, John places it as the basis for sanctification in both his epistles and apocalypse. He states of Christ's return,

> And now, little children, remain in him, so that when he appears we may have confidence and not shrink away from him in shame when he comes back. If you know that he is righteous, you also know that everyone who practices righteousness has been fathered by him. (See what sort of love the Father has given to us: that we should be called God's children– and indeed we are! For this reason the world does not know us: because it did not know him. Beloved friends, we are God's children now, but what we will be has not yet become visible. We know that whenever He is made visible we will be like him, because we will see him just as he is. And everyone who has this hope focused on him purifies/sanctifies himself, just as Jesus is pure). (1 John 2:28–3:3)

Indeed, Paul seems very aware that he is going to die. The prophet Agabus tells him news that leads Paul to declare that he might die in the Book of Acts (21:10–14), and he indicates this in 2 Timothy 4:6–8. Peter also indicates this referencing the Johannine scene about which we have discussed before (2 Pet 1:12–15).

So, the apostles know that they are going to die. Yet, they include themselves in the "we," "us," etc., when speaking of something that will happen to other Christians. This is a type of speech that is quite common. The "we" does not necessarily refer to the literal group (i.e., I and you together) but to the representative group. In other words, the "we" and "us" can refer to Christians in general, apostles in general, those who preach the gospel in general, Christians who are alive rather than dead in general, etc.

This is true for any small part of a group that represents the whole in a synecdoche. The part represents the whole, and sometimes the part even represents others in the group. This means that the apostles, both in terms of relating the necessity of looking forward to Christ's return for sanctification and in terms of speaking to all Christians for all time can use language that describes a participation in events or here, an event, in which they will not literally partake.

Hence, Paul can say of Christ's return and the resurrection,

> *We* will not all sleep, but *we* will all be changed—in a moment, in the blinking of an eye, at the last trumpet. For the trumpet will sound, and the dead will be raised imperishable, and *we* will be changed. For *this* perishable body must put imperishability, and *this* mortal body must put on immortality. Now when *this* perishable body puts on imperishability and *this* mortal body puts on immortality, then the saying that is written will happen,
>
> "*Death has been swallowed up in victory.*" "*Where, O death, is your victory? Where, O death, is your sting?*"
>
> The sting of death is sin, and the power of sin is the law. But thanks be to God, who gives *us* the victory through our Lord Jesus Christ! So then, beloved brothers, be firm. Do not be moved! Always be diligent in the work of the Lord, knowing that your labor is not in vain in the Lord. (1 Corinthians 15:51–58; emphasis added)

Notice that this passage conveys the necessity in looking forward both to Christ's return and to the resurrection of this mortal body for purposes of sanctification, and it relates Paul as being one of those people who is alive at the time it occurs using representational language. If the "we" and "this mortal body" putting on immortality while alive were literal, then Paul was simply mistaken as he died before this event took place in everyone's eschatological scheme, preterist or otherwise.

Instead, these verses make up what is likely God's desire to communicate imminence to all Christians in the first century but, knowing that looking forward to Christ's return is a necessary motivation for Christians in general, He has the apostles use language that can apply to every generation of believers. After all, God did not simply wish to sanctify the first generation of believers by continually reminding them of the imminence of Christ's return but somehow did not see the necessity of giving that same motivation to the following generations of believers.

Ladd references Michaelis who argued in *Der Herr verzieht nicht die Verheissung* (1942) that Jesus did not so much emphasize "the futurity and imminence of the Kingdom, but that his emphasis upon imminence had the spiritual purpose of creating a response of watchfulness in the disciples."[22]

Although I think that Kümmel makes a false distinction between apocalyptic speech and eschatology, he notes the main point and use of such eschatological language in the apostles. Ladd sums up Kümmel:

> Eschatology is concerned with the destiny of men in view of the impending judgment. Apocalyptic reveals future events; eschatology prepares men for the future . . . for the significance of his [Jesus'] proclamation of the imminent end of the world does not lie in the apocalyptic description, but in the fact that men are now summoned to prepare for the end, for they are confronted "with the end of history as *it* advances toward the goal set by God." The real meaning of imminence is not in temporality, but in the certainty of the future and its impact on the present.[23]

This is not isolated to the New Testament. God speaks this way to Israel throughout the Old Testament. Again, it is meant to be a motivational tool so that all Israelites, from the time of Moses to the actual event almost a thousand years later, might be more on guard against idolatry and remain faithful to YHWH. For instance, in Deuteronomy 4:25–31, the following exhortation is made.

> After you have produced children and grandchildren and have been in the land a long time, if you become corrupt and make an image of any kind and do other evil things before the Lord your God that enrage him, I invoke heaven and earth as witnesses against you today that you will surely and swiftly be removed from the very land you are about to cross the Jordan to possess. You will not last long there because you will surely be annihilated. Then the Lord will scatter you among the peoples and there will be very few of you among the nations where the Lord will drive you. There you will worship gods made by

---

22. Ladd, *The Presence of the Future*, 5–6.
23. Ladd, *The Presence of the Future*, 30.

human hands—wood and stone that can neither see, hear, eat, nor smell. But if you seek the Lord your God from there, you will find Him, if, indeed, you seek Him with all your heart and soul. In your distress when all these things happen to you in the "last days," if you return to the Lord your God and obey Him (for He is a merciful God), He will not let you down or destroy you, for He cannot forget the covenant with your ancestors that He confirmed by oath to them.

Notice that the "you" here is the Israelites who are about to cross the river Jordan and enter the land. It is the Israelites of Moses' day to whom this exhortation is given, and it sounds like it is these very people that this punishment will come upon if they are unfaithful. However, we know that this is actually referring to the Israelites of either the Assyrian or Babylonian exiles (perhaps both) hundreds of years later. The "you," therefore, is representative, and it functions to warn not just the Israelites of Moses' day but all Israelites from that day forward. Indeed, it even has application for the believer today, who understands that land is a microcosm of the larger earth that will be inherited if one remains in the faith.

Isaiah 61 speaks of Israel's future ruling over the nations after they have been disciplined by God through deportation and exile. The generation to whom Isaiah speaks is not the generation that comes back to rule over the nations. In a further fulfillment of this passage, Christ tells the Jews of the first century A.D. that this text has been fulfilled in their presence with His coming. Yet, vv. 7-8 state that "you," the audience in Isaiah's day to whom he is speaking, will experience the future restoration in the land, and yet, the text is also clear that this is a different generation which is experiencing this, evidenced by the use of the third person plural "they" found throughout the passage.

> You will be called, 'the Lord's priests, servants of our God.' You will enjoy the wealth of nations and boast about the riches you receive from them ... Instead of shame, you will get a double portion; instead of humiliation, they will rejoice over the land they receive. Yes, they will possess a double portion in their land and experience lasting joy.

Micah is written to the Israelites in the 8th Century. Notice his language.

> In fact, I brought you up from the land of Egypt, I delivered you from that place of slavery. I sent Moses, Aaron, and Miriam to lead you. (6:4)

Did God bring up the Israelites from Egypt in the 8th Century? Clearly, it is referring to the Israelites of the exodus hundreds of years before. The language, again, is representational rather than literal.

In Acts 7:53, Stephen states that "You received the law by decrees given by angels, but you did not obey it." Was it the first century Jews who received the law in decrees that were given by angels? Again, this representational speech is common and is in no way an argument that because an author speaks to an audience with certain pronouns that would seem to indicate they are the generation upon whom all these things will take place that somehow this means such speech is literally true of that generation. Instead, the language is merely representational because the group being addressed is part of the larger group, past or present, that they represent. The Jews of the first century did not receive the law, the Israelites of the eighth century were not brought out of Egypt, the Israelites of the exodus did not go into exile among the other nations, and Paul is not given a transformed body while he is still alive so as to meet Christ and other resurrected saints in the air at His coming. These are representational types of speech. The "you," "us," "we," "they," refer to Christians as a group or unbelievers as a group or false teachers as a group, etc. It does not mean those literal people are going to experience such and such in their lifetimes.

So, one is given two options with these New Testament passages that speak to the believers in the first century as though they are the ones upon whom all these things will come. Either the apostles are wrong in their guesses that Christ will return in their lifetimes because they did not know when He would return, as the Bible indicates, or they are using language that includes believers (themselves and other Christians who would not see the return of Christ) as representative of all believers who are looking forward to the event.

I personally think that the real answer exists in combining these two. In other words, it is because the apostles did not know when Christ would return that they were free to use language that included every believer of their day, even if they did not believe everyone would live until His coming (hence, they include even themselves, e.g., Paul and Peter). And God, who is the One who inspires the text, gears it this way so that the text will cause all Christians everywhere throughout time to look forward to Christ's return as a central motivation for their sanctification.

But preterist proof texts they are not. The nature of the event negates that idea. The fact that the very apostles using this type of representational language did not live to see A.D. 70 negates the idea that the language is literally pointing to the first century audience, and neither the language nor the nature of inspiration and inerrancy, frankly, demands such an interpretation.

All of these remaining verses fall under this category:

> "For who is our hope or joy or crown to boast about before our Lord Jesus at his coming? Is it not of course you?"
> "...we who are alive, and remain until the coming of the Lord...
> ...We who are alive and remain shall be caught up together with them in the clouds......You, brethren, are not in darkness, that the day should overtake you like a thief." (1 Thes 4:15, 17; 5:4).

> "May your spirit and soul and body be preserved complete, without blame at the coming of our Lord Jesus Christ." (5:23).

> "I charge you . . .that you keep the commandment without stain or reproach until the appearing of our Lord Jesus Christ." (1 Tim 6:14)

> "But the day of the Lord will come like a thief, in which the heavens will pass away with a roar and the elements will be destroyed with intense heat, and the earth and its works will be burned up. Since all these things are to be destroyed in this way, what sort of people ought you to be in holy conduct and godliness, looking for and hastening the coming of the day of God." (2 Pet 3:10–12)

Hence, the attempt of some Preterists, like Daniel Harden,[24] to make texts like these "time indicator" texts simply misunderstands this type of language. If someone were a modern prophet and predicted, "The rhetoric we are seeing now will bring us to the point where we must fight another civil war," it does not mean that he cannot die until a civil war occurs because he includes himself in the statement. The "we" is collective of everyone who makes up the group. Preterists themselves apply this thinking in interpreting these very passages as no one argues that the "we" can only refer to Paul and the Corinthians to whom he is speaking. He does not even technically include all Christians in his own day; but the reader can understand that Paul uses "we" as a group, not "we" as a literal referent, otherwise one should only apply what Paul says to himself and to the Corinthians to whom he is writing at that time and not to other churches. These sorts of statements would also include the apostles Peter and Paul who would not be alive in A.D. 70 so the pronouns cannot be restricted in a literal fashion to only the speaker and his immediate audience.

24. Harden, *Overcoming*, 19–20.

The apostles use this language because they believe these things will occur in their lifetimes, but this is not a belief confirmed by revelation since Jesus made it clear that He would not be revealing the times or seasons or epochs of the final *parousia*. It is instead a belief utilized by revelation for the larger purpose of fueling sanctification among the people. This belief is more of a general feeling of imminence that God wants all His people to have as a primary motivation of living in godliness (Matt 24:45–54; 1 Thes 3:12–13; 5:23; 1 John 2:28–3:3; the entire Book of Revelation). Without it, humans tend to think they have all the time in the world and are, therefore, deceived by a feeling of "remoteness" when it comes to Christ's return. The Scripture counters this feeling by not allowing the apostles to know the time of His return so that they, and all generations of believers which follow, might be stirred to godliness since the time, in their taking upon the language of God's perspective of time, is short. Christians are called to have the eschatological perspective that keeps in mind that the suddenness of His coming can be at any time since it is unknown.

Conclusion

This work has looked at the true nature of biblical eschatology by allowing the ancient paradigm evidenced within the biblical texts themselves to speak in their contexts. It has further evaluated the preterist understanding of these passages in light of their contexts and found them wanting not only in terms of its obliviousness to this ancient worldview but in the eisegetical nature of its biblical interpretation. Instead, as argued throughout the book, biblical eschatology is an inaugurated one that continues in a process of creation toward a completion of that creation in a final, macrocosmic event. This hermeneutic is confirmed by the Lord and the apostles to be the correct one, and the individual passages, taken in their contexts, are consistent with, rather than contradictory to, it. In short, preterism fails to take all of the biblical evidence as it stands in its present form by imposing a foreign hermeneutic on biblical texts and then attempts to change the biblical data gained from passages that may oppose that paradigm by changing the contextual referents. As such, it should be seen not as biblical eschatology but rather as a theological system that is ultimately foreign to the biblical text.

Appendix

A Critique of Preterists' Three Strongest Evidences that the Book of Revelation Is Written before A.D. 70

In his book *Before Jerusalem Fell*, Kenneth Gentry argued for an early date of Revelation that would set it before the fall of Jerusalem in A.D. 70. This is largely due to a belief about the nature and subject of the book as a covenant lawsuit against Israel that God was about to judge. There are three main arguments found within the book and in his lectures that preterists seem to find the strongest for dating the Book of Revelation early. These three arguments mainly have to do with the mention of the temple standing in Jerusalem, the identification of the beast as Nero Caesar in the book, and the time statements concerning these things happening "soon." Other preterists also make arguments concerning the identification of the primary antagonists in the book as Jews coupled with the identification of Babylon in the book as Jerusalem in order to argue that the book is concerned with their judgment through the judgment of their city. I will begin a critique of these interpretations in reverse order, starting with his identification of the antagonists as literal Jews and the identification of Babylon in John's Apocalypse and ending with the argument concerning the identification of the beast and what persecution John is addressing (excepting only the time statement argument that I have already addressed earlier in this book).

Israel in the Book of Revelation

The key to understanding the book of Revelation is understanding who the false covenant members are. Are they literally old covenant, unbelieving Jews or are they new covenant community apostates and compromisers? Preterists tend to hold to the former and see literal references to the Jews conspiring with the Romans against the Christians in 2:9 and 3:19.

> I know your afflictions and your poverty—yet you are rich! I know about the slander of those who say they are Jews and are not, but are a synagogue of Satan.
>
> Behold, I will make them of the synagogue of Satan, which say they are Jews, and are not, but do lie; behold, I will make them to come and worship before thy feet, and to know that I have loved thee.

They also tend to interpret the 144,000 from every tribe as literal Jewish people. They also interpret those who pierced Christ as the Jewish enemies to which John is referring in 1:7.

Alternatively, these references should be understood as part of the book's symbolic representation of compromised and apostate Christians in the first century and not literal Jews at all.

The terminology referring to Jews in the letters cannot decide the referent alone. The letters say that they are not true Jews but a synagogue of Satan. They are not Jews in the sense that all faithful Christians are true Jews. Hence, these statements argue that they are not Jews who are actually working against the faithful church. The point, of course, is that Christians are the true Israel and, therefore, the true Jews.

The question must be answered by the context of the book itself. What is the author's purpose and against what or whom is he writing? What is his primary concern in the book? Hence, the terminology concerning Jews is ambiguous in and of itself as it can refer to false Jews who are ethnically Jewish but do not follow the Messiah, or it can refer to false Christians who are not true Jews because they do not follow the Messiah.

It becomes clear throughout the book that the author is primarily concerned with Christians compromising, not with Judaism, but with their former paganism, specifically partaking in the imperial cult in order to ward off persecution from the Roman government.

The concern is voiced numerous times throughout the book as a warning to those who "worship the beast and his image" as well as an encouragement of reward for those who "do not worship the beast and his image."

Those who end up in the lake of fire are those who "worshiped the beast and his image" and "received his mark."

The confrontation in Chapters 11 and 19 is not one between the beast and Jerusalem or Christ and Jerusalem but the beast and Christ.

The letters also spell this out. The concern is not the old covenant or legalism but antinomian teaching which would allow for compromise in the engagement of cult rituals that included sexual immorality and eating meat sacrificed to idols (2:14, 20).

In fact, if one takes the reference of "Jews" and "synagogue" to be literal, it would be completely out of place as the concern in every other letter, and the book as a whole, is that the church is compromising or fighting the temptation to compromise toward antinomianism.

The Church at Ephesus is praised for fighting against the doctrine of the Nicolaitans (2:6), which, based on v. 15, most scholars argue is an antinomian teaching.

The Church at Smyrna is about to be thrown into prison and perhaps even executed, something only the Roman government can do in Smyrna (v. 10). The crime would not be that they are not practicing Judaism but that they are not paying homage to the emperor by worshiping his image.

The Church at Pergamum has teachers in it that are teaching the people that they may engage in the imperial cult in the same way that Balaam set a stumbling block before the people (vv. 14–15).

The Church of Thyatira has a false prophetess the author calls "Jezebel" who is teaching that Christians can partake in the imperial cult by engaging in sexual immorality and eating foods sacrificed to idols (v. 20). This is the only concern of Jesus as no other burden is put upon them if they reject her teaching (v. 24).

The Church at Sardis is told to repent and to complete their works of obedience to Christ as a few of them have by "not soiling their garments" (3:4). The one who conquers will receive "white clothing" (v. 5), which refers to the imputed and infused righteousness of Christ in the book (7:14; 19:8). The soiled clothing represents their lack of good works and their doing of evil works instead. This means that the church is being told to repent because of their disobedience and compromise not because they are following the law and the old covenant.

The Church of Philadelphia is commended for being obedient to Christ's Word.

The Church of Laodicea is told to repent and that they are naked and in need of "white clothing" (vv. 17–18) meaning that they have drifted into severe antinomianism (they do not even have soiled clothes but are naked).

So, the issue with which the author is concerned does not have anything to do with Judaism and the old covenant. It has everything to do with whether the churches are compromising toward antinomian tendencies (specifically in reference to participating in the imperial cult) due to persecution and the permissiveness of false teachers or whether they are remaining faithful through their obedient works.

This means one of two things for how we interpret the terminology concerning Jews here. Either it is a literal reference to Jews who are turning Christians in so that they can be persecuted by the larger threat of the Roman government or, as is more consistent with the author's use of Israel and related terminology throughout the book, it refers to those who claim to be Christians but are not. Their churches are false churches, i.e., synagogues of Satan. The false Jews here are references to false teachers as the other symbolic designations (e.g., Jezebel, Balaam, etc.) are not literal references but symbolic ones.[1]

Either way, the key to understanding the purpose of the book and what it is doing with its imagery in later chapters is to understand the author's concern. He does not care about Judaism and the old covenant nor its influence in Asia Minor. He is concerned with the imperial cult which has its most potent influence in Asia Minor. He fears the Church's compromise in the area, and so he writes to address it. He is not concerned about the old covenant world coming to an end but the wicked world coming to a final end and how that brings hope to the saints to persevere in their faithfulness to Christ who will rule upon the earth, not temporally as these wicked kingdoms, but eternally as the Empire that will remove all other empires.

The promises in the letters form an *inclusio* with the end of the book so that the entire book must be interpreted along these lines.[2] Any other

---

1. Although the Nicolaitans are interpreted later by the Patristic writers as followers of a man named Nicolas, it should not escape the notice of the Greek reader that the term is *niko laos* "overcomers" or the "group of people who conquer/overcome." It seems too coincidental that Jesus is encouraging the Christians to be true overcomers/conquerors by remaining faithful throughout the letters and the book. It may be that this group, since they are grouped together with the antinomian teachers, overcome the threat of persecution by unfaithfully partaking in the imperial cult. In this way, the term may refer to a group characterized by this, rather than followers of Nicolas. In that sense, even this name is not a literal designation of these specific people.

2. "The one who conquers will inherit these things, and I will be his God and he will be my son. But as for the cowards, unbelievers, detestable persons, murderers, the sexually immoral, and those who practice magic spells, idol worshipers, and all those who lie, their place will be in the lake that burns with fire and sulfur. That is the second death" (21:7–8). Notice that the one who conquers does not participate in antinomian Christianity. There is nothing here about conquering in terms of holding onto the new covenant in contrast to the old. The author is simply not concerned with

framework given to it is nothing more than a solid example of the context replacement fallacy.

As for the 144,000, it is clear that this number refers to the entire faithful church on earth in the book and not just ethnic Jews who are virgins (7:4). Virginity is not literal but a contrast of sexual immorality which represents idolatry in the book. They remain faithful to Christ. They are the one who are called the servants of God and sealed from the judgments of God in 7:3. Are only these Jews protected by God in the book? Christ's name and God the Father's name are written on their foreheads (14:1) to convey ownership in contrast to those owned by the beast (13:16–18). Are only these Jewish virgins on earth sealed and owned by God and Christ? They alone can sing the new song of redemption (i.e., the gospel of the kingdom) since they are the redeemed upon the earth (v. 3)? The book says that these are "the ones who follow the Lamb wherever He goes" (v. 4). Is this not all faithful Christians in the book?

If these symbols are not convincing, then consider that the new Jerusalem, which comes out of heaven, is characterized by the same numbers (i.e., 12 in 21:12–14; 12,000 in v. 16; and 144 in v. 17) and helps to confirm the interpretation that the 144,000 is the faithful church on earth . This city is made up of all faithful believers who are placed upon the earth. It is clear, therefore, that the 144,000 are not literally Jews but Christians from every tribe, nation, and tongue who are upon the earth. This means that the author is using names and imagery that belong to Jews symbolically to describe Christians.

Furthermore, the religious enemy in the book, i.e., the land beast/false prophet, corresponds to the antinomian teachers in the church which the author describes in the letter and are his primary concern (as they are in his Gospel and Epistles as well). He sees their teaching as part of pagan, Roman religion rather than an extension of Christianity. This would not characterize Judaism even if the New Testament sees it as a false religion. It is not an extension of Graeco-Roman paganism, but antinomianism is.

If that is not convincing, then what should be is that the beast is described as having the horns of a lamb (13:11). The imagery of the lamb is only mentioned a few times in the New Testament outside of Revelation, and the term *arnion* for the word lamb is used only once outside of the book (John 21:15, which refers to Christians), but it is used 29 times in the book, and every reference is to Christ. Horns in Revelation, as in apocalyptic literature

---

the old covenant in the book. Instead, he is concerned about giving Christians the understanding that the Old and New Testaments are in continuity with one another, and so antinomianism is a false Christianity.

in general, refer to authority. This means that the beast comes in the name and authority of Christ, but the author tells us that it speaks like a dragon.

Judaism does not come in the name and authority of Christ. The beast is not ethnic Israel. Again, the author is not concerned with ethnic Israel. He is concerned with false teachers in the church. The beast, therefore, is the false church, and hence, it is described as the false prophet who leads the nations in the opposite direction (i.e., to the imperial cult) to where the faithful church leads them (i.e., to Christ). The false church is linked to Satan but the true church to Christ and God. The false church will end up in the lake of fire with the beast and Satan, but the true church will end up in paradise with Christ and God. This is the message of the book, and this is why the book should not be interpreted as some treatise deposing the old covenant and setting up the new.

What characterizes the wicked world and false religion is worship of the beast. The beast is given an entire chapter (13) and is then explained in Chapter 17. The author's continual concern is related to whether one worships the beast or his image or takes upon his mark (13:4, 12, 14–17; 14:9–10; 15:2; 16:2; 19:20; 20:4). Almost half of the book informs the reader of the author's purpose, something which the letters at the beginning also do; and that purpose is to communicate to Christians that they need to remain faithful by seeing God and Christ as worthy of worship and the beast and world as unworthy and under God's judgment. Christ is the Emperor/King of Kings whom God has put on the throne, but the Roman emperor is the temporary king whom Satan has put on the throne. The emperor may be the *autokratōr* "having sole power" of Rome, but God is the *pantokratōr* "having all power" over all creation, a polemical term repeated nine times throughout the book (1:8; 4:8; 11:7; 15:3; 16:7, 14; 19:6, 15; 21:22). Revelation is a polemic against imperial worship, therefore, and has little to nothing to do with the passing of the old covenant and old Jerusalem. In fact, it may simply be that the author desires to use the term "new Jerusalem," not because he is contrasting it with the old Jerusalem which the Romans had wiped away, but because he wishes to show that the true Jerusalem can never be wiped away by Rome; instead, its King will wipe Rome away from the earth. The contrast between two cities, therefore, is between Rome and the New Jerusalem, not the old Jerusalem and the new one.

Is Babylon Jerusalem?

Many Preterists identify Babylon in the Book of Revelation as Jerusalem. Samuel G. Dawson argues, as many Preterists do, that the statement made in

11:8 that the "great city" is "where their Lord was crucified" is a clear reference to Jerusalem as obviously Jesus was literally crucified in Jerusalem. He adds to this the idea that Babylon kills the prophets, and since Rome did not kill the prophets, but Jerusalem did, Jerusalem is the sure identity of the great harlot, Babylon.

> If we know where the Lord was crucified, we know the identity of the religious harlot Sodom. It is Old Covenant Jerusalem. Babylon is spoken of again in Rev. 18:24: 24 And in her was found the blood of the prophets and of the saints, and of all that have been slain upon the earth (*ge*, lit., land—SGD). Thus, Revelation has the great harlot, responsible for killing the prophets and saints, as the great city Babylon. Interpreters of Revelation speculate whether Babylon is literal Babylon in Iraq, or Rome. Neither of those cities slew God's prophets, but Old Covenant Jerusalem certainly did.[3]

Joseph Balyeat argues that "the very first time this phrase 'the great city' is used in Revelation, it clearly describes first century Jerusalem . . .*where also our Lord was crucified* (Revelation 11:8).[4] Chilton argued similarly that the book contrasts two cities, and since the one city is the new Jerusalem, it just makes sense that the other city is the old Jerusalem.

> We have seen that the Book of Revelation presents us with two great cities, set in antithesis to each other: Babylon and New Jerusalem. As we shall see in a later chapter, the New Jerusalem is Paradise Consummated, the community of the saints, the City

---

3. Dawson, *Essays on Eschatology*, 42.
4 Balyeat, *Babylon the Great City of Revelation*, 52.

Balyeat also commits an illegitimate referential transference in his methodology of looking for the term "great city" in other texts that deal with Jerusalem. He states that "the best way to examine that issue [i.e., whether Jerusalem is the great city] is to see if any other cities are called "the great city" in Revelation (or any place in the New Testament); and to see if Jerusalem is referred to as "the great city" anywhere else in the Bible." (Ibid.) The problem with this methodology is that Balyeat already assumes that whenever the phrase is used in Revelation, it must be referring to Jerusalem and so cannot by definition refer to some other city like Rome. It is also faulty to just look to see if Jerusalem is ever called "great city" since, as noted in this study, it just means "capitol city" and refers to whatever capitol city of a nation or an empire is in existence at the time. It is therefore irrelevant to note that at one time Jerusalem was called "the great city." This is much like saying that if an elephant is ever described as a mammal in one text, then any referent to a mammal in another refers to an elephant. By that logic, Nineveh is called the great city and should be identified as the city in Revelation. As will be argued in this study, it has a closer connection to the imagery of Revelation 18 than Jerusalem does. However, each text must be taken separately to entertain the possibility that the authors are referencing different things in each of them.

of God. The other city, which is continually contrasted to the New Jerusalem, is the old Jerusalem, which has become unfaithful to God.[5]

There are numerous problems with this identification of Babylon and the arguments used to establish it. First, it is clear that Revelation is a tale of two cities, but the two cities contrasted are the Renewed Jerusalem and Rome, the former symbolizing the kingdom of God and the latter the kingdom of the wicked world. John is arguing throughout his work that one must choose between them and cannot live in both worlds. One compromises the worship of the Lord Jesus Christ when participating in pagan festivals which are held as worship events dedicated to their gods and emperor.

Second, the description of Babylon does not fit Jerusalem. After surveying this evidence for imports and exports, Applebaum concludes that, although there are indications of limited trade, economic activity in Palestine was "predominantly internal." Likewise, Harland concludes that ancient Palestine would not have been a hub of trade within the Roman Empire.

> But why was international trade not even more predominant in such an economy? The answer appears to lie in the subsistence orientation of much agricultural production in Palestine as in other areas of the empire. According to a qualified primitivist model of economy, the majority of the population lived from the produce of the land with little surplus to sell. As well, the economic situation of the peasantry was not conducive to the regular purchase of imported goods, which would be purchased mainly by the wealthy. Much of the produce extracted by large landowners would be sold to the nonagricultural populations of the city on a local basis, if possible, rather than be exported. Once again, this characteristic seems reflective of other provinces in the Roman Empire, as Garnsey and Saller note, where "agricultural areas inevitably aimed at subsistence rather than the production of an exportable surplus . . . In general, the backwardness and expense of transport and the relatively low level of demand limited opportunities for profitable investment in commerce" (1987: 44). This statement should be qualified somewhat in connection with our earlier discussion of the primitivist model. Still, in light of this picture of the empire generally, the suggestion that Palestine is a special case in regard to limited trade due to religious factors or prohibitions, as Grant and Baron suggested, is unnecessary.[6]

5. Chilton, *The Days of Vengeance*, 422.
6. Harland "The Economy of First-Century Palestine," 520.

Josephus, for instance, states the following:

> As for ourselves ... we neither inhabit a maritime country, nor do we delight in merchandise, nor in such a mixture with other men as arises from it; but the cities we dwell in are remote from the sea, and having a fruitful country for our habitation, we take pains in cultivating that only.[7]

As many have noted, Roman taxation tended to leave most people in cities like Jerusalem with very little, and there was little to tax in the first place. This is part of why the Jews hated Roman occupation and rule and were concerned about whether they should pay taxes to Caesar.

Furthermore, as Josephus notes above, Jerusalem is landlocked. Why would merchants of the sea look upon Jerusalem's fall as devastating to their wealth? If Rome were intact as the primary hub of international trade, Rome would have continued to make all these merchant ships rich. And unlike Jerusalem, Rome actually sits by the sea and had ports off the Tiber which ships would use to unload their merchandise into the city. As the capital of the empire, an empire which heavily taxed its entire kingdom, the city was rich beyond measure. That sailors were bringing gold, silver, and fine linens into Rome, instead of Jerusalem, is a reality more consistent with the economic structures of the day.

Another factor to consider is that the language used of Babylon in this text is actually not used of Israel but of literal Babylon. Whereas it has been argued that the imagery of a harlot could only refer to Israel in covenant with God, this is factually incorrect for two reasons: (1) a harlot is not to be confused with an adulteress, which implies one who was in a covenant of marriage. A prostitute, instead, implies that one has no governing authority (i.e., no father or husband), has no covenant to keep, and acts accordingly. The reason why Israel is called a harlot in the Old Testament is because the term serves as a severely ironic rebuke of Israel's adulteries. She is not only an adulteress but acts like a whore who does not have a covenant to keep with a husband. The attempt by Preterists, like Chilton (*Days of Vengeance* 424 fn. 2), to argue that other nations called "harlots" actually were in covenant with God as His people is unconvincing and unnecessary to the concept which has to do with prostitutes who are usually unmarried and without covenant connections. Chilton has simply confused the term "adultery" with "prostitution." (2) Other nations (e.g., Tyre in Isa 23:15–17) are called harlots, but the imagery in these chapters is likely taken from Nahum 3:4 where Nineveh is called a "madam of harlots."

---

7. C. Ap. 1.60

מֵרֹב זְנוּנֵי זוֹנָה טוֹבַת חֵן בַּעֲלַת כְּשָׁפִים הַמֹּכֶרֶת גּוֹיִם בִּזְנוּנֶיהָ וּמִשְׁפָּחוֹת בִּכְשָׁפֶיהָ:

> Because of the many harlotries of the harlot, the charming one, the madam of sorceries, who sells nations in her harlotries and families in her sorceries.

Notice the similarities in this verse with what John says in the verses concerning "Babylon the Great."

> Upon her forehead a name was written, a mystery, "BABYLON THE GREAT, THE MOTHER OF HARLOTS AND OF THE ABOMINATIONS OF THE EARTH" ... And he cried out with a mighty voice, saying, "Fallen, fallen is Babylon the great! And she has become a dwelling place of demons and a prison of every unclean spirit, and a prison of every unclean and hateful bird. "For all the nations have drunk of the wine of the passion of her harlotry, and the kings of the earth have committed acts of harlotry with her, and the merchants of the earth have become rich by the wealth of her luxurious living ... and the light of a lamp will not shine in you any longer; and the voice of the bridegroom and bride will not be heard in you any longer; for your merchants were the great men of the earth, because all the nations were deceived by your sorcery. (17:5; 18:2–3, 23).

In both of these texts, the "great city," a common term that refers to the capital city of an empire (e.g., Caleh, the older capital city of Assyria, in Gen 10:12, Nineveh, the later capital, in Jonah 1:2; 3:2, and Jerusalem in Jer 22:8), is referred to as a madam of prostitutes who whores out the other nations as her service girls and who deceives the nations into pulling tricks for her by her sorcery. Her nakedness is exposed as a part of her judgment in both Revelation 17:16 and Nahum 3:5.

Notice that in the original context this refers not to Israel but to a pagan nation. This does not mean that this proves that John uses this terminology of a pagan nation here but only that one cannot argue that such language only refers to Israel since it does not even refer to Israel in the original context.

The same can be said for the other verses of the Old Testament applied to Babylon the Great here. In Revelation 18:6–8, John quotes Isaiah 47:7–9.

> Repay her the same way she repaid others; pay her back double corresponding to her deeds. In the cup she mixed, mix double the amount for her. As much as she exalted herself and lived in sensual luxury, to this extent give her torment and grief because she said to herself, 'I rule as queen and am no widow; I

will never experience grief!' For this reason, she will experience her plagues in a single day: disease, mourning, and famine, and she will be burned down with fire, because the Lord God who judges her is powerful!" You said, 'I will rule forever as permanent queen!' You did not think about these things; you did not consider how it would turn out. So now, listen to this, O one who lives so luxurious, who lives securely, who says to herself, 'I am unique! No one can compare to me! I will never have to live as a widow; I will never lose my children.' Both of these will come upon you suddenly, in one day! You will lose your children and be widowed. You will be overwhelmed by these tragedies, despite your many incantations and amulets.

Again, the text refers to a woman who exalts herself as queen, has been harsh with the people of God in her slaughter of them, boasts that she will not be widowed (i.e., abandoned by her protective deity which is viewed as her husband), is characterized by her sorceries, and will have her nakedness exposed as her part of her judgment. She is also said to be one who lives luxuriously. All this imagery in Isaiah is used by John to characterize his Babylon in the Apocalypse.

Yet again, the original text is not talking about Israel but Babylon itself. Again, this does not prove that such is the case here as each context must supply its own referents, but it does prove the point that one cannot assume that this language must apply only to Israel.

Preterists, like Chilton (*Days of Vengeance* 424–27), note that Israel played a harlot and so the connection between Babylon and Jerusalem can be established in this way. However, there is a problem with this oversimplification: the city here is a madam, not just a prostitute, and whereas Israel plays the harlot with other nations, this city causes other nations to engage in prostitution like a madam over a whorehouse. This implies some sort of political authority over other nations as well as the "mother of whores" herself being the central hub of idol worship. In other words, the city that the Apocalypse describes causes other nations to partake in its sexual immorality, which itself refers to idolatry in the book. This simply is not the same imagery as being an unfaithful wife, like Israel, who is described as a prostitute. The idea applied to Israel in the Old Testament is that it is playing a prostitute with the idols of other nations. It is seduced by them and their "immorality." Israel is not the one seducing others to worship its idols as its God is YHWH, and it does not have false gods/idols to share with the nations. This is not the case in Revelation 17–18. Instead, the kings of the earth commit acts of prostitution with Babylon versus Israel committing acts of prostitution with other nations. This trajectory serves as an important point in that, whereas Israel was enticed by the gods of other nations to commit sexual immorality, she was not the enticer as the foreign gods that the sexual immorality symbolizes belong to the other nations, not to Israel. In Revelation, however, the foreign gods belong to Rome, specifically the Imperial Cult described in the book as "worshiping the beast and his image," and the nations partake in that idolatry with Rome. This could not be referring to Jerusalem that is neither given over to idol worship in the first century nor is it enticing others to worship idols, especially enticing others to worship in the Imperial Cult. In fact, the very issue over which it gets into the Jewish wars is, precisely, due to its desire to avoid idol worship. That is the primary source of conflict between the Romans and the Jews in the first century, much of which was stirred up by threats of placing statues on the temple (as with Herod placing the eagle on the temple or Caligula threatening to place a statue of himself within it in A.D. 40), threats to destroy the temple (Caligula again), and the Roman mistreatment of temple grounds and stealing of temple funds under Nero. High tensions came to a boil as the impoverished, overly taxed Roman masses clashed with the pious Jews, who were stirred up by pagan blasphemies against God's temple, resulting in revolt.

In what way does this parallel the description in Revelation 17–18? Jerusalem is described as having been stripped of its wealth by Rome. Babylon here is described as being exceedingly wealthy. Jerusalem is described as being rigidly monotheistic and aniconic. Babylon is described as being idolatrous and causing all of the other nations to partake in its idolatry, i.e., image worship.

Further proof that the city is not Jerusalem but rather Rome is found in that both of the two prominent texts used by John in his description of the city refer not only to pagan cities but to pagan capitals of their respective empires. "Great city" refers to a capital of an empire, whether that of Assyria, in the case of Caleh/Kalhu (Gen 10:12) and Nineveh (Jonah 1:2; 3:2) as earlier and later capitals of the Assyrian Empire, or Jerusalem as the once great capital of the Israelite Kingdom (Jer 22:8). If this is true, then the "great city" in Revelation can only refer to Rome as it is the only capital of an empire at the time that John writes. The city itself seems to be presented as a synecdoche (as it often was in John's day and is in our day) for the entire Roman Empire and its power over the nations as a whole. This would explain why John presents Christ as being crucified in the "great city" in Chapter 11 if the referent for the term is the same in both chapters. The point of stating it this way is to place Christ as having suffered death in the same empire in which His people now suffer, displaying the continuity between His suffering and theirs.

There are ways around this, of course. One could argue that the phrase refers to Jerusalem as the once capital city as Jeremiah does in his book, even though it is no longer such. Another way of interpreting it differently is to see "great city" in terms of the size of the city instead of interpreting "great" to mean "capital." There are large cities that are not capitals that might still be called "great" and would be comparable to capital or royal cities (cf. Gibeon in Josh 10:2). One might also argue that although these are capitals, they might be capitals of nations instead of empires. It must be pointed out, however, that the two texts cited, those to which John alludes, describe the downfall of the two capital cities of the two great empires that attacked and killed God's people (Assyria with its deportations in the north and Babylon in its taking the south into exile). Rome was yet another mighty empire that was attacking and killing God's people, and her downfall is aptly described by these two other empires (i.e., Assyria and Babylon) that succeeded in their brutality only for a time but were then visited by the wrath of God with a cup mixed twice as strong (18:6).

However, since the term can be applied to numerous cities, whether as a capital or simply a reference to how large they are, this means that one cannot automatically assume that the "great city" in Chapter 11 is one and the same as the "great city" in Chapter 18 since the term would only then mean "large city." The large city in Chapter 11, if one does not see the synecdoche, could be Jerusalem (although the term obviously can still refer to Rome), but the one in Chapters 17 and 18 might very well be Rome. The same terminology does not mean that one has the same referent since one could argue that because the word "beast" is used for both the false prophet and the emperor that they are one in the same, even though the book clearly distinguishes them as two distinct beasts.

The identification of each city, then, must be obtained from other contextual indicators if one does not see the terminology of "great city" as referring to the capital of the empire. If one does, however, agree that this refers to a capital of the empire, then the city of Rome is the only possible interpretation. Furthermore, if one sees that the city can be used as a synecdoche for the larger empire, then Rome can be understood as the referent in Chapter 11 as well.

Either way, our discussion of the descriptions of the city as dealing heavily in maritime trade, as ruling over the kings of the nations, as being incredibly wealthy, and as the hub of idolatrous worship and sorcery should be sufficient to argue that such a description cannot refer to Jerusalem before its destruction in A.D. 70; but it rather fits the city of Rome perfectly.

Jerusalem did not make the ship merchants rich, but Rome did. Through its many conquests, Rome would have received treasures from all over the empire. This explains why the merchants were bringing in cargo of gold and silver and fine linens. Rome would have paid to have these transported, and it was more than capable of buying all the luxurious items from around the world from its heavy taxation of the nations over which it ruled.

Jerusalem did not rule over the kings of the earth (the attempt to say that these were kings of the land does not work since there was only one local king of Judea, i.e., Herod, and how exactly would the city be ruling over its own king?) The word is also plural, and so "kings of the earth (not land)" displays that this is talking about a city that stands at the heart of the empire and rules over the other kings of the nations.

Jerusalem was not the hub of the worship of idols and sorcery. That is actually the one lesson the Jews did learn from their many chastisements before the first century. In fact, the Jewish wars were brought on specifically because hostilities grew to a fever pitch due to the possibility of Rome introducing idolatry into the temple as well as looting its treasures to use for pagan purposes. The Jews certainly can be seen as unfaithful to God but idol worshipers who then seduce the nations to worship their idols is hardly something that can be said of them. Rome, however, not only worshiped idols but made the nations participate in their worship for the perceived good of the empire. In fact, this is John's main concern in the book: that Christians will not compromise in the face of death by worshipping idols, the beast, and his image (i.e., participation in the Roman festivals and emperor cult). This is why he rebukes the false teachers in the church who argue that Christians can "worship idols" and repeatedly contrasts those faithful to Christ with the wicked world in terms of whether or not they worship the beast and his image.

What further argues for an identification of the city/whore with Rome is the fact that she sits on seven hills and many waters. Rome was called the "seven-hilled city." Although some argue that Jerusalem was also thought to be built on seven hills, the earliest evidence we have for anyone thinking of the city that way comes from the ninth century A.D. There is no indication, therefore, that John's readers would have thought of Jerusalem in that way. The imagery of the many waters, however, would have immediately brought to mind the seven-hilled city of Rome which sat near the Mediterranean Sea and alongside the Tiber River. Italy itself, of course, is surrounded by water, and this all makes for good imagery of Rome sitting on a lot of water as it sits over many people groups.[8]

---

8. It should be noted that the term "many waters" refers to large amounts of water, not necessarily many individual bodies of water. The fact that this is interpreted by the angel to mean that the city is enthroned over many people groups is yet another indication that this is not referring to Jerusalem, but Rome.

There can be no doubt that Babylon the Great is the city of Rome which functions as a synecdoche for the larger empire and its power. Even the imagery of the city being burned by the beast is taken from the fact that Nero literally burned down a large portion of the city. John uses this to show that the emperor, contrary to common claims that he is the savior of the world, is actually, due to his demonic activity and allegiance with Satan, its destroyer and that worshiping such a one will lead to one's own destruction, not salvation. Hence, as the beast is thrown into the lake of fire, so also the false prophet joins him there. The world will also follow him there, but Christ's elect will remain faithful to Him. He is the true King of Kings and Lord of Lords, i.e., the true Emperor, and His Empire will not come to an end. This is the book's contrast and promise, and it has nothing to do with the destruction of Jerusalem in A.D. 70 as John's concern is not that Christians would fall back into Judaism. Therefore, he is not arguing the difference between the old and new covenants (that is what the Book of Hebrews is about, not the Book of Revelation), but rather his concern is that Christians do not compromise by worshiping the beast and his image, taking upon his mark, which stands as a prime example of participating in the evil activity of the world for the sake of pleasure or saving, only temporarily, their own lives. Hence, he repeats this concern continually throughout the last half of the book (13:).

If this is all true, where do Preterists get the idea that "Babylon the Great" is Jerusalem?

As said before, it seems to stem from two things: (1) the common interpretation of 11:8 as referring to Jerusalem and (2) the alleged parallels between Matthew 24 and Revelation 18.

However, the problem is that Preterists want to read 11:8 very literally in a text that is highly symbolic. Chapter 11 starts out with a temple that refers to the Christian church and not the literal temple. It refers to John's protection of it by measuring it, since measuring conveys the idea in the Bible of guarding/watching over something, but he did not literally measure it. It continues to talk about two witnesses who are personified representations of the whole Word of God (Old and New Testaments, i.e., Moses representing the Law, Elijah representing the Prophets and their fulfillment in dying for three days, being resurrected, and ascending into heaven as the representation of the gospel). None of this is literal. The beast is also said to overcome them in this city, but the beast is clearly in Rome. If one were to take it absolutely literally, Christ was not crucified in Jerusalem but outside the city walls. He was crucified within its domain, and the domain of a city can be described as the city itself. Hence, since John seeks to comfort those who are being killed by Rome, he is more likely saying that Christ was killed within the domain of Rome and not referencing Jerusalem at all.

Furthermore, Dawson's argument that Rome did not kill God's prophets is based on the assumption that Revelation is talking about Old Testament prophets; but it is made clear that this is talking about those killed due to the persecution that took place in the first century for not worshiping the beast and his image. The apostles are prophets, not to mention that even elders and other church leaders are considered in the office of prophet in the first century (e.g., the way the Didache talks about church leadership). On top of this, there are numerous Christians who are identified as prophets in the New Testament. Finally, John actually says that the testimony of Jesus is the spirit of prophecy, which would mean that everyone who testifies of Christ is also prophesying. The book itself is identified as "prophecy," which means that John is identifying himself as a prophet. We also know that these prophets existed during the time of the New Testament because Revelation 18:20 declares about Babylon, "Rejoice over her fate, O heaven and also the saints and apostles and prophets! For at last God has judged her with the judgment she gave to you." Notice that she is being judged for killing apostles. Yet, we only know of one apostle killed in Jerusalem, James, and that was by Herod. Most of the other apostles are said to have been killed by Rome or the governing Gentile authorities representing it. The book does not leave its readers in doubt as to why they are being killed. In 20:4, it makes it clear.

> Then I saw thrones and seated on them were those who had been given authority to judge. I also saw the souls of those who had been beheaded because of the testimony about Jesus and because of the word of God. These had not worshiped the beast or his image and had refused to receive his mark on their forehead or hand. They came to life and reigned with Christ for a thousand years.

It was for not partaking in the imperial cult that these saints, apostles, and prophets were killed. This pressure to compromise or die is a mounting concern in the book. Hence, John writes in Chapter 13 and following that Christians are being killed for this reason (13:15), and that is the reason why Babylon is being judged by God. The receiving of the mark of the beast by worshiping him and his image is interpreted in 14:8 as Babylon causing the nations to drink of the wine of her sexual immorality/prostitution. Hence, Rome did kill many prophets, saints, and apostles for the testimony of Jesus which would not allow them to partake in the imperial cult. This is all about Rome and nothing about Jerusalem.

Some argue based on parallels that Revelation must be talking about Jerusalem and its condemnation in the changing from the old covenant to the new. Chilton argued that "while all readily admit that the *Little Apocalypse* is a prophecy against Israel, few seem to make the obvious connection: The *Big Apocalypse* is a prophecy against Israel as well."[9] In his book, *Who Is This Babylon?*, Don Preston lays out his argument for why he thinks Matthew 24 parallels the Book of Revelation as a whole and, therefore, concludes that Babylon is the old Jerusalem. He lists the following.

Both speak of the judgment of a sinful city following the completion of the world mission.

Both speak of the Great Tribulation

Both speak of the Abomination of Desolation

Both urge the faithful to flee from the city

Both speak of false prophets and workers of false miracles

Both speak of the coming of the Son of Man on the clouds

Both speak of the sounding of the Trumpet at the time of the end

Both speak of the salvation of the elect

Both speak of the gathering of the birds to feast on the carcass of the dead

Both predictions were to be fulfilled soon.[10]

Preston, then, sums up his conclusions by stating:

> These, and other similarities, show that the Olivet Discourse and Revelation are parallel . . . If Revelation is parallel to Matthew 24, and Matthew 24 speaks of the impending judgment on Jerusalem, then Revelation must speak of the fall of Jerusalem.[11]

Now, there are several exegetical and logical fallacies here, the foremost being one of ignoring the differing referents in each context. What Preston has essentially done is reduce the two texts to common motifs without noting their respective contextual referents. This leads him to conclude a further non sequitur that if a text has many similar motifs with another text, both texts must be referring to the same thing.

The problem is that one can essentially do this with almost any two texts that have similarities between them, especially if they are of the same genre and are written by authors who come from a similar context using similar imagery.

In fact, many of these things are said of Israel at the time of the exile. By Preston's logic, one could argue likewise, "If the prophetic texts concerning

---

9 Chilton, *Days of Vengeance*, 182–83.
10 Preston, *Who Is This Babylon?*, 2–3.
11 Preston, *Who Is This Babyon?*, 3.

Israel's judgment to exile are parallel to elements in Matthew 24, and those texts speak of Israel going off into captivity by the Babylonians in 586 B.C., then Matthew 24 is about Israel going off into captivity by the Babylonians in 586 B.C. Of course, this is an absurd conclusion because it ignores the contextual referents in each individual text. Matthew 24 is not about the exile in 586 precisely because the context refers to Jerusalem in the first century. Yet, one only knows this by paying careful attention to the context, noting to what the text is referring. Preston simply ignores this vital step in exegesis, and he is thus led to a conclusion that does not follow the premise.

As I have argued, Revelation is not about the destruction of Jerusalem in any way, shape, or form; and Babylon is certainly not Jerusalem in the first century either. What Preston essentially wishes to do is replace the context, along with its referents, with Matthew 24. If Matthew 24, along with its referents to the destruction of Jerusalem, becomes the context for Revelation, then Revelation must be referring to the destruction of Jerusalem. This is precisely the opposite of a reliable exegetical method. If Matthew 24 becomes the context for any text with parallel themes, then all other contexts are erased/ignored, and these texts are merely flattened out to refer to the same event despite their individual contexts which may display different referents.

If the above were not enough, what Preston attempts to do in showing parallels is to state the parallels generically enough so as to make them sound identical. It should be obvious that many will be identical as a part of stock eschatological and apocalyptic language of the macrocosmic event. However, there are a few "parallels" where I think Preston overstates the similarities.

For instance, when saying that both texts speak of a judgment of a sinful city after a world mission, there are further questions to be asked: To what city does each text refer? To what mission does each text refer? In light of the apocalyptic use of macrocosmic language interwoven with microcosmic language, are they present in both texts because this is part of the macro-event that would then show up in New Testament apocalyptic texts?

When speaking of "the great tribulation," again, it is important to note to what this refers in each text. The terminology "great tribulation" speaks of a horrible time of trouble. Surely, Preston is not suggesting that there is only one. Daniel speaks of Antiochus' slaughter of the Jews in the early second century B.C. as a "great tribulation" (12:1). The woman, Jezebel, in 2:22 is said to be thrown into "great tribulation" in terms of plaguing her with a sickness so that she will repent. The word "tribulation" just means "trouble," "distress," and refers to a time of difficulty. The adjective "great" simply refers to the greatness of the difficulty. The phrase in our modern era, unfortunately, has taken upon itself connotations of some unique time period in history, but it merely refers to a horrific time of trouble which can be described as more horrific for a particular people than ever has been or will be again;[12] but it certainly does not limit a time of great trouble to that particular group or era.

In fact, the people who are undergoing the time of great tribulation in Matthew 24 are the Jews under judgment, not Christians. Yet, in Revelation, the people undergoing this great tribulation are Christians (7:14). This is why paying attention to the referents in each context is so important to exegesis. Without doing so, one is led to make dubious connections that the author himself and, therefore God Himself, never intended to make.

The methodology of minimizing differences in Preston's "parallels" continues as he associates the "abomination of desolation" spoken of in Matthew 24 with the image of the beast in Revelation 13. However, the abomination of desolation in Matthew 24 has to do with the defilement and destruction of the temple whereas the image in Revelation is made to cause all nations to bow down to it, including Christians. Nowhere in the text does it refer to this image as the "abomination of desolation" nor is there any reference to the defiling of the temple with it. In fact, even in Matthew 24, this is simply a figurative application to the defiling of the temple and not a literal image as Titus never sets up an image in the temple nor does he make all nations, including Christians, bow down to it under pain of death. Luke even associates it with the armies surrounding Jerusalem. In Revelation, the image of the beast is a threat to Christians. In Matthew, it threatens Judaism and the temple. Again, the contextual referents are not the same. In fact, it is rather odd that a book that alludes to Danielic language so much does not make reference to it in Chapter 13 by calling the image the "abomination of desolation" or referring to it as an image that makes desolate, etc.

Preston, then, simply makes note of the macrocosmic language, language often used in apocalyptic speech in general, regardless of the situation and thinks that this means that his parallels refer to the same event or at least the same people. Hence, the coming of the Son of Man in the clouds, the gathering of God's people, the sound of a trumpet, etc., are all themes found in apocalyptic speech with different microcosmic events as their referents (e.g., Daniel and the persecution under Antiochus IV, 1 Enoch's connection to the flood story and the author's own time in the second century B.C., the destruction of Jerusalem in the Olivet Discourse, and the Roman persecution of Christians under Domitian in Revelation). These themes do

---

12. For instance, Jeremiah 30:7 says of the Babylonian siege and exile, "How awful that day will be! No other will be like it. It will be a time of trouble for Jacob, but he will be saved out of it."

not carry their contextual referents with them. What they refer to in any given context must be supplied by the contexts themselves.

Preston slips in a smaller argument under point nine when he speaks of birds devouring carcasses as a judgment of Israel in the Bible. Actually, the devouring of carcasses by birds is a common theme in war contexts. Hence, when God goes to war with His own people, He uses this descriptor a couple times (Deut 28:25–26; throughout Jeremiah, etc.). It is, however, also used in His judgment against Gog in Ezekiel 39:4 and against the Philistines in 1 Samuel 17:46, displaying that this is not exclusively language about Israel (nor would it be an argument if all other uses had been of Israel since it is the immediate context of each individual text that provides the referent).

Furthermore, Preston must increase the compared text not just to Chapter 18 but to the entire Book of Revelation due to the fact that the description of Babylon in Revelation does not contain most of the parallels mentioned (i.e., points 1, 2, 3, 5, 6, 7, 8, 9, and 10 do not appear in the description of the city's fall in Chapter 18). Point four (the idea that people are told to flee—though which people and what each text means by telling others to get out of the city is ignored) remains somewhat similar although one says "when you see the abomination of desolation, flee to the mountains," and the other says, "come out of her, My People, that you might not partake of her sins," which are not exactly parallel in wording, intent, or even meaning. The description of the city's fall in Revelation 18 actually does not parallel the description of the Jerusalem's fall in Matthew 24.

Finally, Preston states that both prophecies were to take place "soon." Even though I have agreed that Revelation likely says that the events will happen "suddenly" and without warning, the tribulation under Domitian does take place in the first century. This means that even if one were inclined to take both declarations as teaching that the events are imminent, this still does not mean that the historical events to which the texts refer are the same as both events occur in the first century about twenty years apart from one another.

In short, the preterist argument that Matthew 24 is the "Little Apocalypse" in parallel to Revelation is riddled with exegetical and logical fallacies. The events to which its common apocalyptic language refers in each text are completely different, and we know this due to the differing referential indicators in each context.

Instead, the true comparison should be between the text of Revelation 17–18 and the two cities of Rome and Jerusalem. We must ask the question, does this text describe Rome or Jerusalem in the first century A.D.? As argued before, when we compare them to the text, Rome is clearly being described, and Jerusalem is not.

What one can see instead is the preterist tendency to tie conceptual associations between words, phrases, etc., that different texts may have in common and relate their referents to one another, even if those texts do not share the same referents. In doing this, one can make any two different events of which Scripture speaks into a singular event simply because the contextual referents that would distinguish them are ignored or altered. As stated before, if one changes what the words refer to by trading contexts, one can make a text refer to anything, thus altering the meaning of a text and writing a completely different Bible than the one revealed by God. This type of exegetical fallacy, then, is not just a mere difference in interpretation but a rejection of God's revelation in favor of a different one. This type of fallacious interpretive methodology is common among topical Bible studies and systematic theologies. It is, perhaps, the greatest irony of all that while having the words of the Bible before him, he ends up reading and believing a completely different one.

Another common misunderstanding of apocalyptic literature is when a reader takes the "literary present" in the book as the actual time of writing. In Revelation 17:10, the author tells us that five kings have fallen, one is, and a seventh is to come. Readers who are unfamiliar with the genre's use of the literary device where the author goes back to the past to project into the future and, therefore, depicts the past as his present, have concluded that the book can be dated to the sixth king since that king currently, at the time of writing, is living. However, even a basic knowledge of the genre helps illumine the fact that such use of time is a literary device and that the real present of the author is the projected time of the future about which he is "prophesying." This is a common element of apocalyptic literature where "apocalyptic writers frequently present the history of the past right up to their own present time in the form of prophecies."[13]

The apocalyptic works of Enoch are not written by the actual Enoch in the antediluvian period but by a Jewish author in the second century B.C. Likewise, the apocalyptic works of Adam, Abraham, Shem, Moses, Elijah, Zephaniah, Ezekiel, and Ezra (all works considered pseudepigrapha for good reason) are not written by any of these ancient authors but instead go back in time to prophesy of the author's present time or what he thinks will occur in the immediate future. Although many misidentify Daniel as a prophetic book written by a prophet in the exile, it is clear that the author lives during the time of Antiochus IV's persecution of the Jews in the early second century B.C. Apocalyptic is a subgenre of prophetic literature, but reading it is a bit different than reading a regular prophetic book.

---

13 Schneemelcher (ed.) *New Testament Apocrypha*, 547.

Transporting oneself back in time, and sometimes, person is a common device used in apocalyptic literature. It is not seen as a deception any more than a monologue presented by Abraham Lincoln in a play written by a modern author would be considered deception. It is a way to present an argument, and since God uses every genre in the ancient world to communicate truth to His people, apocalyptic literature is no exception.

It must, however, be made clear that there is a distinction between apocalyptic literature and apocalyptic speech. Apocalyptic literature tends to use this device in its presentation whereas apocalyptic speech can be interwoven into any genre of literature (e.g., thematic narrative like the synoptic Gospels or epistolary like 1 Thessalonians or 2 Peter).

Hence, it is in apocalyptic literary works that one finds this device used, although it is not exclusive to this genre either (i.e., there are many literary works within the pseudepigrapha/apocrypha/Bible that are not classified as apocalyptic but still use a major religious figure of the past to comment upon contemporary life—Ecclesiastes, the Wisdom of Solomon, the Testament of Moses, etc.).

Hence, if one were to conclude that the presentation of John writing during the sixth king's reign is literal because the book presents him as doing such, it would simply be due to his misunderstanding of the genre of literature that he is reading. The author, whether it be John or someone within the Johannine school as some authors surmise, lives during the time of the eighth king, i.e., the second beast, with whom the author is truly concerned. Since the author is writing during the persecution of this eighth king, therefore, one must realize that the book can only be understood as written during the time of Domitian since he is the only king that fits the description of the second beast who makes war with Christ through His apostles and prophets because of their testimony about Jesus (Rev 1:9; 12:17; 17:6; 19:10; 20:4).

Those "who had the mark of the beast and who worshiped his image" (Rev 16:20), i.e., the Romans, are the ones who are viewed as putting Christians to death (16:6). Again, the Jews rejected the idolatry of the imperial cult. Instead, this Christian rejection of the imperial cult was among the reasons Domitian viewed Christians as adopting "Jewish sentiments," and they were persecuted by the emperor who hated the Jews for their unyielding monotheism.[14] Hence, describing Jews as those who worship the image of the Roman emperor simply makes no sense.

---

14. Dio mentions that, in the year 95, Domitian brought about a prosecution of all who adopted "Jewish customs." The fact that the Christians were seen as a distinct sect coming out of Judaism by the time of Nero does not lessen the idea that they would have still been considered a sect within Judaism, or at least a religion heavily influenced by Judaism, even at the end of the first century.

Does Revelation 11:2 Literally Refer to the Second Temple in Jerusalem?

Gentry argues that the city and temple mentioned in Revelation 11:1–2 should be taken to refer to the literal city and temple of Jerusalem. He argues this because later in the chapter John uses symbolic descriptions for the capital city that Gentry thinks is also Jerusalem.

> Furthermore, what should be a blatantly obvious contextual clue specifically designates the city as the place "where also their Lord was crucified" (Rev. 11:8): "And their dead bodies will lie in the street of the great city which mystically is called Sodom and Egypt, where also their Lord was crucified." This modifying clause ("where also their Lord was crucified") seems to be given to insure the proper identifying of the city that is referred to mystically as "Sodom and Egypt" (v. 8). The greatest crime of all history was perpetrated at Jerusalem, for "the Lord of glory" who "came unto His own" was crucified there (Matt. 16:21; Mark 8:31; 10:32–34; Luke 9:22; 13:32; 17: 11; 19:28). Through spiritual metamorphosis the once "holy city" has been transformed into an unholy "Egypt" and "Sodom." The *symbolic* references are: "Egypt" and "Sodom." The *literal,* geographical referent here is not another symbol, but the historical city Jerusalem.[15]

It should be said that the argument that is often made, i.e., that the temple in Jerusalem must be standing at the time the Book of Revelation is written since it must exist in order for John to measure it, is a non-argument. The measuring of the temple motif comes from Ezekiel 40–42 where an angel measures the city temple, the outer walls, the inner courts, etc. Yet, this was done during the 25th year of the exile when there was no literal temple standing. The city and temple had been destroyed. Instead, the city in Revelation 11 is the eschatological city and temple that Ezekiel envisions. So, this is something occurring within a vision in Ezekiel, not something that is literally happening to a temple complex that actually exists at the time. The same is obvious in the Apocalypse as this is clearly something that is done in a vision, and John would not literally be measuring the city and the temple.

Instead, since the scene is heavily symbolic, it is likely that the city and temple are also used symbolically here. If this is the case, one might ask what they represent within the book. A survey of how the temple/tabernacle symbolism is used within the book, therefore, might be illuminating.

15. Gentry, *Before Jerusalem Fell* 170.

The temple in Revelation 15:5–16:1 refers to the dwelling of God in heaven. This is referred to as both God's temple and His tabernacle of testimony. It does not refer to the literal temple that is standing in Jerusalem. However, when John refers to the tabernacle as God's dwelling in heaven again in 13:6, he clarifies that this is not referring to some physical place but rather "those who dwell in heaven." In other words, the community of God, specifically those who have been faithful to Christ and are now in heaven because of their faithfulness, are the tabernacle of God. It may be that the temple is both the presence of God in heaven and the presence of God with His people wherever they may be, or the book may be consistent throughout to define the temple/tabernacle only as God's people. Either way, it is not the literal building in Jerusalem.

The understanding that the temple/tabernacle refers to the community of God is vital to understand what John is saying in Chapter 11. The imagery of measuring the city and the temple is taken from Zechariah and Ezekiel.

> "Therefore this is what the Lord says: 'I will return to Jerusalem with mercy, and there my house will be rebuilt. And the measuring line will be stretched out over Jerusalem,' declares the Lord Almighty . . . Then I looked up, and there before me was a man with a measuring line in his hand. 2 I asked, "Where are you going?" He answered me, "To measure Jerusalem, to find out how wide and how long it is." While the angel who was speaking to me was leaving, another angel came to meet him 4 and said to him: "Run, tell that young man, 'Jerusalem will be a city without walls because of the great number of people and animals in it. 5 And I myself will be a wall of fire around it,' declares the Lord, 'and I will be its glory within.' (Zech 1:16, 2:1–5)

In these texts, Zechariah envisions Ezekiel's city to be without walls due to the great number of people that make it up. What this means is that the city is not defined by the structure of a wall but rather by the inhabitants. Since it has no walls, it is without man-made boundaries. Instead, the presence of the Lord Himself will act like a wall around it, and He will fill it with His glory. In this regard, the city functions as a temple, and it is defined by the inhabitants, not the structures that surround or make it up. Notice also that the measuring line refers to the protection of God's people who are owned by God as His very possession. This scene mimics the vision of Ezekiel where the angel measures the eschatological temple.[16] As Richard Bauckham observes:

---

16. Both books stand within the same tradition, and Zechariah is often seen as dependent upon Ezekiel. Bauckham, "The Rise of Apocalyptic," 42.

> ... there is a common conviction that the eschatological promises of restoration in Second Isaiah and Ezekiel remained largely outstanding despite the restored city and temple. In all of these prophecies there is therefore a degree of dependence on and reinterpretation of the earlier prophecies, and all are more or less apocalyptic (according to Wanson's definition) in the extent to which they depict the coming salvation in terms of Yahweh's direct intervention and radical transformation of historical conditions. The distinctive aspect of Haggai and Zechariah (1–8) is that they focused these apocalyptic hopes on the rebuilding of the temple and the leadership of Joshua and Zerubbabel. But these historical realities soon proved incapable of measuring up to the hopes aroused, and so those who subsequently kept alive the eschatological expectation were not opponents of Haggai and Zechariah but successors who sought to remain faithful to their prophecy.[17]

This conviction led the biblical authors to understand that the fulfillment of this temple and city were not just literal but also metaphorical of God's new creation and people. In other words, the temple and the city represented the covenant community which dwelled around and within it. John takes this imagery and applies it to the community of God, whether visible or invisible. Hence, in the Apocalypse, where John wishes to contrast the faithful church with the world and the false church, he depicts the people of God as the tabernacle, temple, city of Ezekiel's and Zechariah's visions. For instance, the eschatological community (that has been purified from the unfaithful who are removed from their presence) is depicted as the New Jerusalem in Chapter 21. The city represents the new Israel, and hence, the names of the twelve tribes are written on the twelve gates (v. 12). The numbers mimic the 144,000 (12,000 from each tribe x 12 = 144,000) that represented the faithful church on earth in 7:3–8 and 14:1, 3–5, and are now used to depict the measurements of the city (12,000 stadia with 12 names on each stone, 144 cubits), i.e., the people of God who become and enter God's dwelling in the eschatological age of the new cosmos. In fact, the city is 144,000 stadia horizontally or vertically (v. 16). Its borders are made up of the names of the twelve apostles, presumably referencing the fact that faithfulness to the teaching of the apostles makes up the boundary marker for those who are granted access to the city (v. 14; 22:14). All the faithful will dwell inside of the city that comes out of heaven and rests forever on the new earth. The city/temple is cleansed as the unfaithful are cast outside (22:15).

17. Bauckham, "The Rise of Apocalyptic," 42.

What this means is that the New Jerusalem is the community of God. Zechariah's and Ezekiel's visions of the city temple refer to the people of God. God will "tabernacle" with them and among them (21:2–4) and remove all chaos from their midst.

The temple is used in the book, therefore, to refer to God's eternal dwelling place, the place from which He rules. Revelation 21–22 make it clear that this throne and His presence will be upon the earth forever as will be his people who have been faithful through the fire that was the great tribulation. In 7:13–17, these people are said to be in God's presence and serve Him in His temple forever. Since God dwells forever in and among them, the people and where they reside are the tabernacle/temple.

> Then one of the elders asked me, "These dressed in long white robes—who are they and where have they come from?" So I said to him, "My lord, you know the answer." Then he said to me, "These are the ones who have come out of the great tribulation. They have washed their robes and made them white in the blood of the Lamb! For this reason they are before the throne of God, and they serve him day and night in his temple, and the one seated on the throne will shelter them. *They will never go hungry or be thirsty again, and the sun will not beat down on them, nor any burning heat*, because the Lamb in the middle of the throne will shepherd them and lead them to springs of living water, *and God will wipe away every tear from their eyes*." (emphasis added)

Notice the parallel between what is said here of these people and what is said of the people in Chapters 21 and 22. They are faithful. They have washed their robes in the blood of the lamb. They will never hunger or thirst again. The sun will not beat down on them. They will partake of springs of living water, and God will wipe away every tear from their eyes. The throne to which this refers is God's throne which is represented by the Lamb's throne and His presence is through the presence of the Lamb. The temple here, therefore, refers to the eternal dwelling of God through the Lamb upon the earth in the New Jerusalem. Since the city is both the place in which the people reside and the people themselves, the temple refers to the faithful people of God and their dominion over the earth and its natural elements as the dwelling place of God through the Lamb.

Again, in 3:12, the believers in Philadelphia are told that they will be made a part of the temple structure and the city if they are faithful.

> The one who conquers I will make a pillar in the temple of my God, and he will never depart from it. I will write on him the name of my God and the name of the city of my God (the new

Jerusalem that comes down out of heaven from my God), and my new name as well.

Likewise, the seven churches in the beginning of the book are represented by golden lampstands, which are furnishings in the temple (1:12–13, 20; 2:1). The Son of Man is dressed as the high priest in His temple (v. 13). The unfaithful church is warned that they may have their lampstand removed if they do not repent (2:5) which displays the contrast, once again, between the faithful and unfaithful churches.

These all make up the sum of how the temple/tabernacle/city of Jerusalem are used in the book. Notice that not once does the city or temple ever refer to the literal city of Jerusalem or literal temple in Jerusalem.

This is helpful to understand since it gives insight into why John would be measuring only the inner sanctuary and not the outer walls or city. Since the city and temple represent the community of God, it can also represent the visible covenant community and in doing so can represent both the faithful and unfaithful churches as they exist in this world. One of John's primary points is to show that there are three groups in the world: the world itself, the true church, and the false church. This was his point in contrasting the woman, the beast from the sea, and the beast from the land that had horns like a lamb but spoke the words of the dragon. As such, the city and temple are used to represent the visible church made up of both true and false Christians, but John divides the outer walls and city from the inner sanctuary, the place of God's throne and presence where the faithful stay close to God. He measures only this area and not the rest which communicates that John and his teaching in the book are only meant to protect the true believers from the corruption of the world. He is only responsible for the faithful, not for the false Christians who compromise with the world and are thus trampled by it. The rest of the complex is given over to the pagans.

Scholars are somewhat in agreement that John is using imagery from the destruction of Jerusalem to make his point but has radically transformed it. If taken literally, John's transformed imagery does not depict the destruction of Jerusalem at all since the inner sanctuary is preserved by John's protection, something that is not true of the literal temple in Jerusalem. Hence, John is not describing the literal temple in Jerusalem at all. He is using that imagery to refer to the visible church and the inner sanctuary to divide the true church from the false. This text, therefore, cannot be used to argue that the literal temple in Jerusalem is still standing at the time of John's penning of the book.

Even Gentry admits that the inner temple that is preserved, i.e., what John measures, is not the literal temple but the faithful church.

> In the second place, the measuring of the Temple is for the preservation of its innermost aspects, i.e., the ναός, altar, and worshipers within (Rev. 11: 1). This seems to refer to the inner-spiritual idea of the Temple in the New Covenant era that supersedes the material Temple of the Old Covenant era. Thus, while judgment is about to be brought upon Israel, Jerusalem, and the literal Temple complex, this prophecy speaks also of the preservation of God's new Temple, the Church (Eph. 2: 19ff.; 1 Cor. 3:16; 6:19; 2 Cor. 6:16; 1 Pet. 2:5ff.) that had its birth in and was originally headquartered at Jerusalem (Luke 24:47; Acts 1:8; 8:1; 15:2). Notice that after the holocaust, the altar is seen in heaven (Rev. 11:18), whence Christ's kingdom originates (John 18:36; Heb. 1:3) and where Christians have their citizenship (Eph. 2:6; Col. 3:1, 2).[18]

I would suggest that the hermeneutic Gentry must develop to maintain his position is a bit odd. The temple and city are literal but not the inner sanctuary/core of the temple since that is symbolic of the church. Which is it exactly? Why must we accept that the temple and city here are literal referents to a city and temple standing at the time of John's writing when this is a vision? John cannot literally measure either what he is told to measure or what he is told not to measure, and the temple never refers to the literal temple in the book otherwise. Clearly, when he is told not to measure the outer courts, it means that John is responsible only for the inner sanctuary and people therein, but would anyone think that John would be responsible for either the inner or outer courts of the literal temple in Jerusalem anyway? It seems obvious that the entire structure represents the church that is filled with true and false believers, some remaining faithful and some not, as evidenced by the very letters to the seven churches in the beginning and the point that is being made by John throughout the book.[19]

What Gentry misses, therefore, is that the contrast is not between the literal building of the temple and the figurative sanctuary that is the church

---

18 Gentry, *Before Jerusalem*, 174.

19. Some of the DSS envision the worshiping community itself as a kind of temple where the faithful shared in the worship offered in the heavenly temple through their prayers to God (Maier, *EDSS* 2:923–24; Davidson, *Angels*, 237–39). "In Revelation the earthly counterpart to the heavenly temple is the worshiping community, depicted as a temple under siege (11:1–2). The heavenly temple theme shows God's solidarity with the earthly community in two ways. First, the heavenly temple is the place from which plagues are unleashed against the forces of evil (11:18–19;15:5–16:21). Second, the faithful are promised a place in God's temple, where they will be pillars and will serve him (3:12; 7:15). In the end, New Jerusalem has features of a sanctuary, though its only "temple" is the presence of God and the Lamb (21:22)." (Koester 645).

but that the whole temple represents the visible people of God/church on earth so that the contrast is between true and false believers (the external believers represented by the externalities of the complex and the internal represented by the inner sanctuary). This is what John is concerned about in the book, not the judgment of Judaism, but true Christians being tempted by false Christians and false Christian teachers represented by the false prophet (19:20), the beast who comes with the horns (i.e., authority) of the Lamb but speaks like a dragon (13:11), false apostles (2:2), those who teach it is acceptable for Christians to partake in the worship of idols and sexual immorality (Rev 2:6, 14–15, 20–23; 3:4), and those through their teaching who cause the world to worship the beast rather than Christ and are, therefore, to be identified as a part of pagan religion rather than Christianity (13:12ff.).

Chapter 11 is the end of the second cycle in Revelation, and it is parallel not only to Chapters 21–22 but also to Chapter 7 where each passage comments upon the visible church and invisible church. Chapter 7 mentions the 144,000 who are standing with Christ upon the earth (7:1–8) and protected/sealed (v. 3) and then the souls of Christians who have been martyred in heaven with God. Finally, they are brought together as one in the consummation (7:9–17). Chapter 11 also splits the visible church into visible and invisible by presenting them as the temple complex, the inner sanctuary being the faithful and the outer courts being the unfaithful (11:1–2). Finally, the true church is made one in the consummation (11:15–19). This means that the temple in Chapter 11 is doing the same thing by displaying the visible church as a temple but now distinguishes between the faithful and unfaithful as it does in Chapters 21–22 where the faithful and unfaithful are finally separated out. Hence, these function as progressive parallels where at first just the faithful church is mentioned both visibly and invisibly, then the visible church is portrayed as existing both as faithful and unfaithful and, finally, the visible and invisible become one, where only the faithful remain among the people of God, and the unfaithful are cast out (21:7–8; 27; 22:14–15).

Gentry commits the fallacy of context replacement since his imported context has John concerned about the destruction of the old covenant world and Judaism rather than what the context indicates both in the beginning and in the end of the book; chapters 1–3 create an *inclusio* with Chapters 21–22 that display the book's purpose: that John's concern is an antinomian compromise among Christians with the wicked world due to imperial, social, and religious pressures. Hence, John continually condemns those who "worship the beast and his image" and those who partake in the sexual immorality of Rome, which is the true referent for the symbolic description of Sodom and Egypt. It is as sexually immoral as Sodom and as oppressive toward God's people as Egypt was. Hence, the great city later in Chapter

11 is not Jerusalem, but Rome. John wishes to present Christ as crucified within the very jurisdiction of Rome in the same way that His followers are now put to death within that jurisdiction. Again, interpreting the city as literally where Christ was crucified misunderstands the point being made and thus confuses what is a referent to Rome both here and in Chapter 18 as a referent to Jerusalem (see the next section).

Hence, there is no good reason at all to join in with certain scholars who create a false inference from the text that the literal temple must be standing in Jerusalem at the time of John's vision. The temple and city are the visible church, and within the visible church are true faithful Christians who do not compromise with the world/beast/false prophet. These true believers are under John's protection and care, and he cares for them by writing to them this very book, warning and encouraging them to remain faithful (1:3). John is not responsible for the false church since it is destined to be trampled by the world of which it so loved to be a part. It belongs to the beast and the devil, not to Christ, and thus will receive the fate of the beast rather than the reward of Christ (19:20; 20:15; 21:8 in contrast to 20:4).

Who Is the Beast?: Should the Kings in the Book of Revelation Begin with Julius or Augustus?

Gentry attempts to make an argument that Nero was the sixth king under which John wrote his work and under whom he was persecuted by starting the count of the kings in the list found in Chapter 17 of the book at Julius instead of Augustus. Since Revelation 17 relates a line of kings, it would make a good argument to show that the sixth king is Nero, the beast with whom John is concerned in the book. One must ask, however, not only whether Julius Caesar was the first emperor of Rome but also whether John begins with him as the first king in the Apocalypse and whether his writing under the sixth king is an apocalyptic literary device rather than a literal description.

Josephus relates a speech given by Gnaeus, an insurrectionist attempting to argue that the senate should govern Rome without the interference of dictators.

> For since Julius Caesar took it into his head to dissolve our democracy, and, by overbearing the regular system of our laws, to bring disorders into our administration, and to get above right and justice, and to be a slave to his own inclinations, there is no kind of misery but what hath tended to the subversion of this city; while all those that have succeeded him have striven one with another to overthrow the ancient laws of their country,

and have left it destitute of such citizens as were of generous principles, because they thought it tended to their safety to have vicious men to converse withal, and not only to break the spirits of those that were best esteemed for their virtue, but to resolve upon their utter destruction. Of all of them, who have been many in number, and who laid upon us insufferable hardships during the times of their government, this Caius, who hath been slain today, hath brought more terrible calamities upon us than did all the rest, not only by exercising his ungoverned rage upon his fellow citizens, but also upon his kindred and friends, and alike upon all others, and by inflicting still greater miseries upon them, as punishments, which they never deserved, he being equally furious against men and against the gods. For tyrants are not content to gain their sweet pleasure, and this by acting injuriously, and in the vexation they bring both upon men's estates and their wives; but they look upon that to be their principal advantage, when they can utterly overthrow the entire families of their enemies; while all lovers of liberty are the enemies of tyranny. (Josephus Antiquities !XX.2)

This text actually does not call Julius an emperor at all. Instead, the word "emperors" is inserted in the English translation. The Greek text merely has the words τῶν ἁπάντων which means "of all." This refers to every tyrant who came after Julius who desired to take the lead over Rome. It may be that it is from this speech that Josephus elsewhere gets the idea that Julius is the first emperor; since Gnaeus begins with the tyranny of Julius as the seed from which the other tyrants have come and undermined the Roman republic, it could be concluded that Julius should be considered the first of Rome's Autokrators. It is understandable for Josephus and others either to purposely set Julius as the first in a line of tyrants in order to make a point about these leaders or to simply mistake him as the first by citing his aggressive actions that led to the organization of the empire under Augustus. Either way, however, it is clear that neither option provides an accurate understanding. The empire does not exist until Augustus organizes it and thus every Roman historian and every emperor to follow considers Augustus, not Julius, the first emperor of the Roman Empire.

Furthermore, Julius is never considered a king over Rome. Cassius Dio writes of a common scene in Roman historic literature where Julius attempts and fails to persuade the senate to see him as their king by manipulating the citizens of Rome who admire him.

> When he had reached this point, the men who were plotting against him hesitated no longer, but in order to embitter even

his best friends against him, they did their best to traduce him, finally saluting him as king, a name which they often used also among themselves. When he kept refusing the title and rebuking in a way those who thus accosted him, yet did nothing by which it would be thought that he was really displeased at it, they secretly adorned his statue, which stood on the rostra, with a diadem. And when the tribunes, Gaius Epidius Marullus and Lucius Caesetius Flavius, took it down, he became violently angry, although they uttered no word of abuse and moreover actually praised him before the populace as not wanting anything of the sort. For the time being, though vexed, he held his peace. Subsequently, however, when he was riding in from the Alban Mount and some men again called him king, he said that his name was not king but Caesar; but when the same tribunes brought suit against the first man who had termed him king, he no longer restrained his wrath but showed great irritation, as if these very officials were really stirring up sedition against him. And though for the moment he did them no harm, yet later, when they issued a proclamation declaring that they were unable to speak their mind freely and safely on behalf of the public good, he became exceedingly angry and brought them into the senate-house where he accused them and put their conduct to the vote. He did not put them to death, though some declared them worthy even of that penalty, but he first removed them from the tribuneship, on the motion of Helvius Cinna, their colleague, and then erased their names from the senate. Some were pleased at this, or pretended to be, thinking they would have no need to incur danger by speaking out freely, and since they were not themselves involved in the business, they could view events as from a watch tower. Caesar, however, received an ill name from this fact also, that, where he should have hated those who applied to him the name of king, he let them go and found fault with the tribunes instead.

Another thing that happened not long after these events proved still more clearly that, although he pretended to shun the title, in reality he desired to assume it. For when he had entered the Forum at the festival of the Lupercalia and was sitting on the rostra in his gilded chair, adorned with the royal apparel and resplendent in his crown overlaid with gold, Antony with his fellow-priests saluted him as king and binding a diadem upon his head, said: "The people offer this to you through me." And Caesar answered: "Jupiter alone is king of the Romans," and sent the diadem to Jupiter on the Capitol; yet he was not angry, but caused it to be inscribed in the records that he had refused to

A CRITIQUE OF PRETERISTS' THREE STRONGEST EVIDENCES   245

accept the kingship when offered to him by the people through the consul. It was accordingly suspected that this thing had been deliberately arranged and that he was anxious for the name, but wished to be somehow compelled to take it; consequently the hatred against him was intense.[20]

But what of the evidence in Josephus and later Christian writers who seem to think Julius is the first "emperor"? Josephus makes the following two statements that are quoted by Gentry as evidence that Julius should be seen as the first in the list of kings in Revelation.

> After him came Annius Rufus, under whom died Cæsar, the second emperor of the Romans, the duration of whose reign was fifty-seven years, besides six months and two days (of which time Antonius ruled together with him fourteen years; but the duration of his life was seventy-seven years); upon whose death Tiberius Nero, his wife Julia's son, succeeded. He was now the third emperor; and he sent Valerius Gratus to be procurator of Judea, and to succeed Annius Rufus.[21]
> So when Tiberius had at this time appointed Caius to be his successor, he outlived but a few days, and then died, after he had held the government twenty-two years, five months, and three days: now Caius was the fourth emperor.[22]

However, Gentry has made a major mistake himself here. He has concluded that Josephus is referring to Julius as the king of the empire by implying that he is the first *Imperator* "emperor" of the Romans. However, the term "Imperator" did not always mean "king of an empire" at the time, as modern readers might mistakenly think. Instead, it often referred to a great general who had become victorious over a people. The term begins to hold those connotations around the time of the Flavian Dynasty, which may explain the mistake being made by Josephus (although even Josephus makes it clear that Augustus, not Julius, founded the empire). When one reads the phrase in Roman history, it should be read as "undefeated commander." It was held by people who were not the king of the empire before and after Julius. For instance, Tiberius' nephew held the title during the period that Tiberius was the ruler of the empire (Tacitus, *Annals* 1.58). Josephus is certainly counting from Julius, as Julius was the first undefeated general and leader in the senate. If Josephus sees him as having a hand in the new empire later organized under Augustus, then he may, in fact, see him as the Roman

20. Dio, *Roman History XLIV*, 9–11.
21 Josephus, *Antiquities*, 18:2.2.
22. Josephus, *Antiquities*, 18.6.10.

ruler. The ambiguity of these statements, however, should give one pause in concluding anything definitive against the vast amount of evidence that presents Augustus as the first true ruler over the empire.

In fact, the very likelihood that John does not include the three usurpers in the year of the four emperors in his list indicates that he is only concerned with making the list about bona fide kings of the empire and not other leaders who may still be considered leaders or even disputed kings in Roman history. Instead, he uses only those who are accepted as such by everyone.

Josephus could be just listing Julius as the first great Imperator general according to his timeline which starts around the beginning of the empire but includes the historical soil in which the empire sprouts. The kings to follow are lined up after him in this way. If Josephus believes Julius is the king, however, he is simply mistaken, as he has been about earlier Roman history time and again. In fact, this is plausible since the word *Imperator* begins to be a title taken on only by emperors in the Flavian Dynasty. Josephus and later Christian writers who do not know better are seemingly making the same mistake that moderns make due to a misunderstanding of the language. Even the Greek word Josephus uses for *Imperator* is not *basileus* "king" but *autokratōr* "sole ruler," which fits what Julius has done and is consistent with what Josephus says if Josephus does not mean that he is king since it is a term that was applied to military leaders as well. It becomes confusing for the modern reader to look back at all of this because the terms eventually do evolve in their meanings, and Josephus seems to have confused them himself. John, in his Apocalypse however, is talking about legitimate *kings* who are also considered Autokrators, and it is clear that he begins with Augustus, as I will argue.

The fact that Josephus is making a mistake, however, is likely since some works that may follow Josephus seem to make this same mistake, and this is likely due to the developing terminology used. Other histories (actual works of ancient and modern Roman historians) that are far more reliable indicate that Julius is in no way a king of the empire. His titles are all those of leaders who came before him, his actions mimic the actions of other leaders before him (e.g., Sulla), and both he himself and other senators of his time explicitly state that he is not the king.

Anyone familiar with Josephus knows that inaccuracies based on sloppiness, misunderstanding, and a purposeful manipulation of historical data are quite common in his works, which is what gave rise to the claim made by ancient historians that his works were unreliable, a sentiment repeated often by modern historians as well. He was particularly sloppy with names and chronologies. The historian is often confused about all sorts of details.

For instance, even in the quote cited above, Josephus has Augustus reign for 57 years, even though he only reigned for around 40. Augustus also died at the age of 75, not 77 as Josephus claims. C. G. Tuland states at the outset of his article that "Josephus, in common with other ancient writers, has never enjoyed the reputation of being a fully reliable or accurate historian."[23]

There is also a question as to whether Josephus may have made this error deliberately since Julius had been congenial to the Jews, and earlier leaders were often used in subtle arguments made to sitting emperors that they should mimic the good leaders.[24] His lack of accuracy when making Julius the first *autokratōr* may be due to his desire to argue that Roman emperors should treat Jews favorably as Julius did. As one modern historian put it, Josephus' works are to be understood more as "propagandistic history."[25]

Likewise, Gentry is likely correct that 4 Ezra 11–12 alludes to Augustus as the second king who reigned longer than the other twelve, although nothing is explicit, and a possibility still exists that the author is mistaken about the length of Tiberius' reign over that of Augustus instead of being mistaken about Julius being the first king.

The question then becomes one of whether John has made the same mistake or has purposely started with Julius for some sort of rhetorical reason. When one actually reads the apocalypse, however, he sees that Nero is the beast who is dead and, therefore, one of the first five kings. In understanding that he must be number five at best, this means that John is starting, rightly so, with Augustus, not Julius, and thus has not made the same possible mistake that Josephus and a couple of later Christian religious works may have made. One merely needs to count back from Nero who is five, Claudius who is four, Caligula who is three, Tiberius who is two, and Augustus who is one.

The fact that our reading of these histories can be confused is demonstrated by Gentry himself, who confuses a statement made by Josephus about Augustus in Antiquities 19.1.11: "These shows were acted in honor of that Caesar who first of all changed the popular government, and transferred it to himself; galleries being fixed before the palace, where the Romans that

---

23. Josephus, *Antiquities*, 166.

24. E.g., Tacitus and Suetonius, especially the latter who uses his work entitled, *De vita Caesarum* "The Life of the Caesars," not to argue that Hadrian and those who may follow him should be like Julius or even to just record a list of Roman rulers but rather to argue that his lust to obtain a kingship he never obtained got him killed and that he should follow the rule of Augustus, the first king, rather than Julius or those who used their power tyrannically.

25 Attridge, *The Interpretation of Biblical History*, 181.

were patricians became spectators, together with their children and their wives, and Caesar himself was to be also a spectator . . ."

Gentry seems to think that this statement is made about Julius, thus evidencing his point that Julius founded the empire, but this statement is actually about Augustus. In fact, Josephus makes this clear in 19.87, "So Gaius came out in a solemn manner, and offered sacrifice to Augustus Caesar, in whose honor, indeed, these shows were celebrated."

Cassius Dio also notes, along with Tacitus, Plutarch, and Suetonius, that Julius Caesar never was the king. It is clear from these texts that Julius did not just shun the title, as Gentry attempts to argue, but that he did not hold the actual position and, hence, got himself killed for seeking a position the republic did not wish him to hold over them. This is quite different from later rulers/emperors of Rome who identified themselves as Jupiter, the king of the gods, because they were the king of the Romans.

Cassius Dio explicitly states that Augustus was the beginning of the monarchy. "In this way the power of both people and senate passed entirely into the hands of Augustus, and from his time forward there was, strictly speaking, a monarch; for monarchy would be the truest name for it, no matter if two or three men did later hold the power at the same time."[26]

I can only conclude that Gentry has made the same mistake some of the non-Roman ancient sources possibly made about Julius Caesar. Indeed, he seems unaware in his book that the term *Imperator* does not mean "emperor" in the later sense of the term but is a designation for earlier victorious commanders under the Republic and early Empire. Instead, being unaware of this, he uses it as evidence that Julius, having the title of *Imperator*, "puts him in line with Augustus and the following emperors."[27] If this statement is true, however, then since it was given to Lucius Julius Caesar (90 B.C.), Gnaeus Pompeius Magnus (84 B.C.), Marcus Iunius Brutus (44 B.C.), and to Lucius Antonius (41 B.C.), all should be considered kings both before and after Julius. In 15 A.D. Germanicus, Tiberius' nephew, was also given the title "Imperator" while Tiberius ruled the empire, so according to this logic, one should consider him co-emperor with his uncle, which throws a wrench in the list as well. However, this title that was given to various generals was possible because the title does not mean "emperor" in the sense that later use of the term, referring to a king that rules an empire, took upon itself. Gentry is simply mistaken that this in any way lends credence to the idea that Julius was the first Roman emperor.

---

26 Dio, *Roman History*, 53.17.1.
27 Gentry, *Before Jerusalem*, 155.

Likewise, he makes the statement that many modern laymen make concerning the name of Caesar. He states:

> Indeed, the following emperors even called themselves by his [i.e., Julius'] name, "Caesar." But more compelling than this are the several contemporary and nearly contemporary lists that include Julius in the line of the Caesars, and as the first of the line. In his Lives of the Twelve Caesars, Roman historian Suetonius (c. A.D. 70–160) begins his numbering of the Caesars with Julius.[28]

In another lecture, Gentry points out that the later development of the word Caesar into Czar somehow gives credence to the idea that Caesar is a title for a king. This, however, is a common anachronistic mistake. Caesar is simply Julius' family name that was then received by Augustus, his adopted heir. When other emperors took upon themselves the name Caesar, they were not taking upon themselves the name of Julius Caesar but Augustus Caesar, which is why they never merely took the name "Caesar" but rather "Augustus Caesar" or just "Augustus." The fact that all emperors took upon the name Augustus, but some did not take upon the name "Caesar" shows that it was the name Augustus that was important and the name "Caesar" did not identify one as the legitimate emperor at all.

Indeed, one could take upon the name Julius without any issue. Caligula's birth name, for instance, was Gaius Julius Caesar Germanicus, named after his father Germanicus Julius Caesar and his great grandfather, Gaius Julius Caesar. He was not the emperor at birth, nor did anyone know he would become so. His father certainly was not the emperor or would ever become so. Yet, their names caused no problem and were not seen as an act of treason because taking Julius' name meant nothing. However, if one took upon himself the name "Augustus Caesar," such was treason as the individual was claiming to be the rightful successor of the first king of the Roman Empire. Caligula added Augustus' name to himself only after he became the king. This is also why all emperors from the beginning of the empire to the fall of the Western Empire at the end of the fifth century adopted the name "Augustus," not Julius. Indeed, their coinage sometimes had Augustus on one side and the image of the current emperor on the other in order to signify in propaganda that the current king was a manifestation of the first king and therefore had a legitimate claim to the throne. Even in the Book of Acts, Luke records Agrippa as referring to Nero as *Sebastos* (25:25), which is a Greek translation of the Latin name "Augustus." Domitian named the

---

28. Gentry, *Before Jerusalem*, 155.

temple dedicated to emperor worship in Ephesus the Temple of the *Sabastoi* "Augusti," i.e., the "Augustuses."

This is an important point because Suetonius, who explicitly recorded the fact that Julius Caesar was not the king, entitled his work, "Life of the Caesars," not "Life of the Kings/Emperors of Rome," which is precisely why any Roman historian will tell us that the book is about Julius Caesar and eleven emperors, not twelve emperors.[29] In fact, it may only include eight legitimate emperors. The work is not meant to be a record of emperors but a polemic against bad leaders who seek to obtain power in an effort to act like tyrants. Julius is a great place to start precisely because he was assassinated for his illegal usurpation of power and the desire to obtain further power as the king within a very committed republic. The fact that the book is about the tragic consequences for society and the individual leaders when they lust after power for self-exaltation, rather than for the good of the people, is also why the three usurpers (Galba, Otho, and Vitellius) are present in the book. It might be more accurate to understand the book as twelve leaders who wanted to rule Rome and what Rome thought of their legacy afterward.

Even Gentry, although rather dismissively, acknowledges that Augustus is the one who organizes the empire, and where lists exist, the lists of emperors begin with him.

> It is true that the Roman empire was officially established as an empire under Augustus, and that there are some scattered lists of the emperors that seem to begin the enumeration with Augustus.[30]

So, although there is a real possibility that Josephus and some Christians (although I would dispute Gentry's use of many of these texts) in later centuries think that Julius was the first ruler of the empire (because he got the ball rolling so to speak), there is the factual history of the Romans, along with the archaeological evidence, that overwhelmingly supports Augustus as the first ruler of the empire. So, we are left with two contradictory streams of thought: one established as the mainstream and one idiosyncratic. Even the reference in Josephus is his quotation of an official making the case that

---

29. Gentry argues that "in his *Lives of the Twelve Caesars*, Roman historian Suetonius (c. A.D. 70–160) begins his numbering of the Caesars with Julius. His first book in his *Lives of the Twelve Caesars* is entitled *The Divine Julius* (*Before Jerusalem*, 155). Gentry makes the mistake in thinking that because Suetonius starts with Julius that this must mean that Suetonius sees him as the first king, something Suetonius explicitly denies. In fact, the only three historians Gentry puts forward to advance his claim are Suetonius, who rejects the idea that Julius is the first king, Dio Chrysostom, who also records that Julius is not a king, and Josephus, who is likely mistaken on the subject.

30 Gentry, *Before Jerusalem*, 154.

tyrants have taken over the republic starting with Julius Caesar. This is not necessarily a claim that Julius was the first king but that he began the current state of affairs by placing himself in a position of power that was not fitting in a republic.

Indeed, what we essentially witness here is that Gentry thinks that (1) he has more sources than he has in arguing for the placement of Julius Caesar at the beginning of the Roman emperors (we see that Tacitus, Suetonius, and Dio Cassius give evidence against his hypothesis, not in favor of it), and (2) that the scarce sources (Jewish and Christian instead of Roman, only one of which is a historical work) that might evidence a belief in this lineage should be somehow elevated above the multiple historians (ancient and modern) and material data we have that overwhelmingly indicate that Augustus was the first king of the Roman Empire.[31]

The real question, however, is which of these does John adopt in his work, the factual history or the mistaken one. Answering this question may make all other speculations irrelevant.

This leads us into what the Apocalypse actually says. Preterists typically cite Chapter 17 as evidence of their early date. The text mentions five kings that have fallen, one who is, and two more to come (the seventh and an eighth).

What many preterists attempt to argue is that Nero is the beast and the sixth king who is still alive. Hence, he is the "one who is." In order to get this interpretation to jive with history, they must change the first king of the empire from Augustus to Julius. Hence, Revelation is written during

---

31. As stated before, even these references should be questioned. Gentry has simply misread many of them. For yet another example, the Epistle of Barnabas 4:4 is quoted as proof that Julius is understood by the author of that work as the first emperor. It states: "And the prophet also speaks in this manner: Ten reigns shall reign upon the earth, and after them shall arise another king, who shall bring low three of the kings under one." Gentry argues that the tenth king refers to Vespasian and the three kings he puts under himself (Galba, Otho, and Vitellius). However, the text actually states that this king will be an eleventh king and is after the ten kings. One now finds himself missing an emperor in order to make it fit. Instead, since the author of the Epistle of Barnabas is proclaiming that the end is upon them, it is likely that he is referring to the reign of Domitian, not Vespasian. Some scholars believe it refers to Domitian's attempt during his reign to delegitimize the three usurpers of his father's time. I would suggest it refers to his three triumphs awarded to him by the senate. The first "triumph" against the Chatti was in the year 83, the second against the Dacians in the year 86, and the third against Germania in the year 89 (Brian Jones, *The Emperor Domitian* 139). Domitian was personally involved in these campaigns to subdue these kingdoms. What this means is that, as the eleventh king, Barnabas would be starting with Augustus in his list, not Julius, which does not make sense of the passage when starting with Vespasian. It should also be noted that Vespasian does not put down the other two emperors but only the last of them, Vitellius.

his reign before A.D. 70. Many laymen are convinced by this because they already have the illusion that Julius Caesar was the first king of the Roman Empire, but this is, as argued before, a historical mistake.

Now, I would dispute the idea that John is writing under the one emperor he says is alive since apocalyptic literature speaks from a historical standpoint into the future (i.e., the author goes back in time to prophesy of his own day that is presented as the future of that past time); but let us pursue the idea for a moment that Nero is the sixth king, who is alive.

Not only does the idea that Julius is to be identified as the first king argue against the evidence we have from Roman historians, past and present, it argues against John, who clearly states that the beast is not the sixth who is alive but one of the five who is dead.

It is agreed that Nero is the beast. The number of his name also corresponds to the word "beast," which is a common use of gematria.[32] But he is the first beast mentioned, and what most Preterists fail to note is that there are two manifestations of this beast, one in the fifth king and one in an eighth. Unfortunately, preterists never seem to cite the verse that says the beast, i.e., Nero, is dead. That information is found in 17:8–11.

> The beast you saw was, and is not, but is about to come up from the abyss and then go to destruction. The inhabitants of the earth—all those whose names have not been written in the book of life since the foundation of the world—will be astounded when they see that the beast was, and is not, but is to come. (This requires a mind that has wisdom.) The seven heads are seven mountains the woman sits on. They are also seven kings: five have fallen; one is, and the other has not yet come, but whenever he does come, he must remain for only a brief time. The beast that was, and is not, is himself an eighth king and yet is one of the seven, and is going to destruction.

The phrase, "was, and is not, but is about to come" is an ironic play on Christ's words earlier in the book when He presented Himself as the "one who is, and who was, and who is to come" (1:8), as well as the phrase, "one who lives, the one who became dead, and, behold, I am alive forevermore" (v. 18). The verb of existence is clearly referential to life and the negation of that existence is an allusion to death. Hence, the word "was" refers to the fact that the beast was alive, but the phrase "and is not" refers to the fact that he is no longer alive but dead. The idea that he is about to have a pseudo-resurrection in terms of returning in the spirit of another emperor is consistent with John's idea that one can be in the world in terms of having

---

32. Bauckham, *The Climax of Prophecy,* 381–452.

the same spirit to their activity (cf. John's understanding of the presence of the antichrist through the spirit that is in the Gnostic false prophets in 1 John 4:3 or a similar idea in Luke's Gospel of John the Baptist as Elijah come again in terms of his spirit and ministry, Luke 1:17). Hence, Nero, the beast "is not," i.e., he is dead, when John presents himself to be writing, and John's actual concern is not Nero but the eighth king who arises and takes upon his disposition against Christians, persecuting them to a far greater extent than Nero did.

In essence, Gentry's argument rearranges Roman history in order to force his preterist interpretation onto the text of Revelation. But he also must ignore what Revelation says about the beast, i.e., Nero, by his own admission. Nero is dead. John writes, as is common in apocalyptic literature, from the historical past as though Vespasian is currently the king[33] (despite Gentry's claim that the three usurpers would not be passed over, John seems to ignore them and is only interested in the two legitimate dynasties[34]). He

33. Despite Gentry's claim that the three usurpers would not be passed over, John seems to ignore them and is only interested in the two legitimate dynasties, the Julio-Claudian and Flavian. Gentry has to ignore two of the usurpers if he is to make Vespasian the eighth king. Otherwise, he must say that Otho is the eighth king, and this makes little sense. Instead, he attempts to pass over Galba, makes Otho the seventh king and Vitellius the eighth, which is quite a curiosity as Vitellius does not persecute Christians in any way.

34. It was often thought that these three men were usurpers, not a legitimate succession of the true emperor Augustus. Hence, Suetonius calls them *rebellio trium principum* "the rebellion of three leaders." Swete remarks that "It is more than doubtful whether a writer living under the Flavian Emperors would reckon Galba, Otho or Vitellius among the Augusti" (Apocalypse 220). As Arie W. Zwiep sums up: "A solution, which other scholars have advanced as well, is not to include the names of Galba, Otho and Vitellius on the list at all. They were pretenders to the throne in a period of immense chaos after the death of Nero. The Roman historian Suetonius speaks slightingly of the events as "an insurrection of three princes" (*rebellio trium principum*). Galba and Vitellius both ruled (notably with a partial overlap) seven months, Otho only five. In Roman historiography this period is usually remembered as the *interregnum*, as if there were no ruling authorities at all. If John decided to ignore these "kings," whose authority was by all accounts a matter of dispute, no one would blame him" ("Eight Kings on an Apocalyptic Animal Farm: Reflections on Revelation 17:9–11" in Jan Krans et al. [eds.], *Paul, John, and Apocalyptic Eschatology: Studies in Honor of Martinus C. de Boer*, Supplements to Novum Testamentum 159 [Leiden/Boston: E. J. Brill, 2013] 229). This position is further secured by the fact that the New Testament writers, especially John (e.g., John 18:36), do not believe in committing actual treason unless it was a necessity of the gospel. What this means is that John would not purposely include these usurpers in a time of the Flavian Dynasty because it would have been considered treason, i.e., a rejection of the legitimacy of Vespasian by viewing him as a usurper, and subsequently, insinuating that his two sons, Titus and Domitian, were also illegitimate rulers. John, therefore, would not purposely commit treason by including these usurpers in his list. The best way to understand the list, then, is to see these three as absent from it.

then speaks of Titus as the seventh king who reigns for only a little while (Titus reigns for two years, which is the shortest of any emperor within the legitimate dynasties) and lands squarely on Domitian as the eighth king who mimics Nero's persecution of Christians but persecutes them for very different reasons than Nero did. Domitian, then, is the eighth king, the beast come again, who beheads Christians for not worshiping him and his image.

This, along with numerous other reasons noted in this book, means that the preterist understanding of Revelation is based upon a historical and textual mistake.

Was There a Persecution under Domitian?

To remove the likelihood that Revelation was written under the persecution of Domitian, there is an attempt to ignore the evidence that would lead one to conclude that there was a persecution of the provinces of Asia Minor under Domitian. For instance, Mathison argues, "While there is a great deal of evidence for severe persecution of Christians under Nero, no clear evidence has yet been found indicating that Christians were systematically persecuted under Domitian."[35]

Gentry also calls into question the very persecution under Domitian. This is a common ploy of revisionist history as all historical texts that comment upon the situation are ignored or held in suspect, and this gives the ability to the modern historian to replace that reported narrative with their own interpretation of history.

> Furthermore, it is remarkable that though Suetonius credited Nero with the persecution of Christians, he makes no mention of Domitian's alleged persecution . . . Thus, the documentary evidence for a general imperial persecution of Christianity under Domitian is deemed questionable by a number of competent scholars.[36]

Actually, Suetonius only brings up the Neronian persecution to defame Nero as the real culprit of the crimes committed against Rome, not because he cares about what is occurring with Christians, whom he clearly detests. This is not only an *argumentum silentio* fallacy but ignores the purpose of Suetonius's work. Suetonius does not mention Nerva or Trajan either since his purpose is to teach Hadrian and his successors something about men who seek power and how they should conduct themselves. He wishes to do

---

35. Mathison, *From Age to Age*, 645–46.
36. Gentry, *Before Jerusalem Fell*, 289.

this without offending the Nerva-Antonine line of which Hadrian is a part. He is not merely writing a history and biography of people named Caesar. Should one suggest, then, that there was no Nerva-Antonine dynasty because Suetonius, who was alive during it, did not mention it? That would seem like a much larger oversight if one were truly writing a history of the emperors up until his day rather than a polemic geared toward a specific purpose. In fact, there are numerous events that occur during the reigns of the Caesars that are not attested in his work. This has little to do with whether they occurred. It should also be noted that many scholars deny that there was any Neronian persecution at all using the same type of revisionist methodologies. Yet, Gentry does not accept those. He conveniently applies these conclusions to Domitian's persecution but not to Nero's. It should also be pointed out that no known persecution from the time of Trajan would be known if not for Pliny verifying the procedures for dealing with Christians. Without this letter, these scholars would likely dismiss the idea that Christians had been persecuted on a larger scale under Trajan as well.
Gentry again argues:

> We must carefully note that the punishment was exclusively directed against Christians as such—as a genus. Clearly Christians were punished as Christians, unlike the situation with Domitian. Furthermore, the punishment was due to their "mischievous superstition" and alleged "hatred (odium) of the human race." Henderson suggests that the role of the emperor cult in the Neronian spectacle is presumed in the emperor worship sections of Revelation: "The great crime is 'Caesar-worship.' This of course suits Domitian. But from other evidence it suits Nero as well—when the Christians suffered as Christians."[37]

Gentry is sidestepping an important issue and characterizing the persecution as singling out Christians as Christians; but what he fails to note is that they were not being persecuted by Nero because they did not worship the emperor and his image, as Revelation puts it, but for Nero's crime of setting the city on fire. They were surely hated for their piety and lack of participation in the general worship of the gods, but there is no evidence that Nero persecuted them for not worshiping him. In other words, Christians were hated and made for good scapegoats, and so they were put to death for their supposed hatred toward humanity by setting Rome ablaze.

Gentry is correct to say that because the great crime is "Caesar-worship" that this means that Domitian fits the bill. The problem for Gentry is that Nero does not. Nero did not exalt himself as a deity before his death.

---

37. Gentry, *Before Jerusalem Fell*, 278.

He definitely viewed himself as a sort of demigod before his death, as did many emperors, but Domitian was the first emperor to consider himself a living deity, having given himself the title *Dominus et Deus* "Lord and God." Instead, Nero did not persecute the Christians for their failure to worship him but for burning Rome. They were blamed because they were Christians, but they were not being put to death because they refused to partake in the imperial cult, as the saints in Revelation are.

Instead, Domitian is not only suitable to fit this description, as Gentry himself admits here, but is the only one who is suitable out of the emperors in the first century as there is no evidence that any of the emperors in the first century persecuted Christians for not worshiping them and their images, except for Domitian. Domitian would have persecuted Christians for the specific reason that they were committing blasphemy against the gods and treason against the empire for not participating in the emperor cult, as well as not paying respect to the other gods. This would have been seen by Domitian in particular as a destabilization of the empire and his rule over the provinces of Asia Minor, and as we are told by historians, he was a tyrant even over his own people like no other before him. Domitian took any criticism, even of his gladiators, personally "as offending his divinity *(divinitatem)* and his deity *(numen)*."[38] Unlike all other emperors before him who waited until death to be treated as deity, there were "extraordinary claims to divinity made by Domitian during his lifetime."[39]

Gentry seems aware that the nature of Nero's persecution is an issue as he attempts to argue that Revelation does not require Nero's persecution to be a direct persecution due to the fact that Christians will not worship Nero. He argues:

> We note here at the outset that a formal, legal relationship of emperor worship to the Neronian persecution is not absolutely required by the prophetic message contained in Revelation. Two considerations lead us to this statement. In the first place, even upon purely secular (i.e., naturalistic, anti-prophetic) presuppositions the ideas embodied in Revelation 13 can be perceived as subtly lurking behind the persecution of Nero. For the very existence of the emperor cult and its employment by Nero himself surely would suggest to the mind even of a mere non-inspired enthusiast both the religious incompatibility of the Christian faith in regard to the divine pretensions of the emperor, as well as the inexorable drift to deadly confrontation . . . In the second place, it could be that the prophecy of Revelation speaks of the

---

38. *Pan.* 3 3.4.
39. Schowalter, *The Emperor and the Gods*, 54.

underlying philosophical and spiritual issues engaged, rather than the external publicly advertised and judicially sanctioned ones.[40]

The problem with this argument is that Revelation is specifically encouraging Christians to refrain from participating in the cult of the emperor and provides the reason for their persecution and executions as due to their "not worshiping the beast and his image," suggesting that what brought about the sentence of death was their unwillingness to participate in the imperial cult, not because they were a good scapegoat upon whom Nero could blame his destruction of the city. There is simply no evidence and, indeed evidence to the contrary, that Nero would have employed the imperial cult as any sort of litmus test for Christians in Rome since living emperors were not worshiped as gods in Rome during the time of Nero.[41] Since the beast in revelation is being worshiped, John does not seem to be referencing the Neronian persecution.

Furthermore, the litmus test described by Pliny the Younger fifteen years after Domitian's reign suggests that Christians were specifically being put to death in the late years of the first century and earlier years of the second because they did not renounce their exclusive devotion to Christianity by worshiping the gods and the image of the emperor. In his letter to Trajan, he states:

> Those who denied that they were or had been Christians, when they invoked the gods in words dictated by me, offered prayer with incense and wine to your image, which I had ordered to be brought for this purpose together with statues of the gods, and moreover cursed Christ—none of which those who are

---

40. Gentry, *Before Jerusalem Fell*, 277.

41. The Roman worship of emperors is complicated and often misunderstood. Although they were given divine honors during their lifetimes, before Domitian, they did not regularly receive worship from citizens. The titles of deity were largely propagandistic rhetoric used to subdue the conquered states outside of Rome. After the time of Augustus, it was not until after an emperor died that he became truly divine and worthy of worship in the imperial cult. Only during and after Domitian's reign did they seem to demand this type of worship during their lifetimes. Until then, the attitude that is displayed in Augustus, as noted by Henry F. Burton, prevails: "But Augustus refused to accept divine honors at Rome. He allowed no temple to be erected to him in the city. He was under no illusion as to his divine powers" (*The Biblical World*, The University of Chicago Press, 40.2 1912, 82). Roman citizens were even forbidden to partake in the imperial cult, and ironically, Tiberius, Caligula, Nero, and Domitian were not made gods after their deaths by the senate but were only given divine honors during their lifetimes in the Eastern provinces like Asia Minor (Burton, *The Biblical World*, 83). This is the very location of the persecution in the Book of Revelation, as opposed to Nero's persecution in the city of Rome.

really Christians, it is said, can be forced to do—these I thought should be discharged. Others named by the informer declared that they were Christians, but then denied it, asserting that they had been but had ceased to be, some three years before, others many years, some as much as twenty-five years. They all *worshiped your image* and the statues of the gods, and cursed Christ.

The nature of the later persecution appears much more in line with the descriptions the reader is given in the Book of Revelation whereas the nature of Nero's persecution over the burning of the city does not seem like it at all. In fact, there is no indication that those Christians could recant Christ and worship the emperor in order to receive pardon since they were branded as having committed a treasonous and murderous crime punishable by death. John, however, indicates in his book that there are those who are worshiping the beast and his image and, therefore, compromising in order to save their lives.

Furthermore, since Nero did not exalt himself to a living deity, the litmus test would not have been based upon whether these people worshiped his image. This test only makes sense under Domitian's reign.

Even more than this, there is absolutely no evidence that Nero banished people for the crime of burning the city. They were given the death penalty for the crime. Domitian, however, executed and banished Christians. This is significant because John was writing from the island of Patmos to which he had been banished "because of the word of God and the testimony concerning Jesus" (1:9). He was a *sygkoinōnos* "co-sharer" in the *thlipsis* "tribulation/persecution" his recipients were enduring. This makes no sense if he was accused of treason and murder under the Neronian persecution.

It is also a glaring omission that John wrote to comfort the churches under persecution and wrote to the churches in Asia Minor, not once mentioning the church at Rome where the persecution of Nero was largely situated. As G. K. Beale has argued, "There is no evidence that Nero's persecution of Christians in Rome extended also to Asia Minor, where the churches addressed in the Apocalypse are located."[42] Mathison attempts to counter this simply by saying that it is possible for the persecution to have been felt in the rest of the church throughout the empire.[43] Although this is certainly true, neither the vision of Jesus nor John himself make any attempt to comfort the Christians in the Roman church that would have suffered the most. However, the provinces in Asia Minor would have felt the wrath of Domitian the most if they had refused to worship him since the worship of

---

42. *Commentary on the Book of Revelation* (1999), 12.
43. Mathison, *From Age to Age*, 646.

the emperor in that region was historically tied to their political allegiance to him. John's address of these churches under Domitian's reign, therefore, made perfect sense. It is unlikely, therefore, that the Book of Revelation is describing the persecution under Nero.

At this point, it is not even necessary to quibble over this matter as even if one were to concede, for the sake of argument, that the reason given in Revelation for this imperial persecution of Christians is merely a root cause of other reasons Christians were persecuted, the book is clear that Nero (the fifth king who is dead) is not the manifestation of the beast that is persecuting the Christians in Revelation but rather the beast in its manifestation as the eighth king, who clearly represents Domitian. It is the beast manifested in the eighth king who concerns John, not the original fifth one. This eighth king is certainly like the fifth in that he persecuted Christians, but he persecutes them for not worshiping him and his image. much like Pliny, the newly appointed governor of Bithynia-Pontus (i.e., Turkey), described in A.D. 112, in his letter to Trajan, of a persecution that seems to have been going on for some time before him.

Emeka C. Ekeke sums up the historical conditions to which Christians were subject under Domitian.

> Because of this refusal, which in turn occasioned other refusals on the part of the Christians, they were hated, imprisoned, banished to lonely islands, condemned to work as slaves in the mines, cast to the lions as a public spectacle and executed by the sword. . . . Christians were always in danger (p.45). However, the Roman persecutions were generally sporadic, localized and dependent on the political climate and disposition of each emperor.[44]

Ekeke further explains:

> Christians, in their rejection of Roman gods and of many Roman traditions, stood in the way of Domitian and this caused persecution for them. The Jews, however, were not left out as Domitian regarded them as one with Christians. Austin (1983) notes, ―. . .he declared a widespread persecution of Christians and Jews‖ (p. 62). Numerous lies were made up during this time to harm the Christians- such as Christians were responsible for every famine, epidemic or earthquake that afflicted any part of the Roman Empire. III. Nature of Persecution. Domitian was a cruel person, and so in his hatred, he issued an order that no Christian, once brought before the tribunal should be exempted

---

44. "Persecution and Martyrdom" ESJ 8:16, July, 181.

from punishment without renouncing his religion. When Christians were brought before Domitian's council, they were told to swear an oath of allegiance to him and if they refused, they were killed. Among those killed were Domitian's cousins, Flavius Clemens and M' Aciluis Glabrio, both consuls. He also banished Domitilla for atheism. Austin (1983) notes, —Tradition holds it was during the Domitian persecutions that the Apostle John was banished to Patmos‖ (p. 62).[45]

The Romans did not sharply distinguish religion from politics; for religion was a function of the state, and the worship of the gods which were recognized by the state was part of the duty of the citizen. Emperor-worship therefore expressed the attitude of the worshiper toward the emperor as the embodiment of imperial power ... They accepted the religious devotion of the people as an evidence of political loyalty.[46]

Emperors before Domitian, however, accepted only vague titles of divinity. They were afforded honor as one who would become a deity, but even upon his deathbed, Vespasian, the father of Domitian, implied, even if jokingly, that he was becoming a god upon his death and was not one in life.

Mark Galli states reasons why Christians had such conflict with Domitian:

Domitian was the first emperor to have himself officially titled in Rome as "God the Lord." He insisted that other people hail his greatness with acclamations like "Lord of the earth," "Invincible," "Glory," "Holy," and "Thou Alone." When he ordered people to give him divine honors, Jews, and no doubt Christians, balked. The resulting persecution of Jews is well-documented; that of Christians is not. However, the beast that the author of Revelation describes, as well as the events in the book, are perhaps best interpreted as hidden allusions to the rule of Domitian. In addition, Flavius Clemens, consul in 95, and his wife, Flavia Domitilla, were executed and exiled, respectively, by Domitian's orders; many historians suspect this was because they were Christians.[47]

Eusebius confirms that no other emperor persecuted Christians other than Nero and Domitian when he states that "he [Domitian] was the second [emperor] who raised a persecution against us" (Eccl Hist 3:17). He also quotes the earlier work of Melito, who states that in the first century, "Nero and Domitian, alone, stimulated by certain malicious persons, showed a

---

45. Ekeke, 183.
46. Burton, *Worship of the Roman Emperors*, 86.
47. See Galli, "Persecution in the Early Church."

disposition to slander our faith." Tertullian also states that both Nero and Domitian were the first century emperors who "raged with the imperial sword against this teaching." He stated that Domitian was "a good deal of a Nero in cruelty" (*Apol.* 5). Hegesippus states that the persecution ceased when Domitian realized that the kingdom about which Christians spoke was an eternal one not a temporal one that was seeking to overthrow the Roman Empire.

Domitian was the first to declare himself a living god, the manifestation of Jupiter himself and, as such, would have put more stock in the sacrifices made to him as to a deity. To fail to worship him was to fail to worship Jupiter and was a subversive action taken against the stability of the empire. This would have added to his suspicion that Christians wanted to replace the empire with their own. It was not until the end of his reign when he may have learned otherwise and softened his stance against them.
Eusebius gives a lengthy description of Domitian's persecutions and John's punishment due to them.

> Domitian, having shown great cruelty toward many, and having unjustly put to death no small number of well-born and notable men at Rome, and having without cause exiled and confiscated the property of a great many other illustrious men, finally became a successor of Nero in his hatred and enmity toward God. He was in fact the second that stirred up a persecution against us, although his father Vespasian had undertaken nothing prejudicial to us. It is said that in this persecution the apostle and evangelist John, who was still alive, was condemned to dwell on the island of Patmos in consequence of his testimony to the divine word. Irenæus, in the fifth book of his work Against Heresies, where he discusses the number of the name of Antichrist, which is given in the so-called Apocalypse of John, speaks as follows concerning him: "If it were necessary for his name to be proclaimed openly at the present time, it would have been declared by him who saw the revelation. For it was seen not long ago, but almost in our own generation, at the end of the reign of Domitian." To such a degree, indeed, did the teaching of our faith flourish at that time that even those writers who were far from our religion did not hesitate to mention in their histories the persecution and the martyrdoms which took place during it. And they, indeed, accurately indicated the time. For they recorded that in the fifteenth year of Domitian Flavia Domitilla, daughter of a sister of Flavius Clement, who at that time was one of the consuls of Rome, was exiled with many others to the island of Pontia in consequence of testimony borne to Christ.

But when this same Domitian had commanded that the descendants of David should be slain, an ancient tradition says that some of the heretics brought accusation against the descendants of Jude (said to have been a brother of the Saviour according to the flesh), on the ground that they were of the lineage of David and were related to Christ himself. Hegesippus relates these facts in the following words. Of the family of the Lord there were still living the grandchildren of Jude, who is said to have been the Lord's brother according to the flesh. Information was given that they belonged to the family of David, and they were brought to the Emperor Domitian by the Evocatus. For Domitian feared the coming of Christ as Herod also had feared it. And he asked them if they were descendants of David, and they confessed that they were. Then he asked them how much property they had, or how much money they owned. And both of them answered that they had only nine thousand denarii, half of which belonged to each of them. And this property did not consist of silver, but of a piece of land which contained only thirty-nine acres, and from which they raised their taxes and supported themselves by their own labor. Then they showed their hands, exhibiting the hardness of their bodies and the callousness produced upon their hands by continuous toil as evidence of their own labor. And when they were asked concerning Christ and his kingdom, of what sort it was and where and when it was to appear, they answered that it was not a temporal nor an earthly kingdom, but a heavenly and angelic one, which would appear at the end of the world, when he should come in glory to judge the quick and the dead, and to give unto every one according to his works. Upon hearing this, Domitian did not pass judgment against them, but, despising them as of no account, he let them go, and by a decree put a stop to the persecution of the Church. But when they were released, they ruled the churches because they were witnesses and were also relatives of the Lord. And peace being established, they lived until the time of Trajan. These things are related by Hegesippus. Tertullian also has mentioned Domitian in the following words: Domitian also, who possessed a share of Nero's cruelty, attempted once to do the same thing that the latter did. But because he had, I suppose, some intelligence, he very soon ceased, and even recalled those whom he had banished.

After Domitian died, the Roman Senate decided that Domitian's honors were to be cancelled due to his tyrannical rule and that those who had been wrongly banished would be allowed to return to their homes and given back their property. It is at this point, Eusebius tells us, that John returned from his banishment on the island "according to an ancient Christian tradition" (Eus 22.17–20).

Cassius Dio records the punishment of a few people on the charge of "atheism," a term that referenced not a denial of any one deity but a denial of the Roman gods and the deified emperors specifically.

> And the same year Domitian slew, along with *many others*, Flavius Clemens the consul, although he was a cousin and had to wife Flavia Domitilla, who was also a relative of the emperor's. The charge brought against them both was that of atheism, a charge on which many others who drifted into Jewish ways were condemned. Some of these were put to death, and the rest were at least deprived of their property. Domitilla was merely banished to Pandateria. But Glabrio, who had been Trajan's colleague in the consulship, was put to death, having been accused of the same crimes as most of the others, and, in particular, made to fight as a gladiator with wild beasts. (*Historia Romana* 67.14)

In the Chronicles written by Bruttius,[48][5] Eusebius mentions that Domitilla was punished because she was a Christian, evidencing that the term "atheist" referred to Christians, and they were viewed as a sect of Judaism even though Christianity would have been seen as a particularly troublesome sect within Judaism.

Hegesippus is also cited by Eusebius, and he mentions the persecution under Domitian as well. The problem is that modern deconstructionist historians thrive on the fact that many histories are lost to us. Hence, they can cast doubt on works of antiquity as they survive only through the quotations

---

48. Many in the deconstructionist movement within historiography come to the Christian persecutions in the first century with an extreme skepticism that is, frankly, unwarranted. The idea that the lost history was merely a fictionalized account made up by Christians is speculative and a case of confirmation bias. I agree with B. M. Levick and J. W. Rich that "such extreme skepticism is difficult to accept. The supposed literary fabrication seems unnecessarily elaborate, and one might wonder why the perpetrator did not choose a more celebrated family for his fictional historian" ("Bruttius" in T. J. Cornell [ed.], *The Fragments of the Roman Historians: Volume 1: Introduction* 594). The attempt to argue that an "empire-wide" persecution is not evident within any official reports fails to note how the prosecution of individuals would be officially viewed versus how they would have been viewed by the Christians who were being prosecuted. As Paul Middleton ("Christology, Martyrdom, and Vindication in the Gospel of Mark and the Apocalypse: Two New Testament Views," in *Mark, Manuscripts, and Monotheism: Essays in Honor of Larry W. Hurtado*, eds. Chris Keith & Dieter T. Roth [London: Bloombury T&T Clark, 2015], 221) notes, "To insist upon a persecution/prosecution distinction is artificial; to the Romans *all* actions taken against Christians were prosecution for misdemeanor rather than persecution, while Christians would interpret all such action as manifestations of the suffering anticipated in the NT on account of Jesus' name."

of other sources. However, when an argument from silence seeks to counter a report, the report should be given the benefit of the doubt as a report is evidence and speculation is not.[49]

Tertullian (Apol 5.4) mentions the persecution as something Domitian unleashed for a short time but then halted, bringing back many he had banished. Neither the early Christian writers nor the Book of Revelation necessarily refer to a lengthy and widespread genocide. Preterists, like Mathison, however, exploit the deconstructionist view in order to give more weight to their view that Nero is the main beast in conflict with Christ in Revelation. He argues:

> "While there is a great deal of evidence for severe persecution of Christians under Nero, no clear evidence has yet been found indicating that Christians were systematically persecuted under Domitian."[50]

Mathison has fallen prey to the idea that literary evidence is not evidence. These deconstructionist historians ignore the literary evidence when it does not suit their hypotheses, and they make their claims based

---

49. A good example of a wayward deconstructionist history of Domitian is that of Brian Jones, *The Emperor Domitian* (London/New York: Routledge, 1992). Alain M. Gowing sums up the problem with such a history as follows: "It is in Jones' handling of the literary evidence, however, that I find some missed (or perhaps purposefully ignored) opportunities. That evidence, from which we derive our most memorable impressions of Domitian, is of course notoriously difficult to assess, as Jones repeatedly and rightly reminds us. Waters (op. cit.) addressed precisely this problem, with good results: admitting that caution is indeed warranted, he conceded that 'all this smoke must indicate at least a few glowing embers' (p. 50) and managed to extract from the literary sources a credible characterization of Domitian. By contrast, Jones' attitude toward those same sources is seldom expounded and often frustratingly ambivalent. At points he admits that some of the evidence may be reliable ('the view of [Domitian's] reign propounded by Nerva's senate and repeated throughout the dynasty could even be accurate — although inevitably hostile, it was not inevitably wrong', p. 161), yet at other times he implies that it is in fact 'inevitably wrong' ('. . . [Domitian] left no heir to deify him and so, unlike Nerva, he was not able to 'guide' the literary tradition to the 'correct' interpretation of events', p. 163). But the 'inevitable hostility' of writers such as Pliny, Tacitus, or Suetonius is assumed rather than proven in this book. Indeed, with a few notable exceptions, Jones rarely engages in direct confrontation with the literary evidence. Admittedly, it is not his purpose to examine Pliny's or Tacitus' attitude toward Domitian, but in light of the overwhelming and understandable influence these authors have exercised on modern views of the emperor, it seems remiss not to have established with clarity the criteria by which their testimony has been either accepted or rejected. Most worrisome is the fact that the (proverbial) non-specialist who turns to this book for an introduction to Domitian will come away with a very fragmented notion of what the bulk of the literary evidence says about him" (*Bryn Mawr Classical Review* 3.06.10).

50. Mathison, *From Age to Age*, 645-46.

on material culture which almost never yields definitive evidence for any narrative one way or the other. There is no clear evidence that Abraham really existed or that the exodus or Canaanite conquest really took place according to deconstructionist methods. In fact, most of the Bible is wrong in their eyes because it is not substantiated by their interpretations of material culture. What is significant in understanding historical events is the literary witness left behind. The community that would comment upon such an event, like the Domitian persecutions, would be the Christian community who were most affected by it. The Roman historians would have cared little about it. However, even they note the tyranny of Domitian. They just speak about it in generalities and not in the specifics of persecuted Christians.

There is also a moving of the goal post in Mathison's comment as no one needs to prove that there was a "systematic" persecution under Domitian. The Apocalypse describes pressure to partake in the imperial cult and the resulting persecution that leads to death for many Christians. It says nothing about there being official laws and some sort of systematic genocide of Christians occurring. Even the Neronian persecution is thought to be localized to the Christians in Rome, yet the book describes the churches in Asia Minor as possibly going through this persecution. The point that John desires to make in the book is that when Christians are faced with martyrdom or idolatrous compromise, they should choose death because they serve Christ who "holds the keys of death and the grave." His point is not to comment upon how vast the persecution may be.

If Pliny the Younger had not written to Trajan to clarify the correct manner of investigation needed to put Christians to death, modern historians would have never known that a systematic persecution took place under Trajan. Not even the Christians mentioned it. Yet, it is clear from that correspondence that Christians were regularly being put to death for not worshiping the gods and the emperor through his image.

What is also important to note is that this persecution in Revelation, according to the literary sources and the Apocalypse itself, includes not only death but also banishment. John himself is said to be affected by this tribulation and banished for it. Banishment, however, was not a punishment under the Neronian persecution as that persecution was not about worshiping Nero but was a sentence of death placed upon all Christians in Rome for the crimes against humanity, specifically because they were blamed for setting the city on fire. All evidence points to only one punishment, i.e., death, handed out to Christians and only execution, not banishment, would make sense if they were being sentenced for that particular crime. As stated before, the persecution under Nero does not fit the description of the persecution in the Book of Revelation.

Furthermore, Domitian is the only emperor who fits the description of the beast in Revelation 17. Mathison wants to argue that the beast is Rome, but this is a confusion of what John is arguing. The beast, i.e., Rome, is personified in two of its kings. Hence, the "beast" in 13:18 is said to be a man whose number is 666, which Mathison and most scholars agree is the title "Nero Caesar." The beast, i.e., Nero, is dead in Chapter 17 and then comes back in the form of an eighth king.

This calls for a mind with wisdom. The seven heads are seven hills on which the woman sits. They are also seven kings. Five have fallen, one is, the other has not yet come; but when he does come, he must remain for only a little while. The beast who once was, and now is not, is an eighth king. He belongs to the seven and is going to his destruction. (vv. 9–11)

Any attempt to make this about the Roman Empire as a whole fails to deal with what is explicitly said in the book about the beast. Verse 11 calls this eighth king "the beast who was and *is not* and is also an eighth king and yet is one of the seven and is going off to destruction." Notice that the beast who was, i.e., Nero, is no longer alive when John is writing. Instead, as one of the seven kings, he will return again as an eighth king. It is the eighth king with whom John is concerned. It is the eighth king who will persecute Christians and attack Christ not the fifth king, Nero, who has already died. Hence, John cannot be describing the persecution under Nero. If he is not describing that persecution, then there is only one other persecution in the first century that fits the description of Revelation and that is the one under Domitian, and if the usurpers are taken out of the count of legitimate kings, Domitian is the eighth king of the Roman Empire.

Furthermore, the fact that the beast is said to be only one of the seven kings, and not all of them, informs the reader that they do not represent the Roman Empire nor all of the kings as a whole. Instead, only these specific two kings, which are presented as two manifestations of the same demonic forces coming up from the abyss, are said to be "the beast." So, when John moves from the generic empire to the specific kings, he is no longer speaking in generalities. The depiction of the empire as the beast is meant to move the reader from generalities to specifics not to confuse the general with the specific. What this means is that one cannot attempt to make the text about the Roman Empire when it is, in fact, describing these two kings specifically as the text itself states.

Instead, all these sources combined present a picture of the following: (1) There was, indeed, a noteworthy persecution under Domitian. (2) This persecution included executions of Christians. (3) It included banishing Christians. (4) It included impoverishing Christians by seizure of their property. (5) It likely included a litmus test where the accused, if they denied being Christians, were made to worship the pagan gods, repudiate Christ, and worship the emperor through his image. (6) Christians were given a time of relief from the persecution. (7) This persecution was only one of two brought against the Christians in the first century, the first being under Nero for different reasons and with only one judicial sentence for the crime of treason via arson, i.e., death.

This evidence fits the description in the Book of Revelation as there are two manifestations of the political beast in the book who persecute Christians, not one. Nero is the proto-beast who is already dead in the book whereas Domitian becomes the eighth beast with which John is primarily concerned. He returns in the demonic spirit of Nero and is presented as one who ascends from the place whence the demonic forces ascend to persecute Christians and oppose Christ. It is the persecution under this beast, therefore, that provides the background for John's Apocalypse and removes it from any concern about an impending destruction of Jerusalem.

Bibliography

Adams, Edward. *The Stars will Fall From Heaven: Cosmic Catastrophe in the New Testament and its World*. London/New York: T & T Clark, 2007.
Attridge, Harold W. *The Interpretation of Biblical History in the Antiquities Judicae of Flavis Josephus*. Missoula, MT: Scholars Press, 1976.
Aune, David. *Apocalypticism, Prophecy, and Magic in Early Christianity: Collected Essays*. Ada, MI: Baker Academic, 2008.
Balyeat, Joseph R. *Babylon the Great City of Revelation*. Sevierville, TN: Covenant House Books, 1995.
Bauckham, Richard. *The Climax of Prophecy: Studies on the Book of Revelation*. Edinburgh: T & T Clark, 1995.
———. "The Rise of Apocalyptic." In *The Jewish World Around the New Testament*, 42. Grand Rapids, MI: Baker Academics, 2010.
Bauers, Walter, *A Greek-English Lexicon of the New Testament and other Early Christian Literature*. Third Edition. Chicago/London: The University of Chicago Press, 2000.
Beale, G.K. *The Book of Revelation: A Commentary of the Greek Text*. Grand Rapids, MI: Eerdmans, 1999.
Best, Ernest. *A Commentary on the First and Second Epistles to the Thessalonians*. Blacks New Testament Commentary. 2nd Edition. London: Continuum, 1977.
Birks, Kelly. "What is the Nature of the Resurrection?" The Second Coming Series, volume 9. 2021, YouTube.
———. "The Sheep and Goat Nations." The Second Coming Series, volume 20. 2021, YouTube.
Botterweck, Johannes G., Fabry, Heinz-Josef, Ringgren, Helmer, eds. *Theological Dictionary of The Old Testament*. Grand Rapids, MI: Eerdmans, 1988.
Box, George Herbert. *The Apocalypse of Abraham*. London: MacMillan, 1918.
Bridge, Steven L. "Where the Eagles Are Gathered: The Deliverance of the Elect in Lukan Eschatology." Journal for the Study of the New Testament Supplement Series 240 (2003) 115.
Brown, Francis, et al. *The Brown-Driver-Briggs Hebrew and English Lexicon*. Peabody, MA: Hendrickson Academic, 1996.
Broyles, Craig C. "The Redeeming King: Psalm 72's Contribution to the Messianic Ideal." In *Eschatology, Messianism, and the Dead Sea Scrolls*, edited by Craig A. Evans, et al., 24. Grand Rapids, MI: Eerdmans, 1997.
Burton, Henry Fairfield. "Worship of the Roman Emperors." The Biblical World volume 40 Number 2 (1912) 80–91.

Carson, D. A. *Exegetical Fallacies*. Grand Rapids, MI: Baker Academics, 1996.

Charles, R. H. *The Apocrypha and Pseudepigrapha of the Old Testament* in English. London: Oxford University Press, 1913.

Chilton, David. *The Days of Vengeance: An Exposition of the Book of Revelation*. Fort Worth TX: Dominion Press, 1987.

Clines, David J. A. *Dictionary of Classical Hebrew*. Sheffield: Sheffield Phoenix Press, 2019.

Collins, John J. *Daniel: A Commentary on the Book of Daniel*. Philadelphia, PA: Fortress Press, 1993.

———. "The Expectation of the End in the Dead Sea Scrolls." In *Eschatology, Messianism, and The Dead Sea Scrolls*, Edited by Craig A. Evans, et al., 76. Grand Rapids, MI: Eerdmans, 1997.

——— eds. "Primary and Secondary Apocalyptic Discourse." In *The Oxford Handbook of Apocalyptic Literature*, 222, 224. Oxford: Oxford University Press, 2014.

Crossley, James G. *The Date of Mark's Gospel: Insight from the Law in Earliest Christianity*. London/New York: T & T Clark, 2004.

Davidson, Gustav. *A Dictionary of Angels including the Fallen Angels*. New York: The Free Press, 1971.

Dawson, Samuel G. *Essays on Eschatology: And Introductory Overview of the Study of Last Things*. 2nd Edition. Bowie, TX: SGD Press, 2013.

DeMar, Gary. *Last Days Madness*. Powder Springs, GA: American Vision, 1999.

———. *Why the End of the World is Not in Your Future*. Powder Springs, GA: American Vision, 2008.

Dio, Cassius. *Roman History*. XLIV 9–11 London: William Heinemann, 1916.

Dodd, C. H. *The Johannine Epistles*. Whitefish, MT: Kessinger Publishing, 2008.

Ekeke, Emeka C. "Persecution and Martyrdom of Christians in the Roman Empire from AD54 to 100: A Lesson for the 21st Century Church." European Scientific Journal 8 volume 16 (2012) 181, 183.

Flint, Peter W. "The Daniel Tradition at Qumran." In *Eschatology, Messianism, and the Dead Sea Scrolls*. Edited by Craig A. Evans, et al., 52–53. Grand Rapids, MI: Eerdmans, 1997.

Flusser, David. *Judaism of the Second Temple Period, volume 1: Qumran and Apocalypticism*, Translated by Azzan Yadin. Grand Rapids, MI/Cambridge: Eerdmans, 2007.

Galli, Mark. "Persecution in the Early Church: A Gallery of Persecuting Emperors." Christian Institute 27 (1990)

Gentry, Kenneth L. *Before Jerusalem Fell: Dating the Book of Revelation*. Chesnee, SC: Victorious Hope Publishing, 2010.

Goldingay, John E. "The Book of Daniel: Three Issues." Themelios 2.2 (1977) 47–48.

Harden, Daniel E. *Overcoming Sproul's Resurrection Obstacles: The First Century Fulfillment*

———*Of The Parousia of Christ and the Resurrection of the Dead*. Philippines: World Without End Ministries, 2007.

Harland, Philip A. "The Economy of First-Century Palestine: State of the Scholarly Discussion." In *Handbook of Early Christianity: Social Science Approaches*, 520. Walnut Creek: Altimira, 2002.

Jones, Brian. *The Emperor Domitian*. London/New York: Routledge, 1992.

Jones, Henry Stuart, Liddell, Henry George, and Scott, Robert eds. *Liddell-Scott-Jones Greek English Lexicon*. Oxford: Oxford University Press, 1940.

Flavius, Josephus. *The Works of Josephus*. Translated by William Whiston. Peabody, MA: Hendrickson Academic, 1987.

Kelly, J. N. D. *Epistles of Peter and Jude*. Grand Rapids, MI: Baker Books, 1981.

Kim, Seyoon. *The 'Son of Man' as the Son of God*. Tubingen: J. C. B. Mohr, 1983.

Kittel, Gerhard. *Theological Dictionary of the New Testament*. Grand Rapids, MI: Eerdmans, 1977.

Koehler, Ludwig, et al. *Hebrew and Aramaic Lexicon of the Old Testament*. Study Edition. Leiden: Brill, 2001.

Koester, Craig. *Revelation and the End of All Things*. Grand Rapids, MI: Eerdmans, 2018.

Ladd, George E. "The Kingdom of God in I Enoch: Part 4." Bibliotheca Sacra 110 (1952) 34.

———. *The Presence of the Future: The Eschatology of Biblical Realism*. Grand Rapids, MI: Eerdmans, 1996.

Leithart, Peter. *The Promise of His Appearing: An Exposition of II Peter*. Moscow, ID: Cannon, 2004.

Lieu, Judith M. *I, II, & III John: A Commentary*. Louisville, KY: Westminster John Knox, 2012.

Manson, T. W. *The Son of Man in Daniel, Enoch and the Gospels: Studies in Gospel and Epistles*. Philadelphia PA: Westminster Press, 1962.

Mathison, Keith A. *From Age to Age: The Unfolding of Biblical Eschatology*. Philipsburg, NJ:P&R, 2009.

———. *Postmillennialism: An Eschatology of Hope*. Phillipsburg, NJ: P & R, 1999.

Middleton, Paul. "Christology, Martyrdom, and Vindication in the Gospel of Mark and the Apocalypse: Two New Testament Views." In *Mark, Manuscripts, and Monotheism: Essays in Honor of Larry W. Hurtado*. Edited by Chris Keith, et al., 221. London: Bloombury T & T Clark, 2015.

Mitchell, David C. "The Message of the Psalter: An Eschatological Programme in the Book of Psalms." Journal for the Study of the Old Testament Supplement Series 252 (1997) 19.

Moffitt, David M. *Atonement and the Logic of Resurrection in the Epistle to the Hebrews*. Leiden: Brill, 2011.

Morris, Leon. *The Epistle to the Romans*. The Pillar New Testament Commentary. Grand Rapids, MI: Eerdmans, 1988.

Nickelsburg, George W. E. *1 Enoch I: A Commentary on 1 Enoch*. Minneapolis, MN: Fortress, 2001.

Noē, John. *Beyond the End Times*. Bradford, PA: International Preterist Association, Inc., 2000.

Pate, Marvin C. "The Progressive Dispensational View." In *Four Views on the Book of Revelation*. Edited by Stanley Gundry, et al., 92. Grand Rapids, MI: Zondervan, 1998.

Perschbacher, Wesley J. *New Testament Greek Syntax: An Illustrated Manual*. Chicago, IL: Moody, 1995.

Preston, Don K. *We Shall Meet Him in the Air: The Wedding of the King of Kings*. Ardmore, OK: Jadon Management, Inc., 2009.

———. *Who is This Babylon?* Ardmore, OK: Jadon Productions, 2011.

Russell, J. Stuart. *The Parousia*. Bradford, PA: International Preterist Association, Inc., 2003.

Schneemelcher, Wilhelm, ed. *New Testament Apocrypha. Volume 2: Writings Relating to the Apostles, Apocalypses and Related Subjects*. Louisville, KY: Westminster John Knox, 1992.

Schowalter, Daniel N. *The Emperor and the Gods: Images from the Time of Trajan*. Minneapolis, MN: Fortress, 1993.

Silva, Moises. *Biblical Words and Their Meaning: And Introduction to Lexical Semantics*. Grand Rapids, MI: Zondervan, 1994.

Stevens, Edward E. Foreword, In *The Parousia*, X. Bradford, PA: International Preterist Association, Inc., 2003.

Suetonius, Gaius. *DeVita Caesarum*. London: George Bell and Sons, 1890.

Sullivan, Michael. "The Eschatological Madness of Mathison or How Can These Things Be?" In *House Divided: Bridging the Gap in Reformed Eschatology, A Preterist Response to When Shall These Things Be?* Edited by David A Green, 80. Ramona, CA: Vision Publishing, 2009.

Swete, Henry Barclay. *The Apocalypse of St. John*. Whitefish, MI: Kessinger Publishing, 2006.

Talmon, Shemaryahu. *Literary Motifs and Patterns in the Hebrew Bible: Collected Essays*. Winona Lake, IN: Eisenbrauns, 2013.

Ulrich, Dean R. *The Antiochene Crisis and Jubilee Theology in Daniel's Seventy Sevens*. Lieden: Brill, 2015.

Wallace, Daniel B. *Greek Grammar Beyond the Basics: An Exegetical Grammar of New Testament Syntax*. Grand Rapids, MI: Zondervan, 1997.

Wright, N. T. *The Resurrection of the Son of God*. Minneapolis, MN: Fortress, 2003.

Zwiep, Arie W. "Eight Kings on an Apocalyptic Animal Farm: Reflections of Revelation 17: 9–11." In *Paul, John, and Apocalyptic Eschatology: Studies in Honor of Martinus C. de Boer, Supplements to Novum Testamentum*. Edited by Jan Krans, et al., 149. Leiden/Boston: E. J. Brill, 2013.

www.ingramcontent.com/pod-product-compliance
Lightning Source LLC
Chambersburg PA
CBHW071244230426
43668CB00011B/1572